Save Your Business a Bundle

---

202 WAYS TO CUT COSTS AND BOOST PROFITS NOW— FOR COMPANIES OF ANY SIZE

BY DANIEL KEHRER

SIMON & SCHUSTER

New York   London   Toronto   Sydney   Tokyo   Singapore

 **SIMON & SCHUSTER**
Rockefeller Center
1230 Avenue of the Americas
New York, New York 10020

Designed by Irving Perkins Associates
Manufactured in the United States of America

10 9 8 7 6 5 4 3 2 1

Library of Congress Cataloging-in-Publication Data
Kehrer, Daniel M.
    Save your business a bundle : 202 ways to cut costs and boost
profits now—for companies of any size / by Daniel Kehrer.
        p.   cm.
    1. Cost control.   I. Title.
    HD47.3.K44   1994
    658.15'52—dc20   93-27334   CIP
ISBN: 0-671-78893-0

This publication contains the opinions and ideas of its author and is designed to provide useful advice in regard to the subject matter covered. It
is sold with the understanding that the author and publisher are not en-
gaged in rendering legal, accounting or other professional services.

The author and publisher specifically disclaim any responsibility for any
liability, loss or risk, personal or otherwise, which is incurred as a conse-
quence, directly or indirectly, of the use and application of any of the
contents of this book

This one's for my son, Walker.

Contents

3 Manage Lean and Smart   81

6 Marvelous Manufacturing Money Savers   145

7 Terrific T&E for Less   160

8 Make Wise Cost-Cutting Choices with Technology   177

12 Tackle Your Telecom Costs   233

Before you dive in . . .

Save Your Business a Bundle doesn't stop at cost-cutting tactics. It also offers specific names, addresses, prices, and telephone numbers (toll-free wherever possible) that you need to *take action, now.* You'll find these throughout the book and in the "Save-a-Bundle Follow-up Files" to each chapter.

There's a catch to this approach. *Things change.* Companies move, change prices, drop products or services, switch phone numbers, go bust.

Because even the best efforts to provide up-to-date information in any book are doomed, we've included cities, states, names, addresses, faxes, and other details so that if one method fails, there's always another way to track these folks down.

—*D. Kehrer*

Welcome to the Running-Lean Revolution

A Cost-Cutting Renaissance for American Enterprise

The way to do things is to begin.
—Horace Greeley

Something momentous awaits American business. Over the next ten years, the results of a slow-motion cost-cutting revolution will jam the business profitability accelerator to the floor.

Businesses of every size, shape, and station—from the home-based caterer to the corporate colossus—are slimming down, shaping up, and preparing to butt heads as new, more competitive entrants in the commercial arena. Government might yet muck it up by adding still more taxes and more regulations, or by botching fiscal policy. But the running-lean revolution is on.

You see, American business is learning something that Uncle Sam and other levels of government haven't grasped: The path to growth and prosperity comes from living within, even beneath, one's means, not from building epic monuments to debt, deficits, and inefficiency.

Financial patterns have changed in the nineties. Inflation's largely in check. Assets such as office buildings and inventory won't necessarily be worth more tomorrow. That puts a premium on the value of cost-cutting. Many companies are realizing that, today, how the company *buys* is as crucial to profits as how it *sells*.

By making cost-cutting an *ongoing* task, companies can keep prices low and attract even more business. There are literally billions and billions (apologies to Carl Sagan) in cost-cutting dollars aching to be saved. Those savings can then be invested in growth.

DURABLE, DOABLE CHANGE

Granted, this is *not* an all-volunteer revolution. Many corporate participants are fat-farm conscripts, forced to slenderize by competitive pressures. Cut or die. But unlike the undisciplined dieter whose fat always boomerangs, smart businesses today are betting on a long-term, sustainable approach to cutting costs—a new and more disciplined mind-set that will pay dividends into the next century. They know now that controlling costs only when business is bad is a prescription for failure.

This is common sense. No quick-fix gimmicks or management theory mind candy. A successful approach to saving is made up of small hands-on steps—a series of cost-control skirmishes that, strung together, constitute a durable, doable lunge toward a permanently flatter company tummy.

To achieve harder business bodies, small, midsize, and large companies are *permanently changing the way they operate and do business*. They are looking for more flexibility; a lower break-even point. They are not reinventing the cost-control wheel. They are *managing* costs, not just cutting them. They are bouncing back office overhead; improving productivity with high-tech equipment; managing leaner; traveling smarter; negotiating harder; and, getting more for their money on everything from ad space to Zip + 4.

These 202 tactics are nontoxic to jobs. By spending smarter on telecommunications, postage, printing, freight, technology, accounting and legal services, insurance, benefits, manufacturing materials, and a host of other items, a leaner, more profitable company can retain or even *add* quality jobs, not take 'em away.

From Michigan's manufacturers to Boston's banks, from the computer companies of California and Texas to small retailers in every city across the U.S.A., there's a new clarion call: *Flatter costs mean fatter earnings.* Cutting your break-even by 10%, 20%, 30%, or more quickly transforms *any* sales into profits.

This is only the beginning. These tactics can help put your business—whatever its size, location, or type—in the cost-cutting front line.

—*Daniel Kehrer*

CHAPTER 1

The Ten Greatest Cost-Cutting Tactics for the Next Ten Years

TACTIC #1
Let Your Employees Lead the Way

Eureka! American business is rediscovering the "lowly" suggestion box (now called a suggestion *system,* thank you)—the most underrated cost-cutting maneuver since the cents-off coupon. Suggestion systems are saving business *billions*—yes *billions*—of dollars yearly and are poised to perform cost-cutting miracles over the next ten years. Some stats from the Employee Involvement Association (EIA), formerly the National Association of Suggestion Systems, a fifty-year-old Arlington, Virginia–based group:

- The one thousand organizations belonging to EIA report combined savings of $2 billion to $2.5 billion *per year* from employee ideas, double the mid-1980s level.
- Average per-idea savings: $6,000 to $7,000.
- Today, 37% of suggestions are adopted, up from 25% in 1985.

Despite those numbers and a suggestion box face-lift (most are now computerized), only about 3% of U.S. companies have respectable suggestion systems in place.

Employee suggestions offer a windfall of *highly specific ideas that only an insider could know.* This is the best, nay the only, way to generate gobs of nuts-and-bolts notions that seem unspectacular alone but can add up to major savings. What's more, company size doesn't matter. Pound for pound, a business with ten employees can benefit just as much as a company with ten thousand. Some examples:

Tom Matykiewicz, Jr., an employee at CertainTeed Corp., a smallish roofing materials manufacturer in Shakopee, Minnesota, suggested a new part to use in making specialty shingles. That part is now saving CertainTeed at least $15,000 annually. CertainTeed encourages ideas with a system called WATT (Working And Thinking Together) that pays employees $5 just for turning in a suggestion (no duplicates, and other rules apply) and 5% of first-year cost savings for those that are accepted. WATT generates about five hundred ideas yearly.

Cleveland-based Ohio Bell's suggestion system, Enter-Prize, saved the company $4.8 million in one year from 102 adopted ideas. Example: Two employees teamed up to invent a movable curb that allows manholes to remain in place when a street is widened, ringing up six-figure savings. The idea's been patented and marketed elsewhere. Ohio Bell's savings are over $2 million.

A suggestion to boost recovery of a solvent and make more of it recyclable saved Indianapolis-based drug company Eli Lilly about $700,000 the first year.

A loan manager at BankAmerica in San Francisco suggested a *free* source of property tax information that BofA was paying for. Savings: $363,352.

IBM netted first-year savings of $1.4 million when an employee devised a tool to produce specialized computing cables in-house. Before the suggestion, IBM was paying an outside supplier $5 apiece to make the cables, now produced for pennies.

In 1992, American Airlines christened a new Boeing 757 in a special ceremony. The plane was purchased entirely with savings flown in by the company's IdeAAs in Action employee suggestion system, launched in 1987.

Designing Your System

- Make a firm commitment to starting and continuing a *serious* program. It takes a lot more than offering a slotted box. To freshen the approach, give it a name like "Valued Ideas Plan" (VIP), "Aim for Ideas," or something similar.

- Ask specifically for *cost-cutting* ideas, not just ideas in general. One terrific way to encourage good ones is to clue workers in on how much things cost. A small West Coast manufacturer makes a game of having employees guess prices on components. Workers invariably underestimate by wide margins. Once they find out what critical items cost, money-saving ideas start flowing.
- Offer rewards for ideas that are used. Cash is popular. Some companies use a percentage of first-year savings. If calculating savings is difficult, consider a flat dollar award for each usable idea ($50 to $100 will usually do). Other firms reward employees with merchandise, tickets, or getaway weekends. Or try entering all suggesters in a periodic prize drawing.
- Make a big deal about presenting awards. Recognition encourages participation. Take photos. Send a letter of appreciation to the employee's home.
- Put someone in charge of the program, but *not* yourself. Let a small management/employee group screen ideas for the best candidates.
- Communication is critical. Set goals, publicize the program, and keep employees informed about ideas that are adopted, those that aren't, and why. A regular notice in the company newsletter or on a bulletin board helps.
- Respond quickly to every idea, good or bad. Let employees know the ideas are appreciated. The first fifty may not fly; the fifty-first may be your diamond.
- Keep accurate records to make sure awards are handed out equitably.

Step back and let things happen—not overnight, but over time. Many of them will be little things that you can't read about in any book or manual—a special rack to hold parts; an unnecessary piece of record-keeping paper eliminated; a dumb ordering procedure exposed. Encourage the little ones and the big ones will come.

SAVE-A-BUNDLE FOLLOW-UP FILE

• The National Association of Suggestion Systems (NASS), a membership group of companies with active suggestion systems, is *the* source for information. EIA runs seminars around the country that are open to nonmembers, offers guidebooks on setting up and operating suggestion systems, and publishes a newsletter. Membership is $220 per year. Contact EIA, 1735 North Lynn Street, Suite 950, Arlington, VA 22209-2022; (703) 524-3424; fax (703) 524-2303.

TACTIC #2
Dodge Litigation Lunacy
with Free-Market Justice

Clogged courts, sue-happy humans, and frightfully high legal fees have spawned a fast-growing, free-market, *lower-cost* answer to litigation lunacy called alternative dispute resolution (ADR). Private, for-profit companies and a variety of non-profits such as the Better Business Bureaus (BBBs) are offering money-saving solutions to costly litigation. What started as a quiet legal revolution is catching fire: One private ADR firm, U.S. Arbitration & Mediation, has been growing at a 20% to 30% annual rate in the 1990s. The oldest and largest private mediator, Orange, California–based Judicial Arbitration & Mediation Services, Inc. (JAMS), referees tens of thousands of cases yearly.

Whether it's a warranty dispute with a customer, a more complex spat over product liability, a self-insurance problem, or countless other legal traps, ADR is the answer to solving your business beefs at bargain-basement rates. It offers prompt, confidential, and cost-effective relief from spiraling legal fees. Whew!

ADR is rapidly leading U.S. business toward its own private judicial system. Little wonder. On cost, quality, or any other yardstick you care to use, private justice beats litigation. Variables abound, but best estimates say that ADR will cost at least 50% less than what a standard lawsuit would run. Not counting your Pepto-Bismol tab during litigation.

Judicate, Inc., another private ADR firm, retains over six hundred former federal, state, and local judges to mediate and arbitrate (I'll explain the difference in a moment) business brouhahas using rules and procedures culled from the public courts. Disputants can choose a particular Judicate judge with expertise in specialized areas of law.

Basically, under *arbitration*, also known as binding arbitration, the warring parties agree to let an arbitrator hear the arguments, look at the evidence, and decide. Arbitration awards are final and binding on the parties involved, because they've agreed to that ahead of time. Disputed sums are often put in escrow before the decision. High/low arbitration is a hybrid that limits any award to maximum/minimum amounts.

Mediation is a less formal, nonbinding settlement conference. Parties try to settle differences themselves, with a professional referee, or mediator, helping. The mediator strives for conciliation. But the disputants, who take part voluntarily, make the final decision.

In any case, speed is a huge cost saver. Mediations can run an hour, a half day, or longer, and can be scheduled quickly. Hourly mediation rates can run $100 to $200, while a local BBB dispute resolution service typically charges $50 to $200 per session.

SAVE-A-BUNDLE FOLLOW-UP FILE

• American Arbitration Association (AAA) is *the* premier resource for information on business arbitration and mediation. Whatever you need to know on the subject, AAA can tell you. AAA is a New York–based nonprofit group that handles arbitration and mediation cases from thirty-six offices nation-wide. This group also offers a huge selection of publications and videos on all aspects of dispute resolution, including some geared to specific industries, such as construction, or professions, such as accounting. Request the group's catalog, *Commercial Dispute Resolution: A Guide to AAA Resources*, from American Arbitration Association, Publications Department, 140 West 51st Street, New York, NY 10020-1203; call (212) 484-4000; fax (212) 765-4874.

• The American Bar Association (ABA) has an excellent directory of nonprofit, religious, educational, government-funded centers and community mediation programs. Write to the ABA's Standing Committee on Dispute Resolution, 1800 M Street, N.W., Washington, DC 20036; (202) 331-2258. The Washington office can send you the pages with listings for your area for free. The entire directory costs $60.

• Most of the 170 Better Business Bureaus across the country now run local dispute resolution programs. Call your local chapter or the national Council of Better Business Bureaus at (800) 537-4600. You can also write to the BBB's ADR Division, 4200 Wilson Boulevard, 8th Floor, Arlington, VA 22203.

• Here are a few selected private ADR firms:

- U.S. Arbitration & Mediation, based in Seattle, has offices in forty-three states and Europe, but can arrange sessions anywhere. Call (800) 933-6348.
- Judicate, Inc., based in Lake Success, New York, has offices in Philadelphia and in Irvine, California. Call (800) 755-7501.
- Judicial Arbitration & Mediation Services (JAMS), based in Orange, California, has over twenty offices across the country. Call (800) 352-5267.
- Endispute, Inc., based in Washington, D.C., has offices in New York, Chicago, Boston, and San Francisco. Call (800) 448-1660.

TACTIC #3
Lease Your Workers

- Dodge mounds of regulatory compliance paperwork (from OSHA, INS, EEOC, etc.) and other red tape.
- Slash your payroll, administration, bookkeeping, insurance, and other personnel costs.
- Get free help recruiting, screening, and hiring new employees.
- Insulate yourself from wrongful-termination lawsuits.
- Offer workers *better* benefits than your firm can afford now.

Those are a few morsels that make employee leasing a good bet to save many small businesses money over the next ten years, and beyond. Employee leasing is one of the fastest-growing business services in America—over a million employees are now leased through some thirteen hundred leasing companies nationwide.

It works like this. The leasing firm either employs or co-employs your workers, along with those of dozens or perhaps hundreds of other companies. The leasing company becomes the legal employer and thus takes full responsibility for payroll and payroll taxes, workers' comp insurance, health insurance, retirement plan, and other benefits. Your company writes one check a month to cover it all, including the leasing company's fee.

Because the leasing company is, in effect, a large employer, it can provide all of that at a vastly lower cost than the typical small firm. The average company spends an *additional* 39% to 50% of its gross payroll on benefits, employee administration, and costs associated with worker turnover. Leasing can lower that cost to 15% to 36% of gross payroll, depending on the benefits included.

Leasing in Action Dothan, Alabama–based Southern Engineered Products—a fifteen-person firm that makes canvas

products such as boat covers and tarps for the trucking industry—may not seem like a cost-cutting pioneer of American
industry. But when co-owner and general manager Jerome
Varnum discovered the leasing concept, it seemed an ideal
way for his fast-growing firm to save money, boost profits,
attract and keep better-quality employees, and be more competitive. "I'd never heard of it before a local rep for the leasing company told me," says Varnum. "Now that we're doing
it, I can't see any down side."

Varnum didn't have to change operations in any way, except to turn his payroll paperwork and related chores over to
the leasing company, National Staff Network (NSN). Workers
wavered for about a week. But when they decided that Varnum was still boss and their benefits were *better*, they were
happy.

Southern Engineered Products compared total before-and-
after costs and concluded that leasing had saved the company
about 5% to 10%. Varnum turns in a time sheet and writes a
check to NSN. That's it, and he couldn't be happier. He's also
thrilled that the leasing firm now helps him find, screen, and
hire new employees—another time and money saver that
doesn't cost Southern Engineered Products an extra cent.
"It's like having your own personnel department but not having to pay 'em," says Varnum.

Finding a Leasing Partner For a while, employee leasing
may be a victim of its own success. The idea is catching on so
fast that some firms' resources are stretched. The inevitable
fly-by-nighters come and go. Some weaker leasing companies
have collapsed, leaving a trail of unpaid medical and other
insurance claims.

Do some research before signing a deal. Here's some key
information to compile. If the leasing company resists providing it, or the information doesn't check out, look for another
company.

- Ask the leasing firm for bank references to verify financial
  stability and for client references. Then call those refer-

ences and ask about the leasing company's performance and customer service record.

- Find out how long the company's been in business. Look for firms that have been around at least five years.
- Ask if the leasing company provides a full range of personnel services, including recruiting, hiring, firing, and administering benefits.
- Ask for certification that the leasing firm meets all IRS and state regulations.
- Will the company provide quarterly, independent audits certifying that all payroll tax, insurance premium, and pension contributions have been paid?
- Are the leasing company's insurance plans backed by strong companies? Check their A.M. Best ratings. The leasing company should readily supply information on its insurance carriers, insurance broker, and the third-party administrator that handles claims.
- Are fees guaranteed for at least a year or longer?

SAVE-A-BUNDLE FOLLOW-UP FILE

- National Staff Network, based in Van Nuys, California, is an umbrella group for four different employee leasing firms operating in a dozen locations, including California, Massachusetts, Colorado, Michigan, Florida, New York, Minnesota, Louisiana, and Alabama. Its founder and chairman, Marvin Selter, is credited with inventing the employee leasing concept in 1972. Call (800) 222-6761.
- National Staff Leasing Association (NSLA), in Arlington, Virginia, is a trade group of leasing companies with local chapters around the country. NSLA can provide information on leasing company certification and can help you locate member firms in your area. Call (703) 524-3636; fax (703) 524-2303.

TACTIC #4
Send for Mailroom Savings

With postage rates ever rising, business is getting the message: This ain't no nickel-and-dime deal anymore! Fortunately, the United States Postal Service itself has concocted a complex brew of ways for companies to cut their postage costs by helping the P.O. do its job more efficiently.

Behind those windowless walls of your mailroom, countless dollars are probably a-wastin'. Mailing has more money-saving moves than David Letterman has wisecracks. Doesn't matter how big you are; savings are proportionate. A home-based biz can lop $400 off a $2,000 postage bill; or a major mailer could save a six-figure sum.

The big surprise is all the great deals now available from the USPS. Odd goings-on at the P.O.—all that talk about automation and greater efficiency is showing results for business mailers. The USPS has introduced an extensive though complicated menu of graduated price breaks for business mail that meets preset conditions. Savings start small, around 5% or so, but can stretch to over 35% in some cases. Ignore mailing costs and you'll pay, pay, pay.

Chapter 5 has more details on individual postage-saving tactics. But if you do nothing else in this area, at least make one phone call: to a USPS "Business Center." They're new, created in the early nineties to service business mailing customers—more specifically, to help 'em save money on mailings. More are being added all the time (there are about one hundred at this writing), so there's probably one near you.

Ask your local P.O. for the number of the nearest Business Center and request information on postal discount programs and other money-saving services for business. It may be the most lucrative call you make this week.

Gary La Haie made the call. He's president of Aussie Connection in Portland, Oregon. Advice he got saved his business over 30% on third-class catalog mailings. "Speed is what really appealed to us," says La Haie. Ironically, *cheaper* mailings, because they are more highly automated, often move *faster* as well. By using Zip + 4 and "Delivery Point" bar coding (it's the latest: see Chapter 5) you can get first-class service at junk-mail rates. "Time is money when you have catalogs sitting in the mail somewhere that are not doing you any good until they reach the customer."

Leslie Brown thought her business was too small to benefit from postal discounts until she met Bill Brock, then manager of the U.S. Postal Service's Business Center in Portland. Brown did know one thing about the mailings her three-person firm had been doing: They were expensive. Her home-based business, Color Fit Systems in Lake Oswego, Oregon, imports and sells fabric liners for closet storage systems. She does at least three to four mailings each year of about eight thousand each.

Some of the first mailings the firm did went full fare because the person Brown had hired to handle mailings never looked into discounts. Now with Zip + 4, Brown's mailings are cheaper and bulk-rate pieces arrive in as little as three days.

SAVE-A-BUNDLE FOLLOW-UP FILE

• A free software program called Mail Flow Planning System is available from USPS. This disk (for IBM) lets any size business easily calculate discounts for any class of mail. Call (800) 238-3150.
   • A few helpful USPS publications include:

   • *Designing Business Letter Mail* (54-page booklet; Publication 25)
   • *Addressing for Success* (9-page brochure; Notice 221)

Ask your Business Center for a free copy of each of the above. Other resources:

   • *The Domestic Mail Manual* is the postal system bible (last count: 833 pages), updated quarterly. Cost: $56/

year. Order from the Government Printing Office (GPO) at (202) 783-3238.
- *Postal Bulletin* has biweekly updates of your favorite regulations. Cost: $81/year from the GPO.

TACTIC #5
Tune In to Telecommuting

Most big companies with telecommuting tendencies don't like to talk about it. "They consider it such a competitive edge that they don't want others to know what they're doing and how they're doing it," says Jack Nilles, president of JALA International, a California firm that helps companies set up telecommuting programs.

Nilles (some credit him with coining the term *telecommuting*) helped Pacific Bell launch a telecommuting experiment in the mid-1980s with about forty managerial-level employees participating. Now about two thousand telecommute at Pac Bell, or roughly 10% of the company's managerial work force.

There are some six million telecommuters in the United States. (Basically, a telecommuter is someone on the company payroll who works from home either full- or part-time.) According to LINK Resources, a New York–based research firm that studies the impact of emerging technologies, telecommuting is growing most rapidly among companies with fewer than twenty or more than one thousand employees; business executives and managers; engineers and scientists.

Three key trends will fuel a telecommuting take-off:

- Low-cost, high-tech tools, including more powerful home computers and software, speedier modems, voice mail, fax machines, and new phone features.
- Increasing numbers of employees who *want* to work from a home office.
- A realization by more companies that telecommuting can work.

Cost-cutting is a major reason that tons of companies are tapping in. That's the angle that Baby Bell companies are taking as they aggressively market telecommuting to business. Carol Nolan, Pac Bell's telecommuting specialist, has helped dozens of organizations launch programs and cites these benefits:

- Improved productivity. On average, telecommuters produce 20% more work than their office-based counterparts.
- Absenteeism drops, often by half. Fewer sick days. Fewer emergency child-care situations.
- Reduced overhead for parking spaces, equipment, office furniture, general maintenance, power, lighting, and big potential savings in office space costs. One large employer estimated total annual savings per telecommuter at $2,880; Pac Bell puts the figure at $6,546.
- Higher morale, lower turnover, and thus lower recruiting and retraining costs.
- Geographic barriers to employment are eliminated: Amy Silberbauer, a software developer, travels from home in Modesto, California, to her job in Silicon Valley (a two-hundred-mile round trip) twice a week. The other three days she works at home. New York Life has fifteen computer programmers working from home—one lives in Nevada. The Portsmouth Consulting Group has sixteen partners scattered across the country who meet electronically several times a week.
- Older employees can stay on the job longer; parents on maternity leave can return to work earlier.
- Telecommuters become *better* managers when their subordinates are not always in sight, with more focus on the real priorities: goals, performance evaluation, effective communication.

Rapidly growing companies are great telecommuting candidates. SITA, a California firm that Nolan has worked with, was facing a $400,000 move to larger space but opted to establish a telecommuting program instead. SITA has a contract with the major airlines to provide data transmission services for the flight arrival and departure information you see displayed on monitors at airports. The firm decided it was cheaper to set up some employees at home than to lease more office space.

Other bulging businesses can sidestep expensive expansion by putting employees to work at home, especially those whose jobs are linked closely to the computer, fax, and phone. According to Gil Gordon, a telecommuting consultant, companies that pay close attention both to the technology and the need to *manage* at-home workers well will be most successful.

Telecommuting converts include thousands of small companies as well as biggies such as Digital Equipment Corp., Sears, Johnson & Johnson, and American Express. The Travelers has become a telecommuting leader since first testing the idea in 1987. This Hartford-based insurance giant has developed four criteria for the types of jobs it feels are right for telecommuting:

- The job must be measurable, with specific objectives and performance standards.
- It must be a job that can easily substitute electronic communication for face-to-face communication.
- The job must be truly portable—that is, one that doesn't require access to files and equipment that aren't available on-line.
- The job must involve tasks such as writing, researching, programming, analyzing, and working with information.

J.C. Penney has turned to telecommuting workers to handle telephone sales orders as a cost-effective alternative to in-office employment. Penney has installed phone lines, computers, and other equipment in workers' homes. The employee must provide thirty-five square feet of office space away from home distractions. Penney calculates the cost at less than half that of an office setup. When catalog sales peak and the company needs help, it's a phone call away. Workers are on-line in five minutes, not the hour and a half it took previously.

SAVE-A-BUNDLE FOLLOW-UP FILE

• Carol Nolan, telecommuting manager at Pacific Bell, has a super-helpful information package available to interested companies in Pac Bell's service area. A booklet called *The Telecommuting Research Guide* offers especially useful information on setting up and evaluating a program. Reach Nolan at 1010 Wilshire Boulevard, Suite 1035, Los Angeles, CA 90017. Call (213) 975-7495; fax (213) 250-1248.

• You can reach Jack Nilles, of JALA International, at (310) 476-3703.

• Gil Gordon, of Gil Gordon Associates in Monmouth Junction, New Jersey, publishes a monthly newsletter, *Telecommuting Review* ($157/year), and is coauthor of *Telecommuting: How to Make It Work for You and Your Company* (Prentice-Hall), available from Gordon for $15.95. The newsletter's a must for any telecommuting enthusiast, with pithy profiles of telecommuting programs, news, reviews, and always with contact names and numbers. Call (908) 329-2266.

• Gil Gordon Associates has also cosponsored a variety of telecommuting conferences and Gordon himself is featured in a twenty-minute how-to video on telecommuting produced by Southern New England Telephone. The video, *Telecommuting in the 90s*, is $135 (includes shipping) from Video Copy Services in Atlanta. Call (800) 531-9889.

• LINK Resources Corp., in New York, has done extensive research and consulting in the area of telecommuting. Reach 'em at (800) 722-5335; fax (212) 620-3099.

• *Homework: How to Hire, Manage and Monitor Employees Who Work at Home* is a book by Phillip Mahfood (Probus Publishing, $24.95). Call (800) 776-2871.

• *Creating a Flexible Workplace* by Barney Olmsted and Suzanne Smith (AMACOM, $59.95) offers practical advice on making telecommuting work in the real business world. Call (800) 262-9699.

TACTIC #6
Buy into Bar Codes and EDI

Bar codes are the most humble-looking critters ever to revolutionize business. They aren't just grocery gadgets anymore. Bar codes (basically numbers that computers can read) and a kindred technology called electronic data interchange (EDI) have blasted their way into every conceivable business niche.

Some reasons for the bar code boom:

- *Speed.* Remember when checkers had to enter prices by hand? Slow. Mistake-ridden. Costly. Sounds like a practice from the Jurassic period now.
- *Accuracy/efficiency.* Ditto above.
- *Money* (as in saving much).

EDI has also become an evolutionary catalyst for business cost-cutting and productivity gains. EDI is any standardized, computer-to-computer business transaction. It could be an exchange of money electronically. Or it could be an executed purchase order, invoice, shipping notice, or some other transaction. My firm's computer checks inventory and orders new supplies from your firm's computer automatically.

EDI offers quick, low-cost response, eliminates paper invoicing, and allows companies better inventory control. Low-cost EDI software kits are a terrific help for small companies wanting to do business with giants like Wal-Mart. The range is immense (see the Follow-up File for leads) and the market for EDI software and services will explode worldwide in the next ten years.

Soon, businesses that never dreamed they'd be hooked into bar code technology and EDI will be cutting costs with this stuff—and wondering how they ever did without. So far, the technology and its potential applications are barely out of diapers.

Bar codes let business track products, parts, documents—you name it—superfast and with almost 100% accuracy. EDI takes it a step further by transmitting bar-coded information from your computer to another computer, which then does something in response. For example, a small card shop tracks its Hallmark card inventory with bar codes, then transmits the stock information directly via computer to Hallmark Cards, Inc., in Kansas City, where electronic replacement orders are generated quickly, accurately, and cheaply.

Put bar codes and EDI together and you've got a knockout technology punch that can make a big bottom-line difference in your company.

Management heads are swelling at the Goodyear Tire & Rubber Company's Tyler, Texas, plant thanks to bar codes. A few years ago, tire types were hand sorted off the assembly line. Today they're bar coded so that robots can do that job. Now, due to this and other modernizing moves, the same fourteen hundred employees roll out almost 25% more tires in Tyler than before.

But EDI is still mostly big-biz territory, right? *Not!* Small firms are plugging in, thanks in part to a Small Business Initiative program pioneered by the Electronic Data Interchange Association (EDIA), an industry group based in Alexandria, Virginia. The technology and business uses are advancing rapidly. The best way to get a fix on how your business can benefit and what it will take to get you set up is to talk to vendors in the field (see the Follow-up File).

SAVE-A-BUNDLE FOLLOW-UP FILE

• The best way to locate bar-code equipment and software vendors is to contact their industry trade group, AIM USA (Automatic Identification Manufacturers, Inc.), at 634 Alpha Drive, Pittsburgh, PA 15238; (800) 338-0206; fax (412) 963-8753. Ask for AIM USA's Success Kit packet, which includes a directory of member companies (cross-referenced by product categories), a publications list, and seminar and trade show information. AIM USA is an authority on all aspects of data collection technology, which includes bar codes. Its mission is to provide unbiased information on the choices available to your business.

• Joining the Electronic Data Interchange Association (EDIA) is a perfect way to plug into EDI. This membership group offers conferences and seminars, access to local user groups, EDI software, service/supplier directories and other publications, and audio- and videotapes. The Small Business Initiative program links small firms with larger ones already advanced in EDI. Dues, based on company size, start at $300. Contact EDIA, 225 Reinekers Lane, Suite 550, Alexandria, VA 22314; (703) 838-8042; fax (703) 838-8038.

• AT&T, IBM, and Sears Roebuck and Co., are three giants who've entered the EDI game as service suppliers. Sears and IBM jointly offer EDI services for tracking orders and inventory through Advantis. Call (800) 366-2722. AT&T's EDI goodies are offered through AT&T EasyLink Services. Call (800) 242-6005.

• A good entry-level EDI software package is Trading Partner PC (for Microsoft Windows) from Wilton, Connecticut–based TSI International. Each kit is customized to your business. Prices start at $495. Call (800) 334-2120.

• The *International Guide to E-Mail and EDI Products and Services* ($50) is published twice yearly by EDI Strategies, Inc., Marietta, Georgia. Call (404) 578-4980; fax (404) 973-9984.

• The National Automated Clearing House Association (NACHA), in Herndon, Virginia, offers almost a dozen publications on financial EDI. The group's stated goal: "To make EDI as easy as ABC." Call for a publications list; (703) 742-9190.

TACTIC #7
Cash In on Countertrade

It started with simple barter. Now *countertrade*, as it's known at many companies, has become a more sophisticated and expansive business tactic. Barter is but one variation. Basically, barter is swapping goods and services—something a company has for something it needs—with no cash changing hands. Companies use countertrade—including counterpurchase, compensation trades, clearing trades, and offsets—to facilitate sales that wouldn't otherwise be made. The International Reciprocal Trade Association (IRTA), an association of barter exchanges in Great Falls, Virginia, says that a quarter-million companies now do $6 billion worth of barter trades annually.

With barter, used mostly by smaller companies, goods and services are exchanged at their full customary cost (including your normal markup). Barter works best when you trade your *excess* time and inventory for goods and services that you'd normally pay for with cash and credit. That puts time and inventory that might otherwise sit idle to productive use. It's *most* advantageous for service-type firms with high margins where the cost of extra business is low; *least* advantageous for low-margin businesses such as discount retailers.

Barter takes three basic forms. You can work deals one-on-one, probably with other business owners you know. You can join one of the four hundred or so barter exchange groups across the United States that help facilitate trades valued in the billions of dollars each year. Or, you can do barter business with a trading company that arranges trades or acquires bartered goods and services for its own inventory. The larger, well-financed commercial barter companies are an outlet for big companies to do large, one-shot barter deals through a firm that has more resources than the small local exchanges can usually muster. (The Follow-up File lists examples.)

Big players—such as paper company James River, Coca-Cola, PepsiCo, 3M, Toshiba, and McDonnell Douglas Helicopter—favor other countertrade tactics (like sales linked to purchases) over simple barter. Mesa, Arizona–based McDonnell Douglas Helicopter, in particular, is a countertrade choirmaster. Gary Pacific, manager of countertrade, doesn't normally talk about McDonnell's countertrade activities because the company considers it such an advantage that it doesn't want competitors to know what it's doing. According to Pacific, McDonnell Douglas Helicopter is doing some $600 million in countertrade business yearly, much of it involving international sales.

Example: A customer in Hungary wanted to buy helicopters but had no hard currency to pay. This customer struck a letter-of-credit deal through a Hungarian spark plug maker to sell spark plugs, for hard currency, to McDonnell Douglas, which then sold the spark plugs to the TuneUp Masters chain in the United States. When the choppers were ready for delivery, the Hungarian buyer used the hard currency paid for the spark plugs to pay McDonnell Douglas.

In a domestic countertrade deal, McDonnell Douglas Helicopter horse-traded advertising credits it had "in the bank" for discounts from a major car rental firm with which McDonnell Douglas was doing about $8 million in business yearly. And it once traded millions of dollars' worth of excess inventory in nuts, bolts, washers, and screws for products and services it needed.

According to Gary Pacific, corporate countertrade's biggest sales-boosting, cost-cutting potential is in such industries as construction, power generation, and food.

Black Eye Is Healed Shady dealings in the seventies gave barter a black eye. Dog-nosed IRS agents are always sniffing for deals used only to dodge taxes. But barter's evolution into the more sophisticated field of corporate countertrade, combined with the creation of national countertrade organizations and the entry of many major corporations, has made this a savvy cost-cutting move for the future.

For small companies, joining a group makes it simple. For a sign-up fee of about $300 to $500 and often a 5% to 15% commission on trades (sometimes split between "buyer" and "seller"), exchange groups coordinate all trades, match "buyers" with "sellers," and track down hard-to-find items. The American Commerce Exchange (ACX), a five-hundred-member association launched in 1981 and based in Toluca Lake, California, charges a one-time fee of $300 to join, a 15%

Bartering Up

• Phil Garaway's Aamco Transmissions outlet in Pasadena, California, snags an extra $2,000 per month in business it wouldn't normally get, thanks to barter deals made through American Commerce Exchange (ACX) in Toluca Lake, California. "In return," says Garaway, "I buy office equipment, dentistry, vacations, hotels, and just about anything I would pay cash for. It's worked really well."

• Copier companies Toshiba, Mita, and Panafax did a month's worth of advertising in the New York market without spending a dime. Their commercials aired some two hundred times on eighteen radio stations—the entire campaign arranged through Reciprocal Marketing Sources, a Manhattan-based barter organization. Perry Silver, president of Reciprocal Marketing, has helped barter an entire fleet of new Chrysler cars, an overprint of books, and commercial parking space.

• Cleveland area restaurants are finding barter a menu for success. Jacob Corea, owner of Proud Pony Restaurant in Bedford Heights, Ohio, and a member of American Trade Exchange (ATX), is a big barter believer. He has traded meals for new floor coverings, a copy machine, and a safe. Tom McDowell, president of ATX, based in Euclid, Ohio, says that restaurants belonging to the exchange have traded for dozens of products and services, including entertainment, cash registers, signs, advertising, trash services, window washing, napkins, and snow plowing.

• Through Chicago Barter Corp., with about fifteen hundred members, Clarklift West, Inc., traded forklifts and other heavy equipment for a new phone system and other items in a trade valued at around $100,000.

• The Los Angeles law firm Pachulski, Stang & Ziehl bartered $25,000 in legal services for food credit at Wolfgang Puck's trendy eateries in and around L.A. Seems another partially Puck—owned company needed bankruptcy representation but had no cash. Hence the advice-for-eats swap.

cash brokerage fee on purchases, and a $10 monthly fee. Chicago Barter Corp., in Lombard, Illinois, charges a $500 fee to open an account and start trading.

All barter transactions are documented and total barter dollars earned for the year are reported to the IRS by the trade exchange. Members receive a Form 1099B along with a printout of barter activity for the year. Barter deals should be reported the same way as ordinary cash purchases or expenses.

Four Steps to Countertrade Success

1. *Make sure it fits.* Do you have barterable goods or services? Talking to a local exchange can help you determine if barter can save your business money.
2. *Do some homework.* Get names of exchanges in your area (see the Follow-up File) and check them out. Talk to members; look for an exchange that can tie you into national trades too.
3. *Be willing to switch suppliers.* In order to spend your trade credits, you must be willing to use the suppliers who are members of your exchange. If you are committed to other outlets, your barter credits will be wasted.
4. *Don't overdo it.* Barter can save you money, but don't count on it to run your business.

SAVE-A-BUNDLE FOLLOW-UP FILE

- To find a barter group in your area:
  - The International Reciprocal Trade Association (IRTA) has more than one hundred exchange members. Fax an inquiry to IRTA at (703) 759-0792 or write to 9513 Beach Mill Road, Great Falls, VA 22066. IRTA prefers written requests.
  - Contact the National Association of Trade Exchanges (NATE) at (503) 684-6105. NATE has about fifty members. Les French, based in Portland, Oregon, is chairman.

• UltraTrade, Inc., is a new high-tech trading network (eleven years in the making) designed to give big business daily access to barter. UltraTrade uses supercomputers and sophisticated software to make trade matches instantaneously. For information contact Advanced Artificial Intelligence Systems, 397 Dal-Rich, Suite 230, Richardson, TX 75080; (214) 238-5778; fax (214) 238-7484.

• Countertrade managers at many of the Fortune 500 corporations involved in this tactic belong to the American Countertrade Association, an idea-swapping trade group based in St. Louis. Call Dan West at (314) 727-5522.

• *BarterNews,* a quarterly, is the largest circulation magazine on barter. A subscription is $40 per year from P.O. Box 3024, Mission Viejo, CA 92690; (714) 495-6529; fax (714) 831-8920. A terrific resource for eager barter beavers.

• Four large commercial barter companies:

  · Tradewell, which calls itself "America's trading partner—worldwide," offers a free booklet on barter called *Business of Barter.* Call (212) 888-8500; fax (212) 755-6312, or write to 845 Third Avenue, New York, NY 10022.

  · SGD Corp., 888 Seventh Avenue, Suite 603, New York, NY 10019; (212) 265-9000; fax (212) 265-9123.

  · Icon International, Inc., 220 East 42nd Street, #1601, New York, NY 10017; (212) 972-7373.

  · Reciprocal Marketing Sources, 225 West 34th Street, Suite 909, New York, NY 10122; (212) 244-3562.

TACTIC #8
Move It!

For a while, Tom Zimmerman felt like "Mr. Irresistible." Wooed by state officials from Arizona, Colorado, Tennessee, Mississippi, Ohio, Illinois, and Michigan, among others, Zimmerman could scarcely get through his mail what with the courtship offers pouring in from state business development offices.

He's some big Fortune 500 muckamuck, right? Not quite. Zimmerman is president of Excal, a small foundry, once based in California but now with a Wyoming address. Excal, a marriage of two brass, bronze, and aluminum casting companies around for over forty years, reincarnated itself as a Wyoming corporation based in Mills (near Casper) for one key reason: to save money.

"Brass foundries are a highly competitive, low-margin business," says Zimmerman. "We needed to lower costs to stay competitive; maybe even to stay in business." Excal slashed its taxes, its workers' comp costs, and the cost of its 115-member work force. The company now owns its facilities, paying less to carry them than it paid to lease in California. Excal cut its trucking costs, and Zimmerman figures his new workers are a great deal more productive too.

Let's Make a Deal Boatloads of businesses are pulling out of high-cost states and dropping anchor where everything's cheaper. Others looking to expand are nabbing sweet deals from state and local economic development authorities in exchange for placing new outlets in those areas. Cutthroat competition among states eager to attract businesses of *any* size has spawned a "let's-make-a-deal" market that can prove lucrative over the next ten years. Mississippi dangles tax credits for every new job a business creates; North Carolina will pay to train your workers; Nebraska, Colorado, Wyoming, and a host of other states will sponsor financing. In South Dakota, the Governor's Office of Economic Development touts that state's lack of any corporate income tax, personal income tax, or business inventory tax—a combination that's proving to be a powerful draw for many companies.

Some movin'-on examples:

Harpers, Inc., based in California since 1954, decided to celebrate its fortieth anniversary year by moving to Idaho in 1994. This maker of metal office furniture is a pack-up-and-move-to-save-money paradigm. Why stay where costs are high if you don't have to? Insurance, real estate, taxes, utilities, wages and benefits, permit and licensing fees are all potential cost-saving areas.

Harpers, with about five hundred employees, was *already* profitable in California. The company had a modern, computerized plant and operated efficiently, recycling everything from cardboard to metal scrap. But it took only a semisharp pencil to figure that in Idaho it could be a whole lot *more* profitable. Some estimated savings:

- Same employee benefits at $800,000 less (mostly lower health insurance costs).
- Sewer, water, and other permits: $245,000 per year savings.
- Workers' compensation insurance costs: cut 50%, saving $500,000.

Wyoming, with a national ad campaign and sophisticated computer-generated cost comparisons, is aggressively courting companies. Those considering a move get a customized report comparing us-vs.-them costs. Wyoming officials gloat that while Georgia has a 6% corporate tax, California's tops 9%, and Colorado's approaches 6%, Wyoming has no corporate tax. There is also no personal income tax, no tax on inventory, no tax on goods made for out-of-state sale, and a low 3% sales tax.

The scent was too much for companies such as SafeCard Services, Inc., a credit card registration service that moved in 1992 from Fort Lauderdale to Cheyenne, and for Sierra Trading Post, Inc., a mail-order firm that sells discount outdoor clothing and equipment. SafeCard, with four hundred employees and $152 million in revenues, captured quick seven-figure tax savings from the move, says cofounder and former CEO Steve Halmos.

For over twenty years, SafeCard prospered in Florida. But the fragrance of lower costs 'cross the Wyoming fence was too sweet. A more stable work force; lower taxes; lower real estate costs—all said, "Move!"

Keith Richardson, Sierra Trading's president, was based in Sparks, Nevada, but moved his eighty-employee company to Wyoming in 1991. "In the mail-order business we have to compete with other companies nationwide, so we have to be in the lowest-cost area," says Richardson.

Sierra was fast outgrowing its Sparks facility, so Richardson made his own detailed study of what it would cost to conduct business in other western states. Wyoming won. Because the state is more centrally located, and about 60% of Sierra's customers are east of the Rockies, Richardson figures he's saving over $25,000 annually in UPS costs to ship his products.

Some cities have emerged as cost-cutting havens for specific industries. Omaha, for example, long known as home to the U.S. Strategic Air Command (SAC), has become a magnet for telecommunications companies. Thanks in part to SAC, Omaha's telecommunications infrastructure beats that of just about any other city in the country. Omaha is also centrally located (better for cross-time-zone calling) and offers some of the cheapest incoming and outgoing 800 rates.

This too: Even *thinking aloud* about a move could save your business money. Worried local authorities may offer incentives for your company to stay put. Either way, with a new "Move It!" mentality, you win.

SAVE-A-BUNDLE FOLLOW-UP FILE

• Call the economic or business development office in any state (usually a Commerce Department unit), region, or community for information on incentives for companies thinking of moving or expanding to the area. Counting all levels, there are now an estimated fifteen thousand business development groups nationwide. Some of the more aggressive states will tailor a welcome package, depending on your size and what you need. Look for help in arranging finances, site selection, and other red carpet treatment. You should be able to get a free cost analysis of what a move would mean to your company, including such items as real estate, taxes, labor, and utilities.

• The American Economic Development Council (AEDC) at 9801 West Higgins Road, #540, Rosemont, IL 60018-4726, (708) 692-9944; fax (708) 696-2990, can supply the names of local economic development agencies in areas you may be considering for a move.

• Right Choice, Inc., based in Salem, Massachusetts, provides cost-of-living or cost-of-doing-business comparisons for individuals and companies considering a move. The cost depends on the size and complexity of your business. Call (800) 872-2294; fax (508) 741-2022.

TACTIC #9
Team Up with a Top Travel Firm

For the average U.S. company, travel costs are the third-largest *controllable* expense, behind payroll and data processing. A typical business trip now costs $1,023, the biggest part of it airfare (41%) and hotels (25%).

For companies of all sizes, two simple moves can tote up travel savings pronto: Team up with a top-notch travel agent, and consolidate all of your travel buying there. Actually, the term *agent* is outdated. The major business travel players now do a whole lot more than book tickets and hotels. They've evolved into multiservice travel *management* companies. Over the next ten years, the best of this new breed of travel service vendor will help save companies—perhaps yours included—tens of millions of travel expense dollars.

A good travel company—whether it's a megafirm like Minneapolis-based Carlson Travel Network, aerospace spinoff McDonnell Douglas Travel Co., in Irvine, California, or a small local agency—is worth its weight in free airfare coupons, and then some. These emissaries of travel and entertainment (T&E) savings can be brutal bloodhounds, sniffing out the best airfares from an odoriferous pile of choices, grabbing great hotel discounts and raucous rental car deals. That's for starters. For expense-cutting help that costs your company *nothing*, travel management firms will be the best business T&E deal of the next ten years. Any size company can benefit. Small companies can save hundreds or thousands; giants save millions. General Electric's early nineties move to consolidate its travel buying at Carlson was expected to save GE *$50 million* per year.

Here's some of what you gain:

- Time and improved mental health. Rube Goldberg–like fare structures, frustrating frequent-travel awards, off-and-on-and-off-again discounts, and the meganumber of choices available for going from point A to points B and C make intelligent travel planning impossible for mere mortals.

- A good agency can help your company manage travel costs and identify potential savings. Firms that work mostly with business clients may offer monthly reports on your company's total travel expenses, along with a cost-saving analysis showing published fares and rates compared to what your company paid—a handy tool to keep travel costs in check.

- Your business travel manager can deliver tickets, itineraries, hotel confirmations, and other travel documents directly to your office, on short notice.

- Have you ever stayed at a hotel and *not* received the corporate rate? The difference can be big; one business traveler might pay the $195 "rack rate" for a room while another traveler in an identical room pays the $155 "corporate rate." A travel manager makes sure it's the other person paying top dollar.

- Travel managers can suggest potential savings if your itinerary is flexible. For example, a minor switch of flight time can reduce a fare by hundreds of dollars if all the "cheap seats" are gone on the first-choice flight.

- The business traveler whose plans never change is rare;

agent/managers can help you make changes on the fly at the lowest cost.

All this costs you nothing. Travel agents earn their commissions from the vendors—typically 7% to 15% on plane tickets and hotel rooms.

There are thousands of small and midsized travel firms to choose from. Check out the premium players in your area; see what services they can offer your business.

SAVE-A-BUNDLE FOLLOW-UP FILE

• One of the most quality- and service-conscious innovators in the field—a megaagency that promises to outpunch the travel competition in years ahead—is Rosenbluth International in Philadelphia. This is a hundred-year-old, leading edge, family-run firm. From $120 million in travel sales as a regional firm in the early 1980s, Rosenbluth has exploded into a $1.5 billion leader with some six hundred locations. Hal Rosenbluth, president and CEO, is a maverick whose mission is to find ever-better ways to provide business travel customers with cost-management services. For example, a special hotel savings program, installed in 1991, saved one Fortune 100 client $1.3 million on annual hotel spending of $7 million. Call an office in your area or Rosenbluth headquarters at (215) 981-1700.

• The National Business Travel Association, in Alexandria, Virginia, is a trade group of business travel managers. Membership is $225/year. Call (703) 684-0836.

• Professional certification isn't a must with travel agents, but it's a plus. Only nine states regulate or require agents to register: California, Florida, Hawaii, Illinois, Iowa, Ohio, Oregon, Rhode Island, and Washington. One professional credential of note is the Certified Travel Counselor (CTC) designation, which is awarded to agents who complete a special two-to-three-year, senior-level travel management program. About one in fifteen agents has the CTC degree. For a list of active certified travel agents in your area, call the Institute of Certified Travel Agents at (800) 542-4282.

- Membership in the American Society of Travel Agents is also a good sign. You can reach ASTA at 1101 King Street, Alexandria, VA 22314; (703) 739-2782; fax (703) 684-8319.
- See Chapter 7 for other money-saving T&E tactics.

TACTIC #10
Cost-Conscious ADA Compliance

The Americans with Disabilities Act (ADA) is one of the most expansive laws U.S. companies have faced. ADA requirements touch everything from your hiring practices, to your signs, to your bathroom fixtures.

Compliance will cost virtually all businesses money. Just how much depends in part on how adroit you are at answering the law's requirements without panic spending, and to what extent you take advantage of available financial incentives.

In short: Comply you must, but a cost-conscious approach can save your company cash.

ADA has two basic parts. The employment provisions specify how you must deal with disabled employees or job applicants; the public accommodation rules say how your company must physically accommodate the needs of disabled customers. All companies, no matter what size, must comply with the public accommodation rules. And while businesses with fewer than twenty-five employees were exempt from the employment provisions when ADA became effective in 1992, as of mid-1994 the exemption applies only to companies with fewer than fifteen employees.

When facing bureaucratic bulldogs such as ADA, companies often overspend because they lack information on what's required. Knowledge is the key to cost-effective compliance. Find out what's required, then figure out what changes your company must make and what financial incentives you can tap. The alternative is to risk lawsuits or other costs of non-compliance later.

Tax Breaks and Other ADA Aid Businesses with thirty or fewer full-time employees or revenues under $1 million can take a 50% tax *credit* for money spent on ADA compliance between $250 and $10,250. That could put up to $5,000 *per year* back into your pocket, deducted directly from the other taxes your company owes. It's called the Disabled Access Credit (Section 44 of the Internal Revenue Code).

You can also take a *deduction* for up to $15,000 on the cost of removing barriers to the disabled in buildings, vehicles, or other facilities. This one is called the Architectural and Transportation Barrier Removal Deduction (IRC Section 190). Ask your accountant or the IRS (contact below) for details.

Here's another: the Targeted Jobs Tax Credit (IRC Section 51). You get a credit of up to $2,444 per employee on first-year wages for hiring qualified persons with disabilities. This one's subject to congressional renewal; but it's a good bet to remain.

For details on these and other incentives and tax breaks available to business, contact the President's Committee on Employment of People with Disabilities (see the Follow-up File).

SAVE-A-BUNDLE FOLLOW-UP FILE

• *The Americans with Disabilities Act: A Practical Guide to Cost-Effective Compliance* (Panel Publishers, $69) is one of the few ADA compliance books that focuses on costs. Call (800) 638-8437 to order.

• The President's Committee on Employment of People with Disabilities, 1331 F Street, N.W., #300, Washington, DC 20004; (202) 376-6200; fax (202) 376-6219; TDD (202) 376-6205. Offers a free package of ADA compliance information for business, including *Employer Incentives* with information on tax and hiring credits.

• Goodwill Industries, through 173 local offices, works with businesses to review the hiring process for ADA compliance and to assist with accommodations for disabled employees. Offers a free pamphlet, *The ADA: What It Means for America's Businesses*. Contact a local Goodwill office or the national Goodwill Industries office in Bethesda, Maryland, at (301) 530-6500.

• *What Businesses Must Know about the Americans with Disabilities Act* is a broad look at the ADA published by the U.S. Chamber of Commerce ($21; or $14 for members). Order from Publications Fulfillment, 1615 H Street, N.W., Washington, DC 20062; (800) 638-6582. The Chamber also offers *ADA Consultant In-A-Box* ($99.95), a compliance manual that includes tools for measuring accessibility; a video called *The Basics of the Americans with Disabilities Act* ($49.95); and a computer disk called ADA IQ ($59.95), available for both IBM and Macintosh. To order these three items, call (800) 528-1993.

• The Job Accommodation Network (JAN), (800) 526-7234, has been offering free advice to businesses for years on how to accommodate disabled workers. It is located at West Virginia University in Morgantown. For specific ADA questions, call (800) ADA-WORK to speak to a JAN consultant confidentially. You will receive information about possible solutions to your particular situation, including names and phone numbers of other employers who have made similar accommodations.

• For questions involving public accommodation and other provisions of the law, the U.S. Justice Department's ADA information line is (202) 514-0301.

• The *Americans with Disabilities Act Manual*, published by the Bureau of National Affairs, Inc. (BNA), is eight hundred pages of business guidance on ADA. Costs $375 per year, which includes the manual plus a monthly newsletter and updates. Call (800) 372-1033; fax (800) 253-0332; or write BNA Customer Relations, 9435 Key West Avenue, Rockville, MD 20850.

• *Complying with the ADA: A Small Business Guide to*

Hiring and Employing the Disabled by Jeffrey Allen (John Wiley & Sons, 1993) is $17.95. Call (800) 225-5945.

• *The Americans with Disabilities Act: A Compliance Workbook for Small Communities* ($14.95) is an eighty-page guidebook that emphasizes no-cost and low-cost ways to open up services and employment to persons with disabilities. The advice is readily applicable to small businesses. Order from the National Association of Towns and Townships, 1522 K Street, N.W., Suite 600, Washington, DC 20005; (202) 737-5200; fax (202) 289-7996.

• ADA has also brought out the scam artists. For a pamphlet called *How to Avoid Scams and Schemes Related to the Americans with Disabilities Act*, send $1 with a self-addressed envelope to the Council of Better Business Bureaus, Department 023, Washington, DC 20042-0023.

CHAPTER 2

Back-Office Bonanza

TACTIC #11
Park Your Paper Somewhere Else

The theory behind storing your company's documents at an outside firm is this: *Their* space probably costs less than *yours*.

If you really want to be in the archiving business, go to it. But if you'd rather stick to what your business does best and leave the storage chores to others, you can save yourself some serious cents.

Contracts, invoices, blueprints, manuals, copyrights, licenses, a slew of you-name-it paper—and the newest nuisance, computer disks and other "electronic storage media"—are choking businesses today, despite the hollow promise of the "paperless" office. Still, this is vital stuff. You want it *protected*, you want it *accessible*, and you don't want storing it to bleed you dry.

A good cost-cutting move is to park your paper and deposit your disks at one of the growing number of firms nationwide that specialize in document storage and management. (See the Follow-up File for names and numbers.) Major league paper-pushers such as law firms, architects, accountants, or medical offices can benefit most. Unlike *your* records storage, which is probably less than ideal, storage specialists use high-density racks, state-of-the-art security, and bar-coded access systems that can pull a proverbial needle out of a huge paper haystack.

They also offer custom inventory reports and records management consulting. The major storers have outlets in dozens of larger cities, though you can find local firms that do the same. Boston-based Iron Mountain, with fifteen thousand business customers at about fifty-five sites, is the largest records management firm in the United States. C. Richard

Reese, Iron Mountain's president, says that the average company can cut its document storage costs by 20% to 40% by using a good outside firm. That counts savings on real estate, maintenance, security, and administrative staff.

Safesite, a records storage and management firm based in Billerica, Massachusetts, is particularly smug about its claims of saving almost any business 50% or more on the cost of storing, safeguarding, and accessing documents. So smug that the firm will do a free study of your company's system for managing and storing records, including what it's costing you and what you could save by "outsourcing" the task.

Could be a savings pot o' gold. It was for accounting firm Deloitte & Touche, headquartered in Wilton, Connecticut. A document stored by Safesite in 1988 and easily retrieved three years later was critical in helping the firm avoid a $100,000 claim. Deloitte's administration director fired off a memo to the firm's other offices. "We have found that the mismanagement of records can be very costly to the firm in terms of office space for files and the cost of furniture and equipment to store files. Large offices can probably save $50,000 to $100,000 annually [with an outside records management provider]," said he.

TACTIC #12
Banish "Feel-Good" Service Contracts

Service contracts are cloaked insurance. Large businesses in particular love service contracts—on computers, printers, typewriters, telephones, audiovisual equipment, fax machines, heating systems, or whatever—because the safety net gives 'em a fuzzy feeling. But as good as some service contracts are, left unchecked they mostly serve to suck money from company veins.

Hardly a business exists that doesn't have unnecessary, "feel-good" contracts on some of its office equipment. The salesperson sold the service deal—probably called a service *agreement* to avoid the more legal-sounding *contract*— along with the equipment; and gosh it sounded good at the time. The profit margin on service contracts, compounded by renewals year after year, is often much greater than what the seller made on the equipment itself.

Survey your service deals with these questions in mind:

- Do you really need 'em?
- Are you getting your money's worth?
- Is the equipment still in use? Or (horror of horrors) do you even own it?

No need to banish *all* service contracts. Keep the ones that represent a prudent investment and dump those that are an unneeded expense. Here's some guidance:

Contracts on high-reliability equipment are a waste. Fax machines, telephones, personal computers, electronic calculators, and laser printers rarely malfunction these days unless you use the stuff like Hulk Hogan. A service contract on a typical desktop setup, including computer, monitor, modem, and printer, could easily run $500 or more per year. Consider dumping pricey service deals on high-reliability equipment. You'll end up paying more for the contract than it would cost to repair or replace the hardware.

Keep contracts on larger computers (minis and mainframes), specialized data processing and other custom equipment, as well as machines that have lots of moving parts such as copiers (they're getting better but are still breakdown prone), typewriters, printers, shredders, and mailroom equipment such as sorters, binders, and folders. Copier contracts in particular can be quite reasonable.

Here are some other cost-conscious moves for service contracts:

- Don't pay for more service than you need. For example, a contract might offer to send a technician to your door for one price, or let you carry in or send the equipment for 30% to 40% less. You could end up paying a bundle for the house-call option. And look at the fine print. If your breakdown occurs "after hours" you might end up paying even more.

- Avoid long-term contracts and any that renew automatically. Contrary to what Murphy might say, if an electronic component is going to fail, it will usually oblige within the first year when the equipment is still covered by a manufacturer's warranty. Even if a longer-term deal is cheap, the discipline of reviewing the contract in a year or two will save you money.

- If you have paid-up contracts, take advantage of all service you are due—including routine maintenance and cleaning that may be included. Let people who use the equipment at your company know about any service contracts in force. Put somebody in charge.

TACTIC #13
Fix Your Own Computers and Printers

A booming brigade of businesses both huge and humble have found the ultimate solution to high equipment repair costs: Train a few of your own employees in PC repair.

Sure, you'd expect firms like Apple, Hewlett-Packard, and Xerox to employ their own in-house fix-it folks. But even such smaller firms as Texas Eastern Transmission Corp. in Houston and CES Office Products in St. Paul, Minnesota, are doing it too by signing employees up for a brief course in PC repair. Macintosh and printer repair courses are taught too.

Don Doerr is a repair pioneer. He's also president of Santa Ana, California–based National Advancement Corp. (NAC), which provides computer repair training for businesses—including most of the Fortune 1000. Doerr's boast: "We can show any business how to repair a computer for $5 that would cost $500 to have a repair person come and do it." Nice savings. And repair costs are only part of the expense you avoid. Downtime and shipping costs also suck money each time a PC peters.

One of the most costly and risky things your business can do is box the machine and ship it to a retailer or service center, says NAC. *What goes on in the back rooms of those places anyhow?* According to Doerr, the "repair" often means swapping parts with another machine. And sometimes the computer isn't broken at all—the user simply goofed.

In-house PC maintenance avoids downtime and lowers repair bills. An NAC course costs about $1,600 (see Follow-up File for details) and includes a year of support and a manual. Courses are available in southern California, New York, Chicago, Dallas, Atlanta, Boston, Washington, D.C., and other major cities.

TACTIC #14
Equip Your Company with Auctioned and Secondhand Stuff

As anyone who's done it lately can attest, the price tag for outfitting an office is close to the national debt. One decent desk chair: $600 to $800. Maybe more. If you don't mind furnishings with a mismatched, luck-of-the-gavel look, you can save your growing business a small fortune by purchasing at local liquidator auctions. For $500 you can probably furnish an office with fixtures that would sell for *five times* that much new. At savings that could reach tens of thousands of dollars, do you care if colors clash? (Remember, the previous owners were probably businesses that bought the stuff at full price and went bust!)

Sure, if you're a hotsy-totsy law or other professional firm looking to impress clients, this tactic's not for you. But if money in your pocket is more important than designer drapes on your walls, here's what you can do:

- Plan ahead—weeks or even months before you need the goods. This isn't a buy-for-delivery-tomorrow deal. Check out local newspapers for office liquidation notices. They're actually quite common. Get details on what's available that meets your needs—brands, sizes, condition.

- Before you buy anything, *find out what the items you're interested in would cost new.* Essential! Without this info you're bargain-hunting blind. You can't be sure what a bargain really is.

- Show up. Get the feel with a couple of small purchases. The basic rule of all auction buying applies: *Don't get carried away.* Decide what's a good deal and pay no more. Beg or borrow a truck to cart your cache back to the office yourself.

- If you plan regular purchases, get to know the people who do liquidation sales. Let 'em know what you're interested in and they'll call you when new sales are coming up.

Finding good secondhand stuff is the bulk of this battle. See the Follow-up File for some good resources, including the Machinery Dealers National Association in Silver Spring, Maryland.

When it comes to sniffing out good used equipment in the farming, construction, trucking, aviation, and related areas, a terrific resource is Heartland Communications Group, Inc., in Fort Dodge, Iowa. Heartland publishes a bumper crop of used-equipment *Hot Line* directories sold by subscription. From cranes to forklifts, combines to spreaders, tractors to punch presses, Heartland's directories are a mother lode of good leads. As Heartland's CEO Joseph Peed likes to remind people, "Many new machines are lemons. Just poor design and workmanship. Smart buyers can buy and utilize good used equipment just as well as new equipment, without putting a lot of dollars into the investment." Reach Heartland at (800) 247-2000.

Cost-Cutting at Dell

Cut-rate computer maker Michael Dell of Austin, Texas–based Dell Computer is one small-company-turned-big that worries about office bloat. As a result, this $1 billion company has dumped executive credenzas (who needs 'em?) and buys only *used* furniture. Dell faced up to cutthroat cost-cutting in the PC biz by aggressively cutting costs himself as a percentage of his company's sales.

TACTIC #15
Coax New Life from Old Computers

Obsolescence is a fact of computerized life. Yesterday's state-of-the-art systems quickly become sniveling heaps of scrap.

But many businesses trash cash by junking computers before their time is really up. There are several ways to upgrade those old workhorses in your computer stable and squeeze out a few more years of labor. In some cases, you can even turn the old geezers into powerhouse studs. For example, you can:

- Install more microchips or a hard disk to expand memory. This lets your computer handle more sophisticated software applications. If you're working just with floppies, adding a hard drive will move you into the computing big leagues.
- Install a video display card to add color and graphics capabilities. A quick and easy upgrade.
- Install an accelerator card. Speeds things up; lets your old computer run newer, more powerful software.
- Install advanced operating software to teach your computer new tricks.

- Install a "prosthetic" device—a souped-up monitor, fax modem, or disk drive—to give the computer more over-all reach.

You can turn an old, upgraded machine into a dedicated workhorse by assigning it a single, designated task. For example, an old PC and printer setup, equipped with mailing list and label-printing software, could be the workhorse for pumping out your company's mailings. That lets you sidestep the time-wasting process of switching paper and labels in your other equipment and gives this machine something to do. Or, by adding a special circuit board to the machine's brains, you can turn an old PC into a fax or a telephone answering machine.

A local computer vendor can install the upgrades for you. Or if you're the tinkering type (or you employ one), a good move is to get one of the books listed below. This approach isn't for computerphobes, though you needn't be a techie to tune in to the value left in old machines.

Books and videos on upgrading:

- *New Life for Old PCs* is published by BusinessOne Irwin and costs $29.95 in paperback in bookstores, or order from the publisher at (800) 634-3966. Author Alfred Poor is a contributing editor of *PC Magazine*.
- *Upgrade or Repair Your PC and Save* by Aubrey Pilgrim (TAB/McGraw-Hill, $19.95). Call (800) 822-8138; fax (800) 932-0183. A good book for the non-nerd.
- *The ABCs of Upgrading Your PC* by Dan Gookin (SYBEX, $21.95). Call (800) 227-2346. Another good treatment of the subject for the computer novice.
- *The Complete PC Upgrade and Maintenance Guide* by Mark Minasi (SYBEX, $29.95). Call (800) 227-2346.
- *Upgrading and Troubleshooting PCs* is a forty-five-minute video with a forty-eight-page booklet. Cost is $24.95 from M-USA Video. Call (800) 933-6872.

TACTIC #16
Discover the Deals in Used Computers

If upgrades won't do, here's another cost-conscious way to get what you need. Sell what you have for cash and buy what you need through the fast-expanding market for used computers. It was a long time coming, but a market for buying and selling used computer equipment is finally taking hold. Firms that broker used equipment—matching buyers and sellers, handling the money, and taking a commission for their trouble—are in place and growing fast.

These used-equipment exchanges are taking the stigma, and a bit of the risk, out of buying used equipment. Buy/sell prices are widely published. The exchange puts a buyer's money in escrow until the buyer receives the equipment and has a chance to verify its condition. Discounts generally range between 25% and 50% off what the equipment would cost in a store.

You can exploit this new market in two ways. It's a great place to sell equipment you're no longer using or have outgrown. And you may be able to find some bargains on upgraded computers that you need. The key is to have an expert look over a potential purchase before you close the deal. But computers aren't like cars. If they're gonna fail, they'll usually oblige within the original warranty period. There are billions of dollars' worth of perfectly good used equipment that the previous owner has simply outgrown.

The two tough questions—How do you find that equipment? How do you know what it's worth?—are where the exchanges help out. They publish hoards of pricing information on what used equipment is selling for, available (usually for a price) via reports, newsletters, or telephone hotlines. The New York–based National Computer Exchange (NACOMEX USA), for example, is a fast-growing computer brokerage company that has franchised its service nationwide, offering speedy trades, guarantees, service contracts, escrow protection, and pricing information. Another such firm is the

Boston Computer Exchange, which charges a 15% commission (paid by the seller) on sales it arranges. See the Follow-up File for where to reach the exchanges.

TACTIC #17
Tone Up Your Laser Cartridges

Say you pay a dollar for a cup of coffee (it's *good* coffee) at a chintzy eatery that charges fifty cents for refills. Now say you want a second cup. Would you pay the fifty cents for a fill-up or fork over the buck to get your java in a clean cup?

Businesses that pay full price—typically $100—for new toner cartridges each time their laser printer runs low are paying big bucks for a clean cup when a lower-priced refill will do the same job. Trading your empty toner cartridge for a refilled one will cost only $40 to $50 in most areas. The extra $50 to $60 is a hefty price to pay for essentially nothing.

Most laser printers work just as well with refilled cartridges as with new ones. And that includes the most popular brands—Apple, Hewlett-Packard, Canon. All you have to do is locate a recharger in your area. The good ones make house calls to install your new (refilled) cartridge and pick up the old one; many also provide routine cleaning and maintenance for laser printers for an extra charge.

Look in the Yellow Pages, ask other businesses in your area, check ads in local business and computer publications, or ask the dealer who sold you the printer for recommendations. If that doesn't work, the International Cartridge Recycling Association at (202) 857-1154 can provide a list of cartridge rechargers in your area. Fax (202) 223-4579.

Also of interest to card-carrying skinflints is Discoversoft, Inc.'s program TonerSaver, a PC software utility that saves about a penny per page each time you print by reducing toner usage about 50% to 70%. The type looks gray, so it's only good for printing drafts, not finished pieces. But the savings can add up if your volume is heavy. Suggested retail is $39.95. Call (510) 769-2902; fax (510) 769-0149.

TACTIC #18
Avoid Office Supply Anarchy

Office supplies have a knack for picking your company's pocket. Most businesses waste office supply money in a variety of ways: A sweet-talking salesperson sells 'em supplies that aren't needed. They constantly buy small quantities of supplies and pay the highest prices. They run out of needed supplies and pay for rush orders. They never comparison shop.

To keep a lid on your office supply costs, set up a simple system to track your purchases and on-hand supplies.

- List the items you regularly need and how much of each should be on hand. That helps you prevent ordering in dribs and drabs.
- Consolidate supply purchases for quantity discounts and put one person in charge of all ordering. Funnel catalogs and sale information to that person; have that individual keep a catalog library, available to anyone looking for specific items.
- Compose a brief form (half a page, max) to use internally for supply requests. This avoids costly ordering errors and makes sure people get what they want.
- Order as much as a year's worth of cheap, low-usage items at a time. High volume lowers price and avoids constant reordering. Schedule seasonal buys (holiday greeting cards, for example) well in advance to get the best price.
- Establish an ordering schedule—quarterly; once a month; every second Friday; etc. Easier to consolidate orders; saves on shipping.

- Keep supplies in a single location with labeled shelves or bins. Lock bulk supplies in storage; leave only short-term quantities open and available.
- Order in standard round lots. For example: Envelopes generally come five hundred to a box. Ordering, say, twelve hundred splits a box, costs more, and risks damaged or lost supplies due to open packages.
- Keep an itemized copy of each order; check it against supplies received. Follow up immediately on any errors.

Cost-Cutting at Quill

Quill Corp., an office supply distributor with a thousand employees, not only preaches office supply efficiency, the company eats its own cost-control cooking. With competition from office supply superstores chomping at Quill's coffers, Jack Miller, president, and his brothers Harvey and Arnold installed a new cost-cutting mind-set at Quill. Their attack included these moves:

For a distributor such as Quill, order processing accounts for a huge expense. So Miller looked there for savings. The company cut sixteen hundred desk trays (unnecessary) and replaced an entire sales manual with a condensed single laminated sheet. *Estimated material savings: $2,700.*

Quill negotiated a lower price for shipping cartons, *saving $25,000 annually;* and a new cleaning contract for a *$7,000 savings.* The company cut costs yet another *$7,000* by switching to a new copier maintenance firm for the company's fifteen machines.

Designing and printing smaller forms (Tactic #30 has more cost-cutting ideas on printing) helped save Quill *$90,000* in that category. And a new desktop publishing system (Tactic #105) for the advertising department is expected to save Quill a hefty *$150,000 monthly.*

TACTIC #19
Go for "Fighting Brands" and Private Label Products

Buying office supplies is a lot like buying groceries or prescription drugs. You can pay top dollar for national brand names, or buy similar stuff in a private label or generic package for a lot less. The object is to skip the brand-name items when all you're paying for is their advertising and marketing budget.

What most business buyers don't know is that many brand-name office supply producers have a "fighting brand"—a relabeled version of a brand-name product priced lower to "fight'" the discount competition. For example, this strategy lets 3M (its fighting brand tape is called Highland) boost sales without damaging the hallowed 3M name.

If you're concerned about quality, sample house or fighting brand products before you make any larger orders. If the products measure up, you can probably save 10% to 25%.

TACTIC #20
Pick the Right Supplier for *Your Business*

Organize a vendor search. If your company has grown, you may have outgrown your previous office products supplier. Target three to five choices from among these categories, then compare prices (on items you actually *use*, same brand names and quantities), service, selection, shipping, and other terms:

- Small local vendor or office supply dealer.
- Office supply superstore or warehouse store.
- Large contract stationer/vendor.
- Mail-order supply house.

If your company is small, you'll probably find the lowest prices at a superstore or by mail order. Shopping in person saves you shipping costs. A single supplier may not have the best price on all items that you need. So don't rule out splitting your orders between more than one supplier—taking advantage of each firm's best prices for what you use. Larger companies do best at a contract vendor that carries enough inventory to avoid any "stockouts" that leave your order hanging.

Selling office supplies is highly competitive. Prices can easily differ by 10% to 20% between different office supply outlets. Have you compared prices lately? If not, you could be passing up huge savings on the items you use most. Catalogs make comparisons easy. They usually price items individually, then show discounts or unit prices for quantities.

Don't waste your time comparing prices on seldom-used items. Focus on the handful of items that account for the bulk of your office supply costs. Buy from suppliers that allow full refunds for returns made within ninety days.

TACTIC #21
Seek Out Sales, Combine Purchases, and Ask for Quantity Quotes

---

Watch for sales *on items you regularly order*, and stock up. Make it a practice to inquire about any current or upcoming sales whenever you order—including sales on other brands.

For items ordered separately at different locations, combine purchases and ask for a large-quantity quote. Some vendors offer additional discounts beyond what you'll see in their catalogs or price sheets, but you'll need to ask; and you'll probably save shipping costs too. The Dallas-based Rosewood Hotels & Resorts, which owns or operates luxury hotels in the United States, London, and elsewhere, rolled up some serious savings on toilet paper when it started consolidating purchases for quantity discounts. When Rosewood grouped its TP purchases at a single supplier, instead of the many it had been using, the price savings hit an estimated $15,000.

TACTIC #22
Factor In Freight

Be sure to factor in shipping costs. Cheap supplies don't mean much if you get fleeced on delivery charges. Unless you shop retail or your supplier is local, freight costs can be factored a zillion different ways. Before you order, check the cost of getting the goods to your door. Add that to the price for your *real* cost.

According to Quill Corp., the office products firm in Lincolnshire, Illinois, shipping ranges from 2% to 5% of the total cost for a lightweight, high-value item such as a calculator, to as much as 40% of the price for a low-cost, bulky item such as a filing cabinet. For large items that must move by truck, there's usually a minimum charge of perhaps $30 to $50 for shipping. As long as you're forking over that freight fee, any additional items you add to your order to bring it up to the weight limit for the minimum fee can ride free!

TACTIC #23
Quash Unneeded Quality

Jack Miller of Quill Corp. sees it daily: Businesses waste big money on quality they don't need and don't use. "The big savings come by knowing when to buy a different item or brand that will still get the job done," says Miller.

Example: To mail a sixteen-page letter-sized document, a twenty-four-pound gummed flap envelope will get it there just as well as a thirty-two-pound clasp envelope—*at 33% less cost*. Ditto for calculators. Why pay $100 for a souped-up calculator with fancy algebraic functions if all you need it for is basic math? A solar-powered, low-end Canon model for around $10 will do the job beautifully.

TACTIC #24
Foil These Photocopying Follies

Don't photocopy high-volume items that you should be printing. Copies typically cost a company five to fifteen cents each—including paper, toner, the labor for someone to stand there and feed the machine (especially on slow copiers), maintenance, and other overhead costs. Printing can lower your cost to as little as three cents each. Also remember: The more copies you make on a leased machine, the more they might cost if you exceed the lease contract's maximum. A typical overage charge: a penny and a half per copy.

The biggest cost culprits are various forms, notices, and form letters that are used in *seemingly* small quantities. Maybe your business uses only, say, ten form letters per week. So someone simply photocopies thirty or forty at a time. That's still over five hundred per year, and at that level you can save time and money by having it printed. Printed items look better, too. You may be able to upgrade the paper and still come out ahead.

Most company copiers are grossly overused—a document that three people should see is distributed to twenty. To break the excess-copying habit, post a copy-conservation notice at the machine and periodically ask employees to think twice about copy volume. Every copy made should be *necessary*, not merely habitual.

Photocopying for personal use is another expense. To

thwart that costly practice, install a tracking system—perhaps just a sign-up sheet—to see where copies are being made. Or ask employees to pay a small honor-system charge.

Copying on two sides of the paper saves money. That can be a pain since many copiers force you to feed it through twice to achieve this. If your company is particularly copy-intensive, consider buying or leasing a high-speed "duplex" copier (for us low-tech folks, that's a two-sided copier). The dramatic paper usage reduction helps offset the higher cost of the machine. See the Follow-up File for two great copier-buying resources, *What to Buy for Business* and *UPDATE: The Executive's Purchasing Advisory*.

TACTIC #25
Think Small

Here's a penny-pinching tip from Sally Cunningham of Orion Rifle Barrel in Kalispell, Montana: "In our mail-order business we found that 90% of our customers were buying only one item and [so] a smaller invoice would do the job and save us money. We were buying bound books of invoices at $4.75 for fifty, but by going to a smaller size we now pay $3.40 for fifty—a 28% savings."

TACTIC #26
Always Use Purchase Orders

Purchase orders are a cost control *must*. Few cash-conscious companies make significant purchases without a P/O. But many businesses—especially fast-growing companies—tend to view 'em as unnecessary paperwork. Buy a standard pack of P/Os from any supply outlet for under $10, and keep a tight lid on who's allowed to use them.

More paperwork, yes—but of the vital variety. A purchase order system helps focus all supply buying in a single location, with a single person in charge of authorizing the expense. Don't let individuals or different departments in the company buy their own supplies. That's horribly inefficient and ends up costing your business dearly.

TACTIC #27
Make "Rush" a Purchasing
Four-Letter Word

Okay, so it already *is* a four-letter word. Make it a *dirty* four-letter word. Rushing isn't something that should have to occur when ordering materials and supplies from your company. Some local suppliers—of office products and other business consumables—now offer a value-added service: They'll check your stock and reorder for you.

Sounds like putting the fox in charge of the chicken coop. But don't dump the idea so fast. You'll still check the bills and watch what the vendor is doing. At the same time, you get free labor to monitor supply levels and make sure the business doesn't run out. The vendor may even offer valuable advice on available discounts and purchasing efficiencies.

TACTIC #28
Enlist Employee Help for "Little Things"

Everyone who takes home a paycheck from your company can help cut overhead expenses with a little nudge from the paycheck provider. Here are a few of the best ideas:

- Enlist everyone's support in an annual Office Supply Roundup. Make a game of it. The challenge: Find as many usable supplies as possible lying around in storage cabinets, on shelves, in desk drawers, or other out-of-the-way places. You may be surprised. When Memphis-based Champion Awards, Inc., did it, the company collected enough to last for months. Give a prize to the winning supply scavenger.

- Use company letterhead for outgoing materials only. Send internal notes on plain paper or on the back of a sales letter that would be trashed anyway. Also, type two short memos on one page, then cut the page in half. Better yet, post a single memo on a bulletin board rather than copying dozens of handouts. Best of all, if your company has an electronic mail system, use that.

- Use a plain, small fax cover sheet. Since the fax machine reads every mark on the page, eliminating unnecessary boxes, rules, characters, and designs cuts transmission time. Or dump the cover sheet entirely.

- To save money spent correcting mistakes, make sure everyone can operate the office equipment. Experienced employees can hold periodic in-house training sessions to update newcomers.

- When you add a copier, fax, or printer, make sure that paper and other parts are interchangeable with machines you already have, or can at least be ordered from the same supplier.

TACTIC #29
Scrap Some Subscriptions

Newsletter publishing—a disproportionate amount of it oozing from Washington, D.C.—is a multibillion-dollar industry. And the really big money is in selling industry publications to companies like yours. The more gumption the newsletter publisher's got, the higher the price. The wimps sell theirs for $100 per year; the more brazen for $1,500 or more. Some newsletters deliver your money's worth. Many don't come close. That's your call.

The big question is whether you even read these gilded grab bags of grammar for which you pay so dearly. Many high-priced publications go from doorway to Dumpster with nary a glance. Might as well dump the dough; save time and postage. Trade magazines and newspapers don't usually command the same extortionist prices as some newsletters, but if you're subscribing to half a dozen or more at $40 to $150 per year, you're into serious money here too.

Two steps will help cut your subscription costs: (1) Add up everything you spend on subscriptions. (2) Cut the ones you don't need; or if you're buying multiple subs, at least cut the duplicates. To get more mileage from your subscriptions, set up a company library. Needn't be anything fancy; perhaps a closet or bookshelf. Appoint a "librarian"; make that person responsible for routing publications to those who need to see them.

TACTIC #30
Pursue Cost Cuts in What You Print

All companies waste money on printing. The only question is how much. Here are some things you can do:

- Remember the first cost-control commandment of printing: The more you print, the cheaper it gets. The cost to print five hundred copies of a one-page item in black-and-white is only pocket change cheaper than printing a thousand—roughly $68 versus $77, depending on the paper grade. For another $92 you can get five thousand copies printed—*ten times the volume for one and a half times the price.*

    Economies of scale work better here than in almost any other line of business. Whether you're printing a few hundred or a few million, the more you can combine print runs, the more money you'll save.

The table that follows shows an approximate unit price for each printed piece in different print runs. Order five hundred copies of a four-page marketing brochure in black-and-white and they'll cost you twenty-two cents each. Order five thousand and the price plunges to a tad over six cents.

To bulk up volume for better prices, print items in larger quantities, less frequently. For example, if your company uses a business reply response card in bulk mailings printed six times a year, consider printing a year's worth all at once to save money. Here are actual prices from a Houston-based printer's price list:

SAMPLE PRICE BREAKS ON PRINT VOLUME

| | | QUANTITY PRINTED | | |
| | | 500 | 5,000 | 50,000 |
	Pages	Approximate price per piece		
Black-and-White	1	$0.14	$0.03	$0.02
	4	0.22	0.06	0.05
	8	0.43	0.14	0.11
	24	1.24	0.42	0.33
Two-Color	1	$0.22	$0.05	$0.03
	4	0.35	0.09	0.06
	8	0.72	0.19	0.12
	24	2.15	0.56	0.37
Four-Color	1	$0.42	$0.07	$0.04
	4	0.64	0.13	0.07
	8	1.15	0.26	0.16
	24	3.42	0.77	0.48

- Check out cheaper papers. Companies often spend big bucks indulging in expensive papers that far exceed the needs of the job. Even if your business "has always used this paper," compare price and quality of others that are cheaper. Even a small downgrade in paper quality can mean big savings, and few people will notice any difference. Ask the printer for advice; some offer better deals on paper they regularly stock, even if it's not exactly what you had in mind.

- Be a black-and-white believer. Who says that color always has more impact? Sometimes, yes. Fact is, though, many print jobs use color poorly anyway, so the extra cost of color—especially full color (a.k.a. *four-color*)—is wasted. Black-and-white, done well, can stand out in its own way. And the cost savings (color printing can easily bump costs 300% to 400% or more) by using black-and-white can let you spend more on quality design talent, typesetting, and paper—*and still come away with money in your pocket*.

  If color's in the cards, you might get it for less by bending your schedule a bit. Some small printers use certain color inks on certain days (depending on the type of press, changing inks can require a printer to wash down the entire press; hence a higher cost). If you print on those days and want those colors, you may avoid an extra color charge.

- Lay in this letterhead thrift: Ever use flashy company letterhead for routine or internal correspondence or, worse, note taking? Try printing two kinds. Use the deluxe color version on opulent paper for clients, customers, prospects, and people you want to impress. The black-and-white version can suffice for other needs. It needn't look cheap, however. By selecting a good grade of paper but axing the fancy inks or embossing, you can save a bundle and still show some class.

- Be accurate; be decisive. "Catching mistakes before documents go to the printer can cut publication costs significantly," says *Communication Briefings*, a newsletter based in Blackwood, New Jersey. You avoid the cost of making corrections in the proof stage; or worse, having to rerun the job because there's an error you didn't catch.

  Making changes late in the printing game is also costly. No, make that *horribly* costly. Changes cause a snowball effect. New type has to be set; designs change; overtime is incurred; schedules are blown. It all costs money, so make up your mind!

- Safeguard your "camera-ready art" (the finished material the printer needs to get started) for print jobs that you'll repeat. The second go-round will be cheaper since the original materials can be reused. Also ask the printer to keep film on file for any print jobs that you'll repeat. That'll save another charge.

- Use cost-wise design. The more rules, picture boxes, and tints that a layout person designs into your print project, the higher the cost. Don't give designers or art directors carte blanche to do whatever they want to make it look pretty. Ask them to design with stripping, color separation, and printing costs in mind.

SAVE-A-BUNDLE FOLLOW-UP FILE

- *What to Buy for Business* offers detailed, unbiased (they accept no advertising) comparisons and recommendations on a full range of office equipment and services. A quick read could help you avoid a costly equipment-buying blunder. Each of the ten yearly *What to Buy* issues focuses on a product category such as copiers, fax machines, mailing equipment, computers, laser printers, phone and messaging systems, and other items. If you haven't read *What to Buy*'s analysis, you haven't done your equipment-buying "due diligence." A year's subscription is $112; single issues cost $21 (buy two and get a third free). What To Buy For Business, Inc., One Rebecca Lane, Pleasantville, NY 10570; (800) 247-2185; fax (914) 741-1367.

- *The Office Equipment Adviser* ($24.95), published by What To Buy For Business, Inc. (see above), is an indispensable, 512-page equipment buyer's companion aimed at offices with one to one hundred people. Fantastic what- and how-to-buy advice on copiers, fax machines, PCs, computer networks, laser printers, phone systems, voice messaging, cellular phones, typewriters, postage meter systems, and shredders. This would be a bargain at many times the price. Don't miss it. Available through bookstores, or call (800) 247-2185.

• *UPDATE: The Executive's Purchasing Advisory* is a sixteen-page monthly newsletter ($95/year), completely subscriber supported, that also gives unbiased reports on products and services for your office. Subscription includes a free problem-solving hotline. Write to Buyers Laboratory, Inc., 20 Railroad Avenue, Hackensack, NJ 07601. Call (201) 488-0404; fax (201) 488-0461.

• For general information on the National Computer Exchange, Inc. (NACOMEX USA), call (800) 622-6639 or write to 118 East 25th Street, 10th Floor, New York, NY 10010. Reach the Boston Computer Exchange at (800) 262-6399. Other used computer exchanges include the Georgia-based American Computer Exchange at (800) 786-0717, and the Western Computer Exchange in New Mexico at (505) 883-8911.

• To find used metalworking or other capital equipment, consider one of the 470 members of the Machinery Dealers National Association, based in Silver Spring, MD. MDNA members abide by an ethics code, are experienced pros who buy, repair, and sell used machinery, and publish a monthly *Locator,* which lists used machines for sale. For a free copy of MDNA's *Used Machinery Buyer's Guide* call (301) 585-9494.

• RE'NU Office Systems, with locations in Santa Ana and Santa Fe Springs, California, remanufactures and sells office furniture to companies throughout the west. The company does all refurbishing work in-house and offers a one-year warranty. Call (714) 259-1440.

• *Used Equipment Directory* (Penton Publications, $45/year) is a monthly that lists dealers and items for sale. Call (800) 526-6052; fax (201) 393-9553.

• For the money ($2), a fifty-page booklet called *How to Save Money on Office Supplies* published by Quill Corp. packs a lot of money-saving punch. Order from Quill at 100 Schelter Road, Lincolnshire, IL 60069; (708) 634-4850; fax (708) 634-5708. Lots of cost-conscious tips on buying specific products—

from ring binders, computer disks, and file folders to calculators and office chairs.

• Here are three leading document storage firms with outlets in dozens of major cities. Call for specifics.

- Safesite: (800) 255-8218; fax (508) 670-5406
- Iron Mountain Records Management: (800) 883-8000; fax (617) 350-7881
- Pierce Leahy Archives: (800) 468-3474; fax (215) 992-8388.

• Xerox Corp., the folks whose machines are responsible for so much of today's document deluge, have jumped in with their own Business Services unit that helps companies store and manage their paper. Grand Metropolitan, a conglomerate that includes Green Giant, Burger King, and Pearle Vision Centers, chose Xerox Business Services (XBS) to manage its computer printing operation. Grand Met's paper output was chopped almost 50%, and first-year savings of about $300,000 paid for nearly the entire three-year contract with Xerox. Call XBS marketing manager Walter Thompson at (716) 383-7746.

• *The Office Expense Reduction System* ($195) by cost-cutting consultant Tod Snodgrass is several hundred pages of highly detailed advice that will quickly pay for itself and then some. As a cost-cutting specialist and seminar speaker in such areas as office supplies, printing, and office equipment, Snodgrass has helped many larger companies snag savings in the millions. Order the book or reach Snodgrass at Cost Control Consultants, 2464 Rue Le Charlene, Suite 944, Palos Verdes, CA 90274; (310) 831-2770.

• National Advancement Corp. (NAC) is headquartered at 2730-J South Harbor, Santa Ana, CA 92704; (800) 832-4787; (800) 443-3384 in CA; fax (714) 754-7166.

CHAPTER 3

Manage Lean and Smart

TACTIC #31
Don't Leave Money on the Table

The cost-cutting revolution in American business has made everything (well, *almost* everything) negotiable. Lease provisions. Legal and accounting fees. Ad agency commissions. Goods, services, and contracts of any kind. If you spend money on it, the price is probably negotiable.

That has placed a premium on business negotiating skills. And the most basic negotiating principle is this: If you don't ask, you don't get. So ask. Got an ad agency? Renegotiate. Push for a lower commission—10% or 12% instead of the "standard" 15. Is your lease coming due? There's another opportunity.

Honing your negotiating skills will save your business money in years ahead. You'll be negotiating with vendors of all kinds, with service professionals, with landlords, with customers and potential clients. I talked to super negotiator Bob Woolf to get his best tips and strategies for business. Woolf has negotiated thousands of deals for some of the biggest names in sports and entertainment—Larry Bird, Joe Montana, Gene Shalit, Larry King, and many others—along with a bevy of more routine business deals. Here's Bob's best advice:

- Leave emotions out of it. Deal making doesn't have to be adversarial. You win by being a nice guy and by treating the other person with respect. Business people often think negotiating is a war. It's not a war. A tough-guy approach usually fails. Celebrity lawyer Alan Dershowitz buys it. "Nice guys *can* finish first if they use Woolf's technique," says he.
- Never use the word "demand." Use phrases like, "Can

you live with this?" or "Am I crazy to suggest this?" Be upbeat and encouraging.

- Always invite the other side to make the first offer. The person who names numbers first usually loses. If both sides balk, Woolf suggests some coaxing: "What are you thinking?" or "Give me some idea of what ballpark we're in." Never raise or lower your price until asked to do so.
- No offer is an insult, and "last offers" often change.
- Don't accept an offer to split the difference. If you're at $9,000 and the other party at $10,000 suggests splitting the difference at $9,500, refuse. Instead, consider $9,500 the other person's offer and split *that* difference to $9,250.
- Prepare your arguments and "giveaways" (items you offer to give up) in advance. Find out early if the person you are talking to is authorized to complete the deal.
- If negotiating by phone, be the caller. In person, negotiate in your office. Negotiate when you look good—that is, when sales are strong, you've won an award, etc.
- Don't let print intimidate. So what if the other guy puts it in writing? *It's still negotiable.*
- Keep records of each conversation. Don't try to tell the other side how to run its business. And don't take anything personally. Woolf says he once sent an NBA player's salary request to the general manager and got back this written response:

  Dear Bob: Hahahahahahahahahahahaha!

  Woolf blew it off and eventually got his way. At an impasse, change something, no matter how minor. Make it clear you want but don't need a deal.

Other Negotiating Tactics to Try

- Bargain hard for something you *don't* want. Here's the logic. Latch on to an item that you know the other party, say a landlord, *thinks* you want but that you are willing to give up. For example, landlords hate giving tenants the right to sublease space. But tenants usually want that option. A business that knows it isn't interested in becoming a sublease landlord can use this for leverage. The tactic: Fight hard for the "dummy" item you've targeted along with the other items you want most. Then, if negotiations snag, offer to give up this item (which you don't really want anyway) in return for something you *do* want.

- Making the first *concession* is okay. While you want the other side to make the first offer, making the first concession can actually improve your position, not weaken it. It creates trust and puts you in control, since it's now up to the other side to make a reciprocal concession.
- Surprise doesn't pay. Again, this isn't a war; there's no need to try to jump the other side. Surprises may throw off the other side briefly, but the result will only be a more lengthy process.

TACTIC #32
Be a Delegator, Not a Dictator

Your time is worth more than your employees' time, right? Presto: you can save money by delegating work from higher-cost people (you) to lower-cost people (employees). Small business owners in particular, and many company managers, are stubborn about doling out responsibility. But it's the only way to grow. And by delegating more, you may find that you don't need the extra person you thought you did. That's money saved.

Delegate routine and especially repetitive tasks. Sure they're things you've "always done." But more profitable efforts await. If you want to grow, prosper, or advance, you can't be a one-person band. Also, employees with more responsibilities tend to be *better* employees.

Here are six steps that can help you become a successful delegator:

1. *Lay it on the line.* Tell employees exactly what's expected of them. Put it in writing. Be specific about what

you want, but be flexible if the other person has different ideas. Don't toss new tasks at an unprepared person.

2. *Walk, then run.* Parcel out authority in small but complete packages. Don't delegate partial jobs; that's not really delegating. Then gauge how the individual is handling it. If the prognosis is good, keep it coming.

3. *Don't be a perfectionist.* Expect mistakes. You make 'em and so will others. Bolster confidence by offering constructive solutions, not recriminations.

4. *Get vertical.* Make your employees specialists; don't delegate willy-nilly. Let one person do more in budgeting and finance, another in advertising and marketing.

5. *Monitor but don't interfere.* You're still the buck-stopper. You need to monitor progress and results, but without interfering.

6. *Give praise for a job well done.*

TACTIC #33
Dump Dysfunctional Forms

Cut your costs by streamlining forms, eliminating outdated forms, or by combining several forms into one. If your business is form-intensive, conduct an annual forms audit. Which ones can be dumped? Which combined? Aren't sure? Try asking employees, customers, clients, vendors, and other folks who must actually *use* the forms. They're the ones who know best where simplifications—and savings—can be made.

A study by the Document Design Center of the Washington, D.C.–based American Institutes for Research reports that more than five billion forms are trashed each year by people who make mistakes filling 'em out. That's usually because the form isn't clear on what it wants.

Faulty forms cost you money three ways: (1) Employees must spend time fixing mistakes or following up on missing information. Their time costs you money and so do the phone calls they must make and letters they must write in pursuit of information the form failed to provide. (2) Form filler-outers must call for clarification—perhaps to your 800 number, which adds another expense. (3) You have to print more forms to replace the ones that are trashed.

Carolyn Boccella Bagin, director of the Document Design Center, claims that a business can save a great deal of money by simplifying forms:

- Use plain English. Dump fuzzy phrases and jargon like "Payment recovery voided . . ." when what you mean is "You can't get your money back."
- Ask only for the necessary information. For example, if someone wants to cancel a membership, don't list six other choices.
- Use headings for clarity. For example: "What we agree to do" and "What you agree to do." This shows readers who's responsible for what.
- Courtesy counts on paper too. For example, ask for a name before a Social Security number. Asking in reverse order makes people feel they're being treated only as a number.

TACTIC #34
Lower the Cost of Your Lease

If you haven't negotiated a commercial lease lately—especially a retail lease—you're in luck. Times have changed. A business that's financially stable gets the red-carpet treatment more often from hard-up commercial landlords who once sniffed at the little businesses while doing backflips for the likes of Wal-Mart.

Commercial rents bend with the local economy. Today's $60,000-per-year prime retail space can be tomorrow's $40,000-per-year space. If you leased your space when commercial landlords were riding high, but the area's economy has turned to mush, bargain for a lower rent. Or, you may be able to upgrade your location for the same money. Some lease-lowering examples:

- A new bakery shop franchise in Evanston, Illinois, got three months free to start (on a $1,600-per-month lease) from a landlord who simply didn't have other takers.
- A travel agency in New Jersey moved to a local mall, doubling its space for 20% less rent. The key: choosing a site that sat vacant for *years.*
- A Chicago skin-care products business secured a lease that allows it to move out if sales don't meet expectations.

Think twice before you buy or build. A Tampa-based restaurant chain called Outback Steakhouse, Inc., has kept costs for its rapid expansion (annual sales gains over 100%) low by *renting* cheap strip mall space and converting it into sparsely furnished, dinner-only restaurants.

Try these tactics:

- Shoot for a walk-away clause in a new lease. Virtually unheard of for smaller retailers in the booming eighties, this option grants you the right to break the lease if your sales don't meet specific targets over the next two or three years. In the nineties, more businesses have successfully inserted this clause into their leases.
- Ask for a rent reduction in an existing lease. You scoff. But it's possible. The owner of a two-outlet Jenny Craig weight-loss franchise in Tucson, Arizona, did it. He heard that his landlord was offering space in a new building nearby at rents *lower* than what he was paying. So he asked for a reduction in return for signing a longer lease. The landlord agreed, and knocked out an automatic 5% annual increase that had been in the original lease.
- Start early. Negotiating a new lease (or finding a better deal elsewhere if the landlord won't budge) can take six months or more. If you wait until a few weeks before your

lease is up to start talking, it's already too late. The land-lord wins.

- Ask for more amenities even if the landlord balks at a rent reduction—parking, build-outs (changes in the office lay-out), moving allowances, better signage. Or agree to a higher rent in return for three or four months free.
- Exercise some due diligence. The landlord's looking at your finances; and you should look at the landlord's. Is the building financed? For how much? Are there vacan-cies? Answer these questions and you can get an idea if the landlord is squeezed for cash. Also, can you realisti-cally get what you want elsewhere? Investigate the mar-ket to find out what other leases are going for.

TACTIC #35
Don't Get Zapped by Deadbeat Dads

Here's a lesser-known law—the Family Support Act—that threatens to cost you dough: If you have a deadbeat dad (behind on child support payments) on your payroll, the gov-ernment says you must withhold child support money from his paycheck and pass it along to the authorities. With dead-beat dads owing an estimated $20 billion nationwide, this law promises major cost headaches for companies large and small.

Find out what's up *before* you get zapped. *If you fail to withhold the deadbeat's wages, your company could be held responsible for the child support payments!* Two key publi-cations can answer your questions:

- *The Income Withholder's Role in Child Support* (sixty-seven-page booklet).
- *Wage Withholding for Child Support: An Employer's Guide* (eighteen-page brochure).

Both are free from the U.S. Department of Health and Human Services, Office of Child Support Enforcement, National Reference Center, Mail Stop OCSE/RC, 370 L'Enfant Promenade, S.W., Washington, DC 20447. Call (202) 401-9383. The shorter brochure includes a complete listing of state child support enforcement offices—a good place to call for information about state requirements that may also apply.

TACTIC #36
Bulletproof Your Business Reimbursables

Many service and professional firms can recoup out-of-pocket expenses and other overhead from customers or clients—phone calls, food, photocopies, mileage, postage, etc. The question is this: *Are you collecting everything you should be collecting?* Are items slipping away because your record keeping is sloppy? It may be happening more than you think, especially under the crunch of deadlines.

"Call accounting" services offered by phone firms are a terrific—and underused—way to track and rebill calling costs to clients. Sign up for the service with MCI, Sprint, or AT&T and, by entering a couple of extra digits when you make a call, your bill will arrive with each call properly flagged by the accounting code you've assigned. All calls on behalf of client #12, for example, will show that number. This extra service usually costs nothing for business customers. Check the Follow-up File for call accounting contacts.

In general, the key to making sure your reimbursables don't go unreimbursed is to install some type of expense-tracking system. Almost any system will do—as long as you have a system. Simpler is better. The basics: Get receipts for *everything*. If you forget to ask for one, write one up yourself later. Mark a job name on each receipt. Don't put it off. If you don't mark something down now, you'll forget about it.

A daily expense log works wonders. A simple, inexpensive notebook will do. You don't need fancy software to do this. Make sure everyone at your company who generates expenses knows he or she is responsible for keeping track of them.

Use business credit cards—American Express Corporate Card, Visa Business Card or MasterCard BusinessCard—for as many business expenses as possible. You can outfit key employees with cards for under $30 per year per person. The advantages are in better record keeping plus the interest-free short-term financing you get on card charges you pay off immediately. The detailed monthly statements you receive can be invaluable in helping you allocate charges to be reimbursed. If you're worried about spendthrift employees, set specific limits on individual cards.

TACTIC #37
Become an Inventory Maniac

Think of your inventory as company cash sitting on a shelf or in a warehouse—*doing nothing*. The costs of carrying excess, outdated, or slow-selling inventory can include storage, insurance, and taxes. Plus, money tied up in inventory is money you can't use elsewhere to build the business.

Inventory wears many masks. Basically, the term includes stocks of anything your company needs to do business; raw materials as well as finished goods. For retailers, inventory contributes to profits only when it's sold. Until then it's a profit *eater*. Bad inventory management—a silent profit killer—sinks thousands of small businesses every year.

The trick is to balance the benefits of inventory (you do need *some*) with its costs. Most businesses play it safe by keeping more than they need. Here are some ways to get inventory under better control:

- Keep good records. Without good information on what you have, your attempts to manage inventory will crash.

Organize your system, either on cards or in your computer. Bar coding can be tremendously helpful (see Tactic #6).

- Take frequent inventory. For some businesses, quarterly or even monthly is best. Doing so lessens the odds of pilferage, lets you know exactly what you have on hand, and allows you to cut costs by carrying less. You may even find that some products are costing you more to inventory than you are making on sales.

- Tour your inventory. Take along a large piece of chalk. Put a mark on machines and materials that aren't producing any money for the business—and look as if they haven't for some time. Then get rid of the stuff. (See Tactic #196 for a great way to do that.)

- Calculate your inventory turnover and compare your rate against the average for others in your business. The basic formula is this:

Turnover rate = Annual cost of goods sold ÷ Average $ invested in inventory.

For example, if your company's cost of goods sold is $1 million for the year, and the investment in inventory is $250,000, the turnover rate is 4.0, meaning that each item in inventory is sold or used four times in a year.

To find what other companies in your industry are doing, check *Annual Statement Studies,* published by Robert Morris Associates (see Follow-up File), which lists comparative financial data for different industries. This is a tremendously helpful book that bankers use to compare a business against others in its industry.

- Regularly root out dead inventory to be discounted, recycled, donated (see Tactic #196), or trashed.

- A. Grant Webb, a partner in the accounting firm KPMG Peat Marwick, says that even a supersimple two-bin technique can be a great way to manage inventories of low-cost commodity items such as small parts for manufacturing. "One container of inventory is opened and material is used only from this container," says Webb. "The second bin remains in inventory, unopened. When the first bin is emptied, the second is opened and an order is placed for a new one."

Webb also recommends the ABC inventory method, which puts primary emphasis on inventory items that cost your company the most. For example, "A" items collectively account for 75% to 80% of the cash your company has invested in inventory. The total value of "B" items is about 15% of your investment, even though they may account for more like 30% or 40% of the total by numbers instead of dollars. The "C" items are what's left. The more valuable the items, the more frequently you should conduct inventory. Store "A" items in the cheapest, most accessible locations.

The just-in-time (JIT) inventory method saves money for some spry manufacturers. This approach keeps materials inventory to a bare minimum. With JIT, materials are delivered only as they are needed.

Leaner in Laramie

For big business or small, inventory control is crucial to cost control. Dell Computer, in Austin, Texas, carries one of the slimmest inventories in the computer business, a tactic that has helped boost its bottom line. But the same goes for a small office supply store in Laramie, Wyoming. Elena Romero, co-owner of Gilette Office Supply & Equipment Co., stopped carrying a wide selection of office furniture even when she and partner Marjorie Williams moved to larger quarters. Now she encourages customers to order exactly what they want, rather than what she happens to have in stock. "The truck comes from Denver once a week and most people are willing to wait," says Romero.

TACTIC #38
Hire Out Your Bookkeeping

One of the first employees many a small business hires is a bookkeeper. But there may be a cheaper—not to mention more accurate and less time-consuming—route. Use an outside bookkeeping service. That's *bookkeeping*, mind you, not *accounting*. You needn't spend the big bucks for highly trained, higher-priced CPAs (though some bookkeepers may have CPA training) to do routine bookkeeping.

Look for a firm that specializes in bookkeeping. Such services can keep a small company's books in tip-top shape for as little as $200 or so per month. Hourly bookkeeping rates average less than $25, compared to $100 and up for CPAs. You still make all the decisions, approve payments, write checks. The bookkeeper simply keeps records of what you do. At tax time, those records—all nicely organized—get passed along to your accountant. And because your records will be in such good shape, you save money on tax preparation time.

TACTIC #39
Tap These Free Management Advice
Resources

- A Small Business Development Center (SBDC) can be a terrific place for small business owners to receive free advice on business plans, legal questions, sales and marketing strategies, financial controls, and more. SBDCs are jointly sponsored by states, private business groups, local universities, and the U.S. Small Business Administration (SBA). There are about eight hundred locations nationwide—many on college campuses—though the program keeps a low profile to avoid overcrowding for its free services. For an overview of how SBDCs work, call the SBA Answer Desk at (800) 827-5722. The automated system tells callers what numbers to press for Counseling and Training, which describes the SBDC program. Other options will help you locate the SBA office nearest you. Or check your local telephone listings.

The Association of Small Business Development Centers, which represents center directors and managers, is at 1313 Farnam, Suite 132, Omaha, NE 68182; (402) 595-2387; fax (402) 595-2388.

- A sister program, called the Small Business Institute, is another resource. The 503 SBI programs are cooperative efforts between the SBA and four-year universities nationwide. Each Small Business Institute uses upper-level business students along with a faculty director to provide free, confidential consulting to small business owners. The goal is to offer more in-depth and longer-term help than that available through SBDCs. For example, Lynn Hoffman, director of the program at the University of Northern Colorado for over fifteen years, has counseled some six hundred small business owners in the Weld County, Colorado, area. Available help there includes financial and debt analysis, accounting, computer accounting systems, computer and software purchases, work flow analysis, and job descriptions.

  To locate a center near you, contact the Small Business Advancement National Center at: College of Business Administration, University of Central Arkansas, UCA Box 5018, Conway, AR 72035; (501) 450-5300; fax (501) 450-5360.

- Business Information Centers (BICs)—another SBA endeavor—are new. At this writing, only five exist, in Seattle, Atlanta, Los Angeles, St. Louis, and Houston. But more are planned. BICs are supposed to be one-stop supermarkets of advice on starting or growing a small business. With help from companies such as Apple Computer, Microsoft, Sprint, and Sony, the BICs showcase some of the latest computer hardware, software, and tele-communications technology. They offer free access to a vast library of helpful business information. Call your nearest SBA office (under federal government listings) or the SBA Answer Desk at (800) 827-5722.

- SBA On-Line is a fast and free way to tap the Small Business Administration's informational coffers via your computer and modem, twenty-four hours a day. To access SBA On-Line, call (800) 859-INFO (for 2400 baud) or (800) 697-INFO (for 9600 baud). In Washington, D.C., call (202) 205-7265 (2400 baud) or (202) 401-9600 (9600 baud).

- The Service Corps of Retired Executives (SCORE) is a network of thirteen thousand retired business professionals who volunteer their services to help small business owners with administration, finance, advertising, personnel, manufacturing, engineering, and other questions. They work from 750 locations nationwide. Consultations are by appointment and SCORE officials say their volunteers will stay with you "as long as necessary." To find the center nearest you call the twenty-four-hour SBA Answer Desk at (800) 827-5722 and request the recording on Small Business Counseling and Training. At the end of that message you can enter your area code and get the phone number of a SCORE center.

TACTIC #40
Turn Service Slips into Opportunities

Every business gets complaints. But business goofs and gaffs (academics call 'em "service recovery opportunities") can be diamonds in disguise. Lose a customer and your business loses money. Salvage a customer and you've *saved* your company money; maybe even made it more. The standard rule of thumb: It costs five times more to replace a customer than to keep one. Many companies spend lavishly to attract new customers, even unprofitable ones, while doing little to keep more valuable *existing* ones.

To mine the diamonds, hone your company's customer recovery skills. *Look* for unsatisfied customers. Complainers are rare. Most people shut up and go elsewhere. You have to make it *easy* for customers to complain—feedback forms; 800 numbers. Seek them out, satisfy them quickly (*call, don't write*), and you've found your gems.

TACTIC #41
Buy Bargains at Government Auction

For bargains on everything from real estate to restaurant equipment, from trucks to telephones, government auctions are great. These are goods that various government agencies have acquired through foreclosures, bankruptcies, seizures, or other methods—all of it regularly auctioned to the public.

Funny thing about auctions, though. The more bidders who attend, the higher the selling prices. The trick is to read up on how it works, where to go, and how to get the *real* deals. Don't attempt the government auction game cold. The buyers who get the bargains are the ones with the most information.

Next to attending lots of auctions yourself, the best way to bone up is through *The Official Government Auction Guide* by George Chelekis (Crown Publishers, $25; (800) 733-3000). This five-hundred-page, phone book–sized directory lays it all out, including what's available, where to find it, how to get the deals and avoid the pitfalls. Chelekis, an auction enthusiast since the mid-1980s, interviewed over two thousand auctioneers, wholesalers, government agency personnel, and regular auctiongoers. Business bankruptcy auctions (they come under the U.S. Trustee's Office) in particular have yielded great bargains in the 1990s, with more to come. Here's advice from Chelekis:

- Look for *unexpected* items. For example, at a welding company or restaurant bankruptcy, dealers will be looking for inventory, supplies, or specialized equipment. That leaves vehicles, photocopiers, furniture, and other items available to the few amateur buyers who bother to show up.
- Go to auctions Monday through Thursday to avoid weekend crowds.
- Before bidding starts, try to spot the dealers. Chat with other attendees; get business cards. Listen. Watch what vehicles people arrive in (read the signs on the door). Going toe-to-toe against a dealer is safer than competing against another amateur who hasn't appraised before bidding. Dealers need a low resale price to guarantee a comfortable profit margin. Up the bid by $25 or $50 until the dealer drops out. Presto, you've got a bargain.
- Hunt for poorly promoted bankruptcy auctions. Get on a local auctioneer's mailing list. Big auction ad budgets mean more competition.
- Attend the inspection—also known as the preview period—and do some comparison shopping. That's the only way you can bid intelligently later.

TACTIC #42
Use Independent Sales Reps

Outside sales reps are independent contractors who serve as your company's frontline sales force—but without all the payroll taxes, fringes, and other overhead that comes with having an in-house staff. You can't have the same degree of control over independent sales agents; nor can you expect to capture all of the reps' time and attention. But for maximum flexibility, a small up-front investment, and the smallest ongoing cost, stitching together your own network of sales agents can help put your company on the growth fast track. Even some companies with sales over $100 million per year insist that reps still offer the most cost-effective method to move their goods.

Finding the best reps for your company, then building a successful long-term relationship, are the biggest challenges. Here are the resources you need:

- The Manufacturers' Agents National Association (MANA) is a trade group for sales reps that's been around since 1947 and has about nine thousand members. MANA publishes an annual *Directory of Manufacturers' Sales Agencies* with detailed profiles of about eight thousand independent reps. The directory, revised each June, costs $85 and includes a subscription to the monthly magazine *Agency Sales.*

  MANA also publishes a three-part series of legal manuals for manufacturers and agents. Manual 1 is on contracts, manual 2 covers state laws, and manual 3 offers advice on avoiding and resolving disputes—$114.50 each, or $313.50 as a package.

  To order or to get more information on MANA's publications, seminars, and other programs call (714) 859-4040 or write to P.O. Box 3467, Laguna Hills, CA 92654.

- The Manufacturers' Representatives Educational Research Foundation will send a free list of industry-specific rep associations. The foundation offers a video on working with sales reps called *The Unique Advantage* ($29.95). Call (708) 208-1466 or write to P.O. Box 247, Geneva, IL 60134.

- A good book on the subject is *Selling through Independent Reps* by Harold Novick (AMACOM, $69.95); call (800) 538-4761.

TACTIC #43
Follow the Five Steps to Better Buying

Start by thinking differently. Consider purchasing to be a source of potential *profits*, not merely a necessary business evil. These five steps can save you money:

1. *Cut back the number of vendors you deal with.*
2. *Look for long-term (i.e., lower-cost) purchasing contracts.*
3. *Negotiate prices whenever you can.*
4. *Nix the mix of business and pleasure.* Suppliers—maybe yours included—love to wine and dine good customers. But cozy up too close and you will jeopardize objectivity. You may not be as tough on prices with your new "buddies."
5. *If you can't manage rules one through four, turn over your purchasing to an outside firm that* can.

Purchasing is another area where outsourcing has arrived. Firms that specialize in buying for other firms have sprung up coast to coast for one reason—they can save their clients money. One such company, Buffalo-based Purchasing Support Services at (716) 631-9441, has documented millions of dollars in purchasing savings for clients in upstate New York. Because such firms are still quite new, you may need to ask around in your area to locate one.

TACTIC #44
Score Stock Offer Savings with SCORs

Pssssst! Wanna raise up to a million bucks for your business without jumping through a bunch of costly bureaucratic hoops? There *is* a way. It's new. It's quick and cheap. It's okay in twenty-six states. And it doesn't involve anybody named Swifty.

The wondrous device that can do this for you is a Small Corporate Offering Registration (SCOR), also known as a Form U-7 filing. Attorney Lee Petillon, a leading SCOR authority, says this is *the* simplest way to publicly issue stock in a small business. State-regulated SCORs are exempt from Securities and Exchange Commission (SEC) regulations. And the Form U-7 is a quick Q&A. "The typical small business owner can fill in most of the form without outside help," says Petillon, who is affiliated with the Los Angeles firm Gipson, Hoffman and Pancione. A small company can complete a SCOR stock offering for as little as $20,000 in costs, compared with over $100,000 *in legal costs alone* for the old, fully registered variety.

The offering limit is $1 million per year. These states have approved SCORs: Alaska, Arizona, California, Colorado, Connecticut, Idaho, Indiana, Iowa, Kansas, Maine, Massachusetts, Mississippi, Montana, Nevada, New Hampshire, New Jersey, North Carolina, North Dakota, Oklahoma, Oregon, Pennsylvania, South Carolina, Texas, Washington, Wisconsin, and Wyoming.

For a SCOR information booklet or diskette (specify size) that includes the Form U-7, send $10 to the North American Securities Administrators Association (NASAA), One Massachusetts Avenue, N.W., Suite 310, Washington, DC 20001; (202) 737-0900; fax (202) 783-3571.

TACTIC #45
Save Time

A good start is to get more organized. Hire a professional organizer if you must. Businesses that specialize in organizing other people's business are now available in many areas. For example, Barbara Hemphill operates Hemphill & Associates,

Inc., an organizing consulting firm in Raleigh, North Carolina. Being "organized" is not a destination but a journey, says Hemphill. The task never ends. Hemphill wrote *Taming the Paper Tiger: Organizing the Paper in Your Life* (Kiplinger Books, $11.95), a worthwhile read and one of the best-organized books on organizing yet published. Call (800) 544-0155.

Hemphill suggests that you ask four questions about every piece of paper that comes your way: Do I *really* need to keep this? *Where* should I keep this? How *long* should I keep it? How can I *find* it? If the answer to the first question is no, you need only master the difficult art of what Hemphill calls waste-basketry. Says she, "Your ability to achieve goals is directly related to your willingness to use the wastebasket."

A good motivator is to keep track of how much time you waste now. Keep a time log continuously for a week. Record what you did in quarter-hour or half-hour blocks. Then take a look at how it shakes out. Look for large time blocks spent unproductively.

To better use your time, schedule it. Use "to-do" lists, with the most important "to-dos" listed first. Refine and update the list as the day progresses.

Learning to handle interruptions can be a huge time saver for business people forced to live in an interruption-rich environment. When you need to meet with someone, go to *his or her* office. You can leave whenever you want. Position your desk so people *can't* see you as they walk by. Out of sight means fewer interruptions.

Adopt a personal call-screening system. If you don't have someone to help screen your calls, use voice mail or an answering machine. Designate a time for taking calls and let the receptionist know. Make your return calls all at once, rather than piecemeal.

Time-saver nuggets:

- Always confirm appointments the day of or the day before. Crossed signals mean wasted hours.
- In the car, listen to tapes of seminars or business books.

- Skip morning coffee-newspaper-conversation rituals. Get right to work and tackle your most difficult tasks first. Finish one task before moving on.
- Close your door when you're under deadline. No apologies needed. If someone enters, standing up will help shorten the stay.

Jeffrey Mayer's bestselling time-management system is appropriately titled *If You Haven't Got the Time to Do It Right, When Will You Find the Time to Do It Over?* (Fireside, $8.95) and shows you how to make your desk, your files—even your to-do list—more effective, helping you to become more organized and meet your deadlines. Call (800) 223-2336 to order.

Another good book is *Organized to Be the Best! New Time-saving Ways to Simplify and Improve How You Work* by Susan Silver (Adams-Hall Publishing, $13.95 plus shipping; (800) 888-4452). Includes hundreds of great time-saving ideas.

Need an organizing pro? Call the National Association of Professional Organizers in Tucson, Arizona; (602) 322-9753 or send a stamped, self-addressed envelope to 655 North Alvernon Way, #108, Tucson, AZ 85711.

TACTIC #46
Miss Your Next Meeting

The greatest business time waster of all time: The Meeting.

Asking, "Is this meeting necessary?" can gain most managers an extra day a week, says Frank Grazian of the management newsletter *Communication Briefings*. Senior managers spend almost half their workweek mired in meetings. "By using phone calls, memos, and one-on-one communication to eliminate just one meeting a day, executives could gain about eight hours a week," says Grazian.

First, chomp into those regularly scheduled meetings. A

simple notice on a memo board or in an electronic mail message can often eliminate the need to meet.

But when a meeting is needed, says *Communication Briefings*, based in Blackwood, New Jersey, these tips can help make it more productive:

- Set goals in writing ahead of time. Putting it on paper helps sharpen everyone's focus and keep the meeting on track.
- Distribute the agenda a day in advance and ask for specific actions. Insist that people come to your meetings prepared to *decide on,* not merely discuss, the agenda.
- Invite only key people.
- Never pass out support materials at the beginning. They let people read, not listen to what's being said. You'll have to call another meeting to clear up the misunderstandings that result.
- People have short meeting memories. Make it clear who's responsible for action. Put it in writing as soon as possible following the meeting.

TACTIC #47
Form or Find a Buyers' Group

Small retailers that can't qualify for quantity discounts on their own are finding joint purchasing power through small business buying groups specific to their industry. Whatever your specialty, be it office products, hardware, furniture, or dozens of other retail areas, there's a buyers' group to join that can help cut your merchandise costs through the power of group buying. Buyers' groups—many structured as tax-exempt cooperatives—are proliferating as small retailers look for survival ammunition to compete against the likes of Wal-Mart and the segment superstores. Cost savings achieved through small business buyers' groups have been the difference between success and failure for many small stores. Check your industry trade publications for listings. Expect to pay a membership fee to join and perhaps monthly fees as well.

SAVE-A-BUNDLE FOLLOW-UP FILE

• *Annual Statement Studies*, published by Robert Morris Associates (RMA), lists key financial ratios for over 350 industries. The book is updated yearly and provides financial comparisons plus historical data. RMA is an association of bank loan and credit officers, who mostly use this book, but it's available for $105.00 to anyone and can also be found in some libraries or maybe in your CPA's office. Reach RMA at One Liberty Place, 1650 Market Street, Suite 2300, Philadelphia, PA 19103; (215) 851-0585; fax (215) 851-9206.

• Here's a small investment that will help save your business many times what it spends, year after year: a membership in the National Federation of Independent Business. Nashville, Tennessee–based NFIB is the largest (over six hundred thousand members), oldest (formed in 1943), and most powerful small business advocacy group in America, with offices in Washington, D.C., and all fifty state capitals. You set your own dues level, with a $100 minimum and $1,000 maximum (to prevent anyone from wielding too much power); all key positions are determined by membership vote.

NFIB has won victory after victory in Washington, sparing small American companies miles of red tape and billions of collective dollars. That's the kind of work NFIB does, quietly and methodically. Members automatically receive *IB* (*Independent Business*)—"America's Small Business Magazine"— which I edit. Call (800) NFIB-NOW ([800] 634-2669) or write to NFIB, Membership Development, 53 Century Boulevard, Nashville, TN 37214.

• For information on call accounting services:

  · AT&T Call Manager, AT&T Small Business Services, (800) 222-0400, or (800) 972-1152.

· MCI Prism Plus or MCI Preferred, (800) 727-5555.
· Sprint Business Clout, (800) 800-2568.

• *Communication Briefings*, a monthly newsletter ($69/ year), covers new ideas and research, including money-saving tips, for some fifty thousand subscribers. Call (800) 888-2086; fax (609) 232-8245. This is sharply focused advice from a group that knows its stuff. A forty-four-page report called *How to Create Forms That Get the Job Done* ($25) is a big help. *The Best Ideas in Time Management* ($25) is also a winner.

• *Friendly Persuasion* by Bob Woolf (Putnam, $8.95) is one of those rare books that combine interesting anecdotes with boxcars of useful advice. Woolf's 101 proven strategies for successful negotiating hit a bull's-eye, no matter what business you're in or how much is involved. In bookstores, or call (800) 631-8571.

• *Smart Negotiating: How to Make Good Deals in the Real World* by James C. Freund (Simon & Schuster, $21.50) reveals real-world negotiating tactics and is written by a big-league negotiator. Available in bookstores, or call (800) 223-2336.

• *Business-to-Business Negotiation* by George Holmes and Stan Glaser (Butterworth Heinemann, $29.95) hammers at the nuts and bolts that you need in specific business situations; call (800) 366-2665.

• Other specialized negotiating books: *How to Negotiate Anything with Anyone Anywhere Around the World* by Frank Acuff (AMACOM, $27.95) offers advice on negotiating with foreign firms; call (800) 538-4761. *The Art of Negotiating* by Gerard I. Nierenberg (Fireside, $7.95) details simple, imaginative strategies and tactics on how to hone your negotiating skills; call (800) 223-2336. *Negotiate to Close* by Gary Karrass (Fireside, $9.95) adds the crucial ingredient—how to actually pin down and successfully close the final agreement; call (800) 223-2336.

• A good book on keeping customers is *50 Simple Things You Can Do to Save Your Customers* by Paul Timm (Career

Press, $6.95). Short, snappy advice in a quick-read package. Call (800) 955-7373.

• Two good how-to books on delegating are: *Delegate: The Key to Successful Management* by Harold Taylor (Warner Books, $8.95), available in bookstores; and *T.E.A.M.S.* by Jim Lundy (Dartnell Corp., $19.95). Call (800) 621-5463.

• A freebie called *30 Ways to Use Less Paper*, one of 3M's Reduce, Reuse, Recycle handouts, is available from 3M's Commercial Office Supply Division. Call (800) 395-1223, or (612) 733-1110.

• How to Organize Your Desk is a thirty-minute problem-solving video featuring several small businesses as examples. The cost is $59.95 plus $3.50 shipping from HTO Enterprises, P.O. Box 1703, Clackamas, OR 97015. Call (800) 225-8755.

• Two government publications worth a look: *The States and Small Business: A Directory of Programs and Activities* (document number 045-000-00266-7; $21) is a one-stop reference guide to small business assistance programs in all fifty states. *Exporter's Guide to Federal Resources for Small Business* (document number 045-000-00263-2; $4.75) describes federal programs that help small companies begin or expand exporting. Available from the Government Printing Office; call (202) 783-3238.

• Jane Applegate's book *Succeeding in Small Business: The 101 Toughest Problems and How to Solve Them* (Plume, $12) is a sure bet to make every small business owner's life easier. Applegate, whose nifty newspaper column, "Succeeding In Small Business," appears in papers across the country, provides real-life solutions to real-life problems, and she writes with wit and style. In bookstores or call (800) 526-0275.

CHAPTER 4

Personnel: Pare Costs, Not People

Attack Absenteeism

When employees are unexpectedly absent, it costs your company money—both directly and indirectly. Vacations are known; they're expected. But *unscheduled* absences cost the average company about $411 per year, per employee, in *direct* costs, according to research by Commerce Clearing House, Inc. But that's a low figure because it doesn't include *indirect* expenses related to "AWOL" workers, such as what you pay others to fill in (overtime; temps, etc.); time spent scrambling to fill gaps left by the absent employee; the cost of additional paperwork; and any lost sales or customer service blunders that result.

Here's what your company can do to attack absenteeism and cut associated costs:

- Consider a revised schedule for the summer, when Friday absenteeism is highest. Some companies let employees work four ten-hour days instead of five eight-hour days. Check state overtime laws and your own overtime policies before you proceed.
- Make employees call in sick to a supervisor, not just anyone who answers. They'll be less likely to concoct tall tales about why they aren't showing up.
- Keep good records on when individual employees are out. Look for a disproportionate number of Monday and Friday absences as an indicator of employees giving themselves more three-day weekends. Asking employees about such a pattern at least notifies them that you are taking notice.
- Revamp your sick leave policy. Instead of a "use-it-or-

lose-it" approach that encourages people to take off, sick or not, consider a system that lets employees bank a portion of unused sick leave to be used later as *scheduled* vacation time.

- Reward employees with top attendance records. Some firms create a small bonus pool to split among workers with a perfect record for the preceding month, or quarter, or some other time period.

TACTIC #49
Cut Pension Costs with a 401(k), SEP, or SARSEP

At large and midsize companies, the 401(k) salary reduction plan is the hottest money-saving pension move going. These plans, named for the tax code section that authorizes them, let companies cut costs by having employees help fund their own pensions through salary reduction. Money diverted to a 401(k) isn't included in taxable wages. To encourage participation, many firms match a portion of each employee's contribution. Additional company contributions can be linked to profits.

More and more smaller companies are using 401(k) plans too. Service-Maintenance Sales, Inc., a ten-person mechanical services firm in Toledo, Ohio, replaced an older plan with a 401(k) in 1991. "I wish I'd done it sooner," says founder Ed Mullin, now in his seventies and semiretired. Service-Maintenance, with about $1 million in sales, matches employee contributions fifty cents to the dollar up to the first 3% of salary. The plan is set up through the Principal Financial Group, a Des Moines, Iowa–based leader in business pensions. Nine out of ten new pension plans opened by the Principal Financial Group are 401(k)s, many for businesses with as few as ten employees.

Still, 401(k) plans are not without costs and paperwork.

Each plan must offer employees a range of investments and materials that help them choose wisely. Officials at Baltimore-based T. Rowe Price Associates, hoping to minimize drawbacks, designed a "plain vanilla" 401(k) for small companies. The T. Rowe Price Century Plan makes the 401(k) as simple and inexpensive as it gets. It comes with its own PC-based software to run it, prototype documents, and choices of T. Rowe Price mutual funds, all aimed at making this a bulletproof plan.

Deborah Shillito, of J. C. Estimating, Inc., in Elmsford, New York, was one of the first small business owners to sign up for the Price plan. Her twelve-person firm, which does construction cost consulting, matches employee contributions dollar-for-dollar. "We're a very employee-oriented company," says Shillito, "and the pension plan with a matching contribution is great for employee relations."

The Super Simple "Business IRA" There's another low-cost, low-maintenance way for even the smallest companies to offer retirement benefits. It's like a "business IRA" that permits deductible contributions far above the $2,000 limit for regular IRAs. This plan, called a simplified employee pension, or SEP, is painless to set up and requires no annual paperwork.

Yet just like the complex programs offered by big corporations, SEPs deliver crucial tax savings to you and your employees. Your business or self-employment taxable income is reduced by the amount of money you put into the SEP. And the money in the plan, including earnings on investments, grows untaxed until it is tapped.

You can contribute as much as 15% of your net self-employment earnings, up to $22,500. (After applying some goofy IRS math, the figure actually comes to about 13%, so use that figure instead.) Contributions can vary year to year. If you have eligible employees, you must contribute to their SEPs each year you contribute to your own. There's just one form for the business to fill out to open a SEP, and all contributions are deductible. Employees make their own investment decisions, so you're relieved of that worry too.

A Streamlined 401(k)   A "salary reduction" SEP (SARSEP) is a streamlined 401(k) available only to businesses with twenty-five or fewer employees. SARSEPs are cost-control cool. They offer a way to install a retirement plan for your company but limit expense by having employees contribute to their own retirement accounts through salary reduction.

In a SARSEP you set up individual accounts for employees who want to divert part of their pay to the plan. The limit is basically 13% for you and 15% for employees, to a maximum amount that is adjusted yearly for inflation (recently between $9,000 and $10,000). Unlike a 401(k), however, no matching contributions by the company are allowed. At least half of your employees must agree to participate, and the amount of money you are allowed to put into your own account is linked to the amount your employees contribute to theirs. Your contribution cannot exceed 125% of the average percentage of pay contributed by employees—if they contribute an average of 5% of their pay, your contribution would be limited to 6.25%.

Sound Propeller Inc., a twelve-employee Seattle firm that makes large marine propellers, is thrilled with the low-cost SARSEP it installed in 1990. "We're a nonunion shop. To attract quality employees we needed a pension plan," says Jackie D'Agosto, who pilots Sound Propeller's plan. The employees also think it's great. And because employee participation is high, the three owners of the business can contribute more to their own nest eggs. Finding the right plan took tenacity. "When we started looking, others told us it would cost too much," says D'Agosto. "A big brokerage firm we called said, 'Sure, we'll come out to see you. But it will cost you a fortune.' We thought there must be something that will work for us, so we did some more searching and came up with the plan we have now. There *are* plans that work for a little business."

Annual contributions to a SARSEP can be highly flexible, the paperwork is simple, and fees are low. Go with a SARSEP if you have fewer than twenty-five employees and don't expect to grow. Choose the 401(k) if you have fifteen to twenty employees and expect to pass the twenty-five level in a few years.

TACTIC #50
Pay Employees Electronically

Cranking out paper payroll checks is a time-consuming and expensive way to pay employees. Paying 'em electronically—by direct deposit—will save your business a bundle, whether you employ four or four thousand employees and whether you deal with a large or small bank, S&L, or credit union. According to a study by KPMG Peat Marwick, the average yearly cost of producing payroll checks is $212 per employee. For a firm with twenty employees, that's $4,240; and if you have a hundred, it's over $21,000.

Susan Busbice, chief accountant for the City of Lubbock, Texas, reckons that Lubbock lopped 30% from its payroll processing costs by going direct deposit—a first-year bundle of over $47,000. Stanford University went to school on direct deposit and cut its payroll processing from twenty-one cents per person to less than five cents.

Direct deposit is a fast-track way to do payroll by electronically depositing employee paychecks directly into their bank accounts. No checks to produce, sign, and reconcile. There's still a cost, but a firm with twenty employees who get paid weekly can save about $100 per month—about $1.25 per employee for every pay period. Also, companies that pay workers via direct deposit report significantly higher employee productivity on paydays than companies that don't. Employees who know their money's in the bank are less inclined to simply kill time waiting for the check to arrive. And they don't have to leave work to deposit their checks.

The National Automated Clearing House Association (NACHA), the nation's largest electronic payments network, offers a free booklet describing the wonders of direct deposit, including materials on how to promote employee involvement. Call (800) 467-2329 (an outside service bureau) or write to NACHA, 607 Herndon Parkway, Suite 200, Herndon, VA 22070. Call NACHA direct at (703) 742-9190; fax (703) 787-0996.

TACTIC #51
Prevent Penalties with Payroll Processing Help

Some things are better left to outside specialists. Handling payroll—including state and federal tax filings—is absolutely one of 'em. Especially these days when IRS rules on depositing payroll taxes may be your company's worst nightmare. Convoluted, ever-changing, and costly, this bear trap snags one out of every three companies each year. Result: penalties for doing what the company thought was right.

Small companies fall prey most often. The IRS is especially hard-nosed about payroll taxes being deposited in full and on time. No excuse for failure is good enough. Consider these firms the IRS zapped:

- Crawford Moving & Storage of Mathews, Virginia, was notified that because its quarterly tax deposit of $10,497.94 was six cents short, it was being fined $106.00
- Salem Welding of Winston-Salem, North Carolina, was hit with $50,000 in penalties for failing to deposit Social Security (FICA) and federal withholding taxes on time when the family member in charge of bookkeeping at this family-owned firm stayed home to have a baby and her replacement didn't make the deposits.

The message is clear and simple: Don't do payroll yourself! The amount you'll pay an outside firm to handle your payroll and payroll tax filings is a pittance compared to what you could save in penalties if you're among the 33% who mess up each year. Automated Data Processing (ADP), which handles payroll chores for about two hundred thousand businesses, says it will pay the penalty for any error it makes. Other payroll services will do the same.

To calculate the economics of using an outside service, answer these questions:

- How much do you now spend to prepare your payroll, issue employee paychecks, reconcile your business checking account, deposit your payroll taxes, prepare and file your quarterly and annual payroll tax returns, and issue W-2s?
- What is the cost of your bookkeeper's time—time that could be spent on other business priorities?
- Can you afford to make a mistake on payroll taxes, which by the time the government discovers it might set you back financially or impair the reputation of your company?
- Do you have the tax expertise to handle payroll? Are you knowledgeable on business tax requirements and do you stay abreast of the ever-changing tax laws?
- Would it be helpful to have a buffer between you and the IRS—someone who will handle the correspondence with the government if it questions something? If there is a mathematical mistake in your payroll tax returns, would you like the payroll service to assume the liability and pay the penalty?

TACTIC #52
Cut Costs with Preemployment Testing and Screening

Preemployment testing and screening have moved center-court as cost-cutting and loss-prevention tools as more companies avoid hiring purely on faith.

Testing Consider Holiday Inn's experience, researched by Reid Psychological Systems (RPS), a major preemployment test publisher in Chicago. Holiday Inn wanted to know how testing could cut the hotel chain's costs due to absenteeism and turnover of entry-level desk clerks, reservationists, and housekeepers. High rates in both areas were draining profits.

A study of 137 new hires showed that by using a personnel selection test called the Reid Report to avoid hiring mistakes, Holiday Inn could reduce absenteeism by over 70% and turnover by 60%. Reid and Holiday Inn execs concluded that the hotel could save about 19.8% on hiring and training costs by using tests to screen applicants—savings that in Holiday Inn's case reach well into six figures per year.

Similar cost-saving studies in other industries produced similar results: Testing can reduce employment costs considerably by weeding applicants who are most likely to show up for work late, be absent frequently, and quit after a short time.

Restaurateur Gilbert/Robinson, based in Kansas City, is another believer that testing cuts costs by lowering turnover and filtering out dishonest job applicants. Gilbert/Robinson tests all of its management candidates as well as hourly employees who are in a position to handle cash. The firm operates over ninety restaurants around the country, including Houlihan's, Bristol Bar and Grill, Darryl's, Charley's Place, and others.

Honesty tests are a big money saver for retail businesses. Stephen Coffman, president of Reid Psychological Systems, says that about a hundred such firms now use Reid tests and find that losses from internal theft are reduced an average of 50% to 70%.

Screening Preemployment screening is another way to head off costly hiring mistakes. According to the Credit Managers Association of California (CMAC), an affiliate of the National Association of Credit Management, dishonest employees cost U.S. companies billions of dollars each year. But trying to verify a job applicant's background is difficult and it's something most companies don't do.

Big mistake, says Jerry Wohl, a leading security consultant to business and a lie detection expert. When Wohl helped a convenience store chain prescreen its job applicants, he says that inventory shrinkage dropped from between 4% and 5% per month to less than 1%. Preemployment screening can definitely save business money, says Wohl.

CMAC has developed an inexpensive applicant screening program—a kind of prepackaged private-eye service—that it offers nationwide. The CMAC "Pre-Employment Applicant Screening Service" verifies past employment, including any record of employee theft, criminal convictions, credit history, and drug use. CMAC is a consumer reporting agency regulated by federal law and has been around for over a hundred years. The in-depth screening reports cost about $110 per applicant, less for an abbreviated minireport. Call (800) 447-3998 for information.

TACTIC #53
Avoid Firing Line Foul-ups

Here's a shocker: Since the early 1970s, lawsuits for "wrongful termination" have exploded by 2,000%. Measure that against a "mere" 125% increase for other civil-type cases and you get an idea of what businesses face. Some three million U.S. workers get canned every year. As you read this, tens of thousands of wrongful-discharge lawsuits are choking state and federal court dockets.

So for heaven's sake, if you've gotta fire somebody, do it right so you don't get sued. There's no way to give you all the legal do's and don'ts of hiring and firing in the limited space here. It's a process that begins with hiring, and extends through your entire relationship with an employee. Telling employees clearly what is expected of them, reviewing performance with them in person, acting quickly on problems, and documenting all of your actions are a few keys to avoiding trouble.

A small investment in time to read up on the legalities of firing can help you avoid costly mistakes. Here are some good resources:

- A concise guidebook on the subject is *Every Manager's Legal Guide to Firing* by August Bequai (BusinessOne Irwin, $45); call (800) 634-3966.
- *Employee Matters: A Legal Guide to Hiring, Firing, and Setting Employee Policies* by E. Kenneth Snyder (Probus, $24.95); call (800) 776-2871. This, too, is a good basic guide on firing line legalities.
- *How to Legally Fire* and *How to Legally Hire* are two companion videos ($79.95 each; $149 together) available from the Friedman Group, 5828 Uplander Way, Culver City, CA 90230; (800) 351-8040. A good compact package on firing/hiring do's and don'ts.
- BNA Plus, the special projects division of the Bureau of National Affairs (BNA) in Washington, D.C., offers an information package called *Termination Procedures* for $25. Call (800) 452-7773.
- *Stay Out Of Court: The Manager's Guide to Preventing Employee Lawsuits* (Prentice Hall, $18.95 in paperback), by attorney Rita Risser, offers practical, step-by-step guidelines on how to prevent lawsuits. Available in bookstores or call (800) 235-3435.

TACTIC #54
Use More Temps

A flexible work force is one key to keeping costs low and being competitive in the cutthroat nineties. What better way to stay flexible than to plug temporary help into your firm's permanent employment mix.

Temping has come far since the days of fill-in typists. In the years ahead, some of the most successful companies will rely *day to day* on temps to give their firms a marketplace edge. Given today's high cost of full-time employment, the once-expensive move of hiring temps has in many cases become a low-cost labor alternative.

"Many American corporations have fundamentally re-shaped their work forces in recent years, establishing a smaller core work force of permanent employees surrounded by a flexible border of temporary and part-time workers," says *The Wall Street Journal*. Results: lower labor costs; more flexibility.

Stuart Olsten, who heads Olsten Temporary Services in Westbury, New York, argues that temping will continue to be a big part of corporate cost control in coming years. "More companies are turning to flexible staffing to maneuver through the ups and downs of the business cycle, avoid layoffs, and transform fixed costs into variable costs."

Temporary workers are also a solution if you can't find the talent your company needs. Business demand for temps with special technical expertise is exploding, and temp firms are responding. For example, Mid-States Technical Staffing Services, Inc., in Iowa's Quad Cities, is a specialist in providing technical temps for manufacturers and other businesses in Iowa, Illinois, and Nebraska. Hiring your own technical expert would cost a small fortune; a temp can be a cost-conscious alternative.

On a strict hour-to-hour comparison, temps seem to cost more than permanent employees. But that doesn't count all the other costs of finding an employee, paying benefits and taxes, and all the other associated paperwork costs that add another 40% or so on top of wages.

Temporary firms are becoming increasingly prolific and competitive, so interview several firms before you move ahead. Look for the best fit with your company in terms of service and type of employees they have, not just at price.

You can check for a local outlet of one of the temp industry majors, including Manpower, Inc., Kelly Services, Olsten Temporary Services, Robert Half International (Accountemps Division), Adia Services, Lifetime, CDI Corp., and Staff Builders. Look for smaller local firms too.

For a free copy of *How to Buy Temporary Help Services*, send a stamped, self-addressed business envelope to the National Association of Temporary Services, 119 South St.

Asaph Street, Alexandria, VA 22314; (703) 549-6287. A helpful book is *How to Choose and Use Temporary Services* by William Lewis and Nancy Molloy (AMACOM, $24.95); call (800) 538-4761.

TACTIC #55
Cut Costs with Apprenticeships and Interns

If your company will have technical jobs to fill in the years ahead—from metalworking machinists to health-care workers to copier repair people—you may find yourself in a tough position trying to attract and train workers or replacements. That's why apprenticeship programs—once *the* key means of passing along trade or professional business knowledge—are staging a comeback. Apprenticeships do two things for your company: (1) get you cheap help now; and (2) help assure you a supply of well-trained workers for the future.

Smaller manufacturing companies in particular, who are finding it increasingly hard to locate experienced metalworkers or fill similar positions, are literally going back to school for help—joining other companies and linking with high schools, vocational schools, and colleges to make students part-time apprentices. New apprenticeship programs are in place nationwide. The students stay in school, learn a trade while earning a small "training wage," and often move into a job when they graduate. Businesses capture the technical help they need and often improve their productivity and bottom lines. See the Follow-up File for more.

Hiring Interns Interns—generally college students you hire for a summer or fresh out of school—can be a terrific source of high-energy, low-cost labor. Green they may be, but an intern's eagerness to learn on the job can be a great asset if tapped judiciously. Many firms large and small regularly hire interns as low-cost help. In exchange, the businesses offer the interns a chance to gain real-life business experience, and in some cases, college credit too.

Jill Marti, owner of a small entertainment production firm called Jazbo, Inc., in Beverly Hills, California, has long relied on interns to help her company compete with deep-pocket competitors in the television, film, and live entertainment areas. Jazbo is just right for using interns—it's small, aggressive, and must be ready to shrink or expand in a flash, depending on whether the latest development deal is a go or a bust.

Talk to the job placement offices at colleges and universities in your area about your plans for hiring an intern. Most schools already have a system in place for helping companies fill such positions. See the Follow-up File for information on internship directories.

TACTIC #56
Use Independent Contractors . . .
Carefully

Warning: Hiring workers as independent contractors instead of regular employees could be hazardous to your bank account. No doubt about it: Business use of independent contractors is under heavy artillery assault from that Constitution Avenue monolith called the IRS. The tax folks want to smoke out companies that evade taxes by classifying employees as outside contractors when in fact they are not. And that makes it sticky for everyone who uses independent contractors legitimately.

The penalties for misclassifying workers are staggering. A company whose $15K per year independent contractor is reclassified by the IRS as an employee could owe $20,000 in taxes, penalties, and interest over a three-year period.

There's nothing shady or illegal about using independent

contractors instead of employees for some tasks. You just have to follow the rules to the T. Each year, the IRS slaps business with over $100 million in penalties and back taxes for misclassified workers. Especially vulnerable types of businesses include construction firms, truckers, couriers, travel agencies, nursing agencies, and consultants.

For some small companies, however, cutting costs via contract labor is the only thing that keeps them in business. Consider Bud's Airport & Taxi Service in Hopkinton, Massachusetts. The IRS wanted to penalize owner George Dusseault $25,000 for classifying his twenty drivers incorrectly as independent contractors. To soften the blow, the IRS offered to waive the hit if Dusseault would make them all employees in the future, reports *The Wall Street Journal.*

Dusseault says he almost took the bait, but did a little ciphering first. To make up for the extra cost of taking on the twenty drivers as employees, he figured he'd have to *double* his fares. That would end his business. So Dusseault documented what his competitors in the Boston area were doing and was able to argue that common, established practice in the livery business was to use drivers as independent contractors. That satisfied the IRS, which canceled the penalties. Dusseault had discovered one of the "safe harbor" exemptions to the rules, which says that if established practice of a particular industry in a geographic region is to use certain workers as independent contractors, the IRS can't complain.

One basic protective step is to have a written agreement (a contract) with all independent contractors. For a booklet on model agreements, contact James R. Urquhart III Business Seminars in Irvine, California (see Follow-up File).

The IRS plays a game of twenty questions, or tests, to determine if a worker is a legitimate contractor or is really an employee. The issue centers on how much control you have over the contract worker, and whether or not that person has anything at risk in the relationship other than the job itself. The IRS considers an abundance of "yes" answers to be evidence of an employer-employee relationship.

1. Do you provide the worker with instructions as to when, where, and how work is performed?
2. Did you train the worker in order to have the job performed correctly?
3. Are the worker's services a vital part of your company's operations?
4. Is the person prevented from delegating work to others?
5. Is the worker prohibited from hiring, supervising, and paying assistants?
6. Does the worker perform services for you on a regular and continuous basis?
7. Do you set the hours of service for the worker?
8. Does the person work full-time for your company?
9. Does the worker perform duties on your company's premises?
10. Do you control the order and sequence of the work performed?
11. Do you require the worker to submit oral or written reports?
12. Do you pay the worker by the hour, week, or month?
13. Do you pay for the worker's business and travel expenses?
14. Do you furnish tools or equipment for the worker?
15. Does the worker lack a "significant investment" in tools, equipment, and facilities?
16. Is the worker insulated from suffering a loss as a result of the activities performed for your company?
17. Does the worker perform services solely for your firm?
18. Does the worker not make services available to the general public?
19. Do you have the right to discharge the worker at will?
20. Can the worker end the relationship without incurring any liability?

TACTIC #57
Consider a State "Work Share" Program

They're still relatively new and only a handful of states have them. But they can be a good payroll reducer and an attractive alternative to layoffs for small companies. Each program works a little differently, but basically they allow companies to reduce work hours by, say, 20% to 50% and have employees receive partial pay for the off time through a state unemployment insurance program. States with such programs include Arizona, Arkansas, California, Florida, Kansas, Louisiana, Maryland, Massachusetts, Missouri, New York, Oregon, Texas, Vermont, and Washington. Check with the state unemployment office for details.

TACTIC #58
Deautomate the Automatic Annual Raise

Who decreed that all employers shall grant annual pay increases? Maybe that worked in the inflationary seventies, but most businesses today can't afford this magnanimous move. Be ready for the argument: *"But we've* always *received an annual raise!"*

This is no longer always. Wage increases every twelve clicks of the calendar are not an entitlement. Merit increases are in; automatic increases out. Here's your key yardstick for considering increases: *Can the company afford it?* And that goes for the higher-ups as well as the rank and file. Base increases on what the business can afford; on real merit (that's *progress*, not merely *survival*); on inflation. Review every eighteen or twenty-four months instead of twelve.

TACTIC #59
Stop Paying Weekly

Do you pay employees weekly? Most small businesses should not be paying employees more often than every other week. The administrative costs of doing a weekly payroll are especially high for small companies. You can cut those costs by perhaps 20% to 40% by reducing your payroll frequency.

TACTIC #60
Age-Weight Your Pension Plan

One of the newest opportunities limiting the cost of providing benefits to employees is the "age-weighted," or age-based, profit sharing pension plan. Such plans, cleared by Treasury Department and IRS rulings in 1992, are well suited to small business owners in their fifties whose employees are younger by an average of ten years or more. Age-weighted plans let small business owners avoid the "top-heavy" rules that otherwise bar them from putting a higher percentage of income into their own pension plans than they set aside for their employees.

You still have to include employees in the plan. But with this strategy you may be able to accelerate your own savings while putting less away for your younger workers. If you think this kind of plan may work well for you, get in touch with an accountant, financial planner, or consultant with experience in small business pensions.

SAVE-A-BUNDLE FOLLOW-UP FILE

• To set up a SEP, request Publications 560 and 590 and either Form 5305-SEP for a basic plan, or 5305A-SEP for a salary-reduction SEP, from a local IRS office, or call (800) TAX-FORM. Complete the form (a mere six lines or so) and you're ready to go.

• Attendance Controller is a simple ring-bound system for tracking who's absent and *why*, produced by G. Neil Companies of Sunrise, Florida. A package of fifty forms costs about $30. Call (800) 999-9111.

• Automated Data Processing (ADP) offers a free *Payroll Tax Guide* for business, updated yearly. Call (800) 225-5237 or write to ADP Response Center, 335 Bishop Hollow Road, Newtown Square, PA 19073. The compact guide briefs you on facts, forms, and figures you need to know about payroll processing and IRS rules. For questions on how a payroll service can help, call ADP's payroll services division in Roseland, New Jersey—(201) 994-5000—or a local ADP office.

• Paychex, Inc., based in Rochester, New York, specializes in payroll services for small business. Call (800) 322-7292.

• Chicago-based Reid Psychological Systems has tons of research on testing in different industries. Call (800) 922-7343; fax (312) 294-0140. Another firm that provides general employee testing services is the Stanton Pinkerton Services Group, based in Charlotte, North Carolina. Call (800) 438-5959; fax (704) 554-1806.

• Jobs for the Future, based in Cambridge, Massachusetts, is a nonprofit organization that works with youth apprenticeship programs throughout the United States. Write to 1815 Massachusetts Avenue, Cambridge, MA 02140, or call (617) 661-3411.

• The National Tooling and Machining Association conducts an annual national apprentice contest. For information call NTMA in Fort Washington, Maryland, at (800) 248-6862; fax (301) 248-7104.

• *Internships* ($29.95), a directory published by Peterson's, an educational publisher in Princeton, New Jersey, lists details on company-sponsored internships. For information on listing a position, call (800) 338-3282.

• The National Society for Experiential Education, in Raleigh, North Carolina, publishes *The National Directory of*

Internships ($29.50) every two years. For information on list-ing a position, call (919) 787-3263; fax (919) 787-3381.

• *Real Jobs for Real People: An Employer's Guide to Youth Apprenticeship Programs*, a handbook published by the Washington, D.C.–based National Alliance of Business, offers some solid advice. Cost is $12.95. Call (202) 289-2910.

• The *Independent Contractor Report* is a monthly news-letter ($95/year) published by James R. Urquhart III Semi-nars in Irvine, California. Urquhart's seminars on independent contractors—including tips on how to safeguard independent contractor status—are super and cost under $200 to attend. Urquhart's book *The IRS, Independent Contrac-tors, and You* ($24.95) is a worthwhile read. Call (800) 262-6554; in California, (800) 826-3830.

• *Employer's Handbook: Independent Contractor vs. Em-ployee* ($297; includes monthly updates for a year) is a com-prehensive manual for protecting contract worker status at your business. From Thompson Publishing Group, (800) 964-5815.

• *Tax Guide for Small Business*, the IRS's Publication 334, includes information on independent contractors. If you're among the gifted few who can actually understand IRS-speak, call (800) TAX-FORM to get a copy.

• No-load mutual fund groups are an excellent place to set up a retirement plan with minimal expense. T. Rowe Price Associates, for example, offers a compelling line of low-cost, low-maintenance 401(k) and SEP plans for small business. Call (800) 638-3006 to reach one of the firm's retirement plan specialists. Other fund groups to consider include Dreyfus, (800) 373-9387; Fidelity, (800) 544-8888; Vanguard, (800) 962-5086; Scudder, (800) 225-2470; and INVESCO, (800) 525-8085.

• The Principal Financial Group, based in Des Moines, Iowa, is one of the nation's biggest providers of pension plans for small business. Call (800) 543-4015, ext. 80505.

• *Employee Performance Appraisal* ($119) is one of the top-selling manuals published by Borgman Associates, 321 Lennon Lane, Walnut Creek, CA 94598. Ask for the firm's free Personnel Department Store catalog, filled with guide-books, how-to kits, videos, software, and newsletters on hir-ing and managing employees. Call (800) 942-4494; fax (510) 988-1888.

• *Getting Results: The Performance Appraisal Process* ($139) is an innovative audiocassette/workbook program avail-able from the American Management Association (AMA). It shows you how to use ongoing performance appraisals to boost productivity and morale, decrease turnover and absenteeism, and improve work quality. There's a 10% discount for AMA members. Call (800) 538-4761. Request publication #80134.

CHAPTER 5

Sending and Receiving Your Stuff

TACTIC #61
Clean Up Your Lists and Add Zip + 4 for Free

Here's a cost-cutting punch that's hard to beat: a free service (updating mailing lists; adding Zip + 4 codes) that can help you save 20% or more on your mailings.

One of the biggest postage wasters for business is mailing to bad addresses. The Diskette Coding Service, from the U.S. Postal Service, will update your commercial mailing lists— correcting most faulty street and city names and Zip codes— and add Zip+4. No charge. "Slip us your diskettes and we'll straighten up your mailing lists," says USPS. Send in your address files on personal computer disk and they'll standardize your address records, correct your regular Zips, and add Zip+4. Call (800) 238-3150 for information. One freebie per customer.

To update your own lists, buy a software program that does it for as little as $35. See the Follow-up File.

TACTIC #62
Presorted Zip and Zip + 4

Presorting mail gets you a discount of about 15% on first-class mailings of five hundred or more and third-class drops of two hundred and up. Presorting basically means that you bundle mail going to the same area. Even the most basic presort level puts $1,500 in your pocket if you've been spending $10,000 per year; $15,000 if your budget's more like $100,000. There are various rules and requirements; ask your P.O. for details or check the publications listed in the Follow-up File.

TACTIC #63
Nonpresorted Zip + 4

With nonpresorted Zip+4 the savings aren't huge, but by converting your lists to Zip+4 you can knock about 1.4 cents per piece, or 5%, off the rate on mailings of 250 or more. A business that does, say, four such mailings a month (1,000 pieces total) would save $156 per year. Again, USPS will convert your mailing list (supplied on computer disk) to Zip+4, and will correct addresses at the same time, for free on a one-time basis. Contact your nearest Postal Business Center or the USPS National Customer Support Center, 6060 Primacy Parkway, #101, Memphis, TN 38188-0001; (800) 238-3150; fax (901) 757-8853.

TACTIC #64
Bank the Bar Code Bonus

When you get to Zip+4 with bar codes you're approaching the Holy Grail of postal savings. Bar-coded eleven-digit Zips (that's Zip+4+2, known as delivery point bar code, or DPBC) earn the biggest discounts—up to nearly 20% for the highest level of sorting. The bar code, by the way, is merely a graphic version of the Zip code number portrayed as a series of long and short bars.

If your firm mails in-house, this will require an investment in equipment and software, or an upgrade of your existing equipment. But the payback can come in less than a year, depending on your volume. When you buy hardware or software, make sure you get the latest upgrades, capable of handling DPBC! If you use an outside mail service, saving money can be as simple as asking them to apply the bar codes.

TACTIC #65
Get Front-Door Pickup of Five Hundred Packages for Under $5

Which service will pick up every overnight or two-day package you've got—whether it's one, ten, or a thousand—for a total charge of $4.50? USPS will. And that's a bargain that can save big money and big time whether your business is big or

> ### *Titans of Postal Tightwadery*
>
> Small business owners Jim and Amy Dacyczyn in Leeds, Maine, are card-carrying tightwads.
>
> They toss around nickels as if they were manhole covers. They should. Their business is publishing a consumer newsletter called the *Tightwad Gazette.* So what do these certified penny-pinchers do to save their own five-employee business some money? They tap the juicy discounts doled out to businesses that use Zip+4 and bar coding on their presorted mail. When the Dacyczyns (the name sounds like "decision") started the newsletter in June 1990 their subscriber list of 130 was below the 200 minimum for bulk-rate discounts. "So we sent extra copies to public libraries in order to qualify—and still saved money," says Jim. After mailings passed 30,000, old methods were too expensive and time-consuming. So Jim looked into bar coding. "The hardest thing was finding the right equipment," he says. Dacyczyn settled on a machine made by RENA Systems (see Follow-up File) that his postal rep had told him about. Dacyczyn figures his savings on a 40,000 mailing were about $1,000 in postage plus the cost of 170 hours of labor. And that'll turn a tightwad's head any day.

small. The charge is $4.50 per *pickup*, not per *package*. Just give the P.O. person $4.50 on your meter and you're set. You can also arrange a regular pickup for Express Mail, two-day Priority Mail, and parcel post. Call (800) 222-1811.

TACTIC #66
Claim Refunds for Meter Mess-ups

Postage meter mistakes happen. The machine may foul up; the operator may goof. Maybe you left something out of the envelope and had to use a new one after meter postage had already been applied. Whatever the source of the error, your business can apply for refunds on unused postage meter mess-ups for up to 90% of the face amount. Get the necessary claim forms at your local P.O. (USPS Form 3533) and put someone in charge of saving the messed-up meter tapes and envelopes. They're refundable for up to a year.

TACTIC #67
Join Forces with Other Mailers

Volume too puny for decent discounts? Find a mailing service or postal "presort" company in your area. These firms collect mail from small businesses, combine the mail for presorting/bar coding, and share in the savings. Patti Carter, owner of the Pony Mailing & Business Center in Oak Harbor, Washington, says that in addition to saving on postage, you will save in other ways as well:

- You'll make better use of employee time. Office managers, secretaries, and bookkeepers shouldn't be stuffing envelopes, licking stamps, or waiting in line at the P.O.

- You'll cut rental and maintenance costs for postage meters and related equipment—and gain more space to use for other purposes.
- Itemized statements showing mail volume and activity can help you better plan your mailings.
- You'll have access to postage experts who know how to jump through all the hoops to achieve the best rates.

Some USPS Business Centers (see Follow-up File) offer a free directory of private mailing and presort services, or check the Yellow Pages.

TACTIC #68
Check Out Express Mail Drop Shipping

Express Mail Drop Ship service is a cheap way to get large mailings to recipients overnight. Works like this: Bundle mail destined for the same city or area together and send the bundles via Express Mail to key cities. P.O. workers at the other end will pop those Express Mail pouches and route your mail immediately. The result is overnight service at a fraction of the overnight cost for sending each piece individually.

TACTIC #69
Speed Your Incoming Cash

If you receive payments and orders from a national customer base, you can accelerate delivery by directing this mail to local P.O. box addresses in key cities or regions. For a small fee, the USPS will package and Express Mail the contents to you. You get your money and orders faster.

TACTIC #70
Lower Overseas Mailing Costs

Check out these money savers from USPS Worldpost Services:

- International Surface Air Lift (ISAL) is cheapest, but slowest. Rates for larger volumes are based on total *weight* rather than the total number of pieces. Pitney Bowes, the mailing machine maker in Stamford, Connecticut, says that forty thousand half-ounce mail pieces (1,250 pounds) can be shipped to England via ISAL for less than half of what it would cost to mail them individually. Delivery time is seven to fourteen days. Pieces that weigh two ounces or less cost thirty-two cents each; per-pound rates for heavier pieces can cut that rate in half. Deposit mailings directly at Worldpost gateways in New York, San Francisco, and Miami and save another thirty cents per pound. Other discounts available. Call (202) 268-2263.
- If you have mailings of at least ten pounds or two hundred pieces of any class of international mail (but not parcel post), International Priority Airmail (IPA) lets you combine your mailings by country and ship at a lower per-pound rate. Delivery time on presorted International Priority Airmail is three to six days; four to seven days for nonpresorted. This may be the best bargain in the U.S. Postal Service's international system. There's a ten-pound minimum, mailings can be different sizes and weights, and there's free IPA pickup in service areas around dozens of major U.S. cities. Call (202) 268-2263.
- Express Mail International Service is a low-cost way to get two-day delivery to major cities overseas. Send up to eight ounces to Europe or Japan for $13. You can pay by postage meter, stamps, or via an Express Mail corporate account. Call your local post office.

BE AN EXPRESS/OVERNIGHT DELIVERY TIGHTWAD

TACTIC #71
Get Unhooked from the Overnight Habit

Does it absolutely, positively have to be there tomorrow morning? Or are we all hooked on the overnight delivery habit? One of today's biggest mailroom money wasters is misuse (morning delivery when cheaper afternoon delivery will do) and excessive use (spending $14 for overnight delivery on a Friday when a first-class stamp will get it there on Monday just as easily) of express delivery services. Ironically, companies that pinch postal pennies let large FedEx charges slip.

Adding up your total express delivery expense for last year is an eye-opener and a good first step toward shaking the overnight habit. Most companies underestimate what they are spending by a factor of *three*.

Then put someone in charge of deciding what needs to go express and what doesn't. Next afternoon and second-day service can trim costs 20% to 50%. Ground service through UPS or RPS (Roadway Package Service) can sometimes deliver local packages within two days at an even lower cost.

Set priorities; *ask recipients when they want to receive your package.* Firms that ask often discover that only about half of the intended recipients say they really need the item the next morning. In fact, some businesses prefer to receive these deliveries in the afternoon rather than early morning.

Say you have a ten-pound package that needs to get from Houston to Chicago by Wednesday and today is Monday. To be safe, you ship it overnight for $26 to $48, depending on the carrier. A two-day service, from UPS for example, could have delivered by Wednesday for around $13, for a hefty savings. And the recipient is just as happy either way. Cost spreads are significant. For example: next afternoon (possible 30% savings); second day (possible 60% savings); ground delivery (possible 80% savings).

TACTIC #72
Consolidate Shipments;
Bargain for Lower Rates

Don't be a right hand that doesn't know what the left hand is doing. Express shipments should be coordinated through one person or department. Those going to the same destination can be combined for savings. You can still combine items going to the same destination even if they are going to different people.

Consolidating with a single shipper also gives you muscle to negotiate a lower rate if your company's volume is large enough. Not all users pay the published rates; there's room here for some bargaining. The key is to arm yourself with complete details of how your company uses express services. That includes not only the number of shipments, but their weights and destinations as well.

TACTIC #73
Claim Your Refunds

Some carriers guarantee delivery by a specified time (10:30 A.M. or 3:00 P.M., for example). If they're late, you're probably due a refund. But one thing you can be sure of: *You won't get it unless you claim it*. Include a standard request in all your express packages asking the recipient to notify your office if the delivery is late. That will help alert you to refunds you're due. Call the express company's toll-free line and request the rebate.

Watch for additional charges that may appear on your invoices. A goofed-up address, perhaps just a missing Zip code digit, can trigger a charge of $5 or more. Dispute those charges if they are irrelevant to the delivery. The delivery firms will often relent and grant credit. But ya gotta ask.

TACTIC #74
Avoid the FedEx Friday Fiasco

How many times have those thriftless cads at your company sent a Federal Express (or UPS overnight, or Airborne, or DHL, or Emery) package for Monday delivery at the full overnight rate? If the answer is even once, you're overpaying by $10 to $15 a pop.

The money-saving solution: When you need Monday delivery and it's Friday, use two-day Priority Mail instead. You'll still get Monday delivery and you can send up to two pounds for a paltry $2.90 (at 1994 rates). Why pay 300%, 400%, or more for the same darned service?

Priority Mail is simple and cheap, but effective. It's great for packages up to two pounds—and much cheaper than both overnight and second-day delivery from the private carriers. Pop whatever you have into a Priority Mail "Flat Rate Envelope," slap on the postage, and your package is on its way.

Still another way to save—let the USPS pay for envelopes instead of your business. Pick up a supply of free Priority Mail envelopes—including the letter-size cardboard jobs and the larger plastic ones—from the post office.

TACTIC #75
Use Express Mail on the Road

Traveling? Need to send something overnight? FedEx, UPS, and some of the other alternative carriers have convenient drop boxes and outlets in major cities and many airports. But they can't match the U.S. Postal Service's nationwide network of sixty-six thousand Express Mail boxes and post offices.

You don't need cash or stamps or meters or any of that stuff. Open an Express Mail corporate account and take a few of the preprinted labels and flat-rate envelopes along—they go for a bargain rate no matter how much you cram into the envelope. Express Mail will forward your package at no extra charge if the recipient has moved. You also get Saturday delivery at no extra charge.

FOCUS ON YOUR FREIGHT

TACTIC #76
Audit Your Freight Bills

If your business does a large volume of shipping and you aren't auditing the bills from your trucker, you may be losing money. Freight bills are notoriously error prone, partly the legacy of massive trucking industry deregulation in the 1980s. Every day, thousands of companies overpay for freight because they haven't checked for accuracy.

You needn't do this yourself. Find a firm that specializes in auditing freight bills and set 'em loose on yours. If form holds, they'll find plenty of unintentional errors that are costing you money. Such audit firms will normally charge a fee plus a percentage (half is not unusual) of any money you recover from errors they find.

The best system, however, is to check invoices *before you pay them.* Verify shipping weights and freight classifications with your own records, dates, and delivery locations. And never pay duplicate invoices (they should be marked "duplicate"); only pay originals. Crank up your calculator. Many mistakes are merely sloppy math.

TACTIC #77
Make Your Freight Claims Stick

Damaged and lost freight shipments—both incoming and out-going—cost U.S. business an estimated $1 billion or more per year. Such losses even drive some small companies into bankruptcy. According to John Price of the Reno, Nevada–based Freight Claims Inspection Bureau, you can capture savings here two ways:

1. By taking steps to avoid the loss in the first place; and
2. By knowing how to document and collect on a freight damage claim.

Price, who has helped many businesses collect freight claims, recommends that only trained personnel be assigned to receive freight and that all paperwork attesting to the safe arrival of the goods be carefully cross-checked with the actual goods. Hurried employees often fail to inspect boxes and sign for items that aren't really there.

Look for little things that may indicate a problem: boxes that are taped shut but have staple holes showing (an indication they've been opened); boxes sealed with different types of tape or different sealing methods (i.e., some shrink-wrapped, some banded); ruptured tape; open, buckled, or crushed boxes. When damage or other problems are found, they should be recorded immediately on the freight bill. Be specific about what the problem is. Take photos of damage. Documentation will be crucial later in collecting any money.

On the flip side, it's critical that *outgoing* packages be properly sealed and clearly marked. The vast majority of all freight claims are caused by faulty packaging or labeling at the point of origin.

A helpful, hands-on guidebook on spotting, documenting, and collecting freight claims is the *Freight Claims Handbook* ($24.95) by John Price. Order from Freight Claims Inspection Bureau, P.O. Box 20008, Reno, NV 89515; call (702) 972-4617.

POSTAL POTPOURRI

TACTIC #78
Collect These Golden Nuggets

- *Get savings by the truckload.* If your business mails or ships parcels by the truckload you needn't pay for your own trucks or a trucking service to haul your mail to the P.O. You may qualify for "Plant Loading," a USPS pickup service. Check with a USPS Business Center near you.
- *Take a ride on RPS.* One of the latest entries in the two-day service derby is Roadway Package System's RPSAir. With this new kid looking to steal market share, there's a bargain to be had here. Reach RPS at (800) 762-3725.
- *Use smaller envelopes.* As editor of *IB* magazine (*Independent Business*), I receive hundreds of pieces of first-class mail each week from small businesses, PR agencies, and corporate PR departments. It's often a heavy-gauge nine-by-twelve or ten-by-thirteen envelope with one to three pages inside. The size and weight of the envelope requires postage for two ounces instead of one. A big waste. And those envelopes aren't cheap.
- *Get tougher on pirated postage.* Remind employees that your postage meter isn't their personal post office. Audit your outgoing mail from time to time to check up.
- *Use a postage scale.* Don't guess at how much your mail weighs—you'll always use too much postage. A small electronic postage scale will pay for itself in savings in short order.
- *Join the postcard renaissance.* Postcards—Cheap City when it comes to mailings—are making a comeback. They're a quick and convenient way to make your point.
- *Put bar codes on return mail too.* Printing bar codes on your business reply cards and envelopes (BRCs and

BREs) will also earn you discounts on postage. Speeds your replies too.

- *For a receipt, use* certified *not registered mail.* Certified costs much less. If you need insurance as well, use registered—the insurance ups the price.
- *Use your lists intelligently.* For example, sending catalogs of gardening products to someone whose street address includes the word "Apt." doesn't make much sense.
- *Don't invoice separately.* If possible, combine invoicing with product shipments to save the additional postage and other costs of mailing separately. This also allows you to eliminate a shipping or packing list that's usually sent with a product. The invoice can serve the same function.

SAVE-A-BUNDLE FOLLOW-UP FILE

- Your nearest USPS Business Center is a terrific source for cost-cutting information. The Business Centers are new, created in the early 1990s specifically to help business customers become more efficient and cost-effective mailers. More Business Centers are being opened all the time (there are about one hundred at this writing). Call your P.O. for the nearest location.
- The USPS's National Customer Support Center has a slew of helpful printed, disk, or CD-ROM directories and other services that can help improve your mailings. For a complete list call (800) 238-3150; fax (901) 767-8853.
- For USPS Priority and Express Mail pickup, the number to call is (800) 222-1811.

Software

- A free program called Mail Flow Planning System is available from USPS. This disk (for IBM) lets any size business easily compare current monthly mailing costs and calculate discounts for any class of mail. Call (800) 238-3150.
- MyAdvancedMailList is a mouthful of a name for a great software deal. Publisher MySoftware Company, of Menlo

Park, California, specializes in small business applications. MyAdvancedMailList (version 4.0 or higher) will apply eleven-digit (DPBC) bar codes to your mail and will automatically generate the eleven-digit codes from existing Zip+4. Suggested retail is $59.95, but you can buy both IBM and Macintosh versions at outlets such as K mart, Wal-Mart, Office Club, Office Depot, CompUSA, and some smaller retailers for around $35. Reach the company at (800) 325-3508.

• Group 1 Software, of Lanham, Maryland, offers several helpful software programs: ArcList ($995) is a powerful mail-handling package for business. AccuMail ($295 per quarter) applies eleven-digit bar codes and comes with national database updates on CD-ROM. Dupe Eliminator ($149) purges list duplicates. Call (800) 368-5806; fax (301) 731-0360.

• Envelope Manager lets you apply bar codes using only a PC and laser printer, no other special equipment required. Available in several versions starting at $79.95 from Envelope Manager Software, Palo Alto, CA; (800) 576-3279; fax (415) 321-0356.

• RateFinder, an inexpensive software program for both IBM and Macintosh, can help manage shipping costs. It offers an easy way to compare rates for FedEx, UPS, Airborne Express, and USPS. Enter the destination Zip code, your Zip code, the package weight and—presto—RateFinder shows you rate comparison tables for the major delivery companies. International rates too. You can also customize the program. The $119 price includes shipping and six months of rate-change updates. After that, updates are $49 per year (or input your own). Call (800) 756-0511; fax (303) 840-7314 or write to West/Marketing Associates, 10940 South Parker Road, #511, Parker, CO 80134-7439.

• Pony Express is a shareware program (see Tactic #112) that will compare the cost of sending a package via USPS, FedEx, or UPS, plus other features. You should be able to find it through a computer users' group in your area. Or get it from Glossbrenner's Choice for $5 (5¼" disk) or $6 (3½" disk) each plus $3 shipping. Write to 699 River Road, Yardley, PA 19067-1965.

• Postbar is an easy-to-use program for around $99 from Electronic Technologies of Rochester, Michigan; call (800) 325-7379.

Hardware

• Two companies that make USPS-certified address/barcoding equipment are RENA Systems—call (800) 426-7905—in King of Prussia, Pennsylvania, and Bryce Office Systems, which markets its equipment through Datatech Enterprises; call (800) 523-0320.

• Pitney Bowes, a leading maker of mailing equipment, is a great source of mailing efficiency tips; the company offers a free booklet: *35 Timely Tips to Get the Most from Your Mailing*. Call (800) MR BOWES.

Seminars

• USPS offers an ongoing series of seminars across the country through its Mailer Education Center. Choose from seven designed to help businesses cut costs. Fees range from $75 for a half-day course to $275 for a two-day marathon. For a complete schedule call (800) 877-7843.

Where to Reach 'Em

• For rate and account information, call:

ADCOM Express:	(800) 747-7424
Airborne Express:	(800) 426-2323
DHL Worldwide Express:	(800) 225-5345
Emery Worldwide:	(800) 443-6379
Express Mail:	(800) 222-1811
Federal Express:	(800) 238-5355
Roadway Package System & RPSAir:	(800) 762-3725
United Parcel Service:	(800) 222-8333

- *MAIL: The Journal of Communication Distribution* is $27 per year (eight issues). Write to Gold Key Box 2425, Milford, PA 18337-9607. To subscribe call (607) 746-7600; fax (607) 746-2750. Terrific little magazine for mailroom managers; includes articles on saving money. Good place to find mail equipment and software vendors.
- Mailcom is a major annual exhibition with dozens of seminars on cost-cutting. Sponsored by *MAIL* magazine and the Mail Systems Management Association (MSMA). For info on the show, write to Four Court Street, Delhi, NY 13753. For membership information on MSMA call (800) 955-6762.
- Curtis 1000 is an Atlanta-based printer and envelope company that specializes in making business reply mail postal-correct. The firm's boast: "If we can't save you postal dollars on reply mail, nobody can!" Call (800) 766-1007.

CHAPTER 6

Marvelous Manufacturing Money Savers

TACTIC #79
Tap High-Tech Help at a Low-Tech Cost

Here's a crafty move that can cannonball small manufacturers into the technological big top. It's a successful, though still little-known, program that brings leading-edge manufacturing technologies to small companies at bargain rates.

Thousands of small manufacturers have already received valuable aid from at least seven (more are being added) manufacturing technology centers (MTCs) now operating across the United States. The MTCs have helped companies cut costs, increase efficiency, and capture new business.

The centers were spawned by a 1988 law that ordered the U.S. Commerce Department's National Institute of Standards and Technology (NIST) to help pass along technology developed by big companies and government research labs to smaller manufacturers. NIST (the old U.S. Bureau of Standards) created MTCs to serve as technology "distribution" centers for small manufacturers.

Yes, that does make this a government-*inspired* program, but not government *run*. The MTCs are linked to technology institutes and community colleges, which deal directly with the company/clients. Some results:

Savings of $220,000 in a Few Weeks Brimfield Precision, Inc., an eighty-five-employee prosthetic body parts manufacturer (replacement hip and knee joints) in Brimfield, Massachusetts, saved $220,000 in the span of a few weeks. The firm was about to drop a quarter million dollars on a mainframe computer to upgrade its computerized design and manufacturing capabilities. The decision to spend such a huge sum was critical to the company's future. The wrong choice could mean financial ruin.

Before making the decision, company president Bill Lyons learned of the MTC program. He called. After meeting with field engineers for the Northeast Manufacturing Technology Center (NEMTC) and reviewing over fifty combinations of hardware and software the MTC had on-line and ready to "test drive," Lyons discovered that a simpler system costing just $30,000 could do the job *and* allow the company to perform custom design and development work for other firms. The savings bowled over Brimfield, and the company went on to tap the MTC's expertise to establish other cost-cutting measures such as computerized production control systems for inventory management and parts tracking.

Fortified at Fortitech   Walter Borisenok, president of Fortitech, Inc., was thrilled by what the MTC program did for his twenty-employee company in Schenectady, New York. Fortitech manufactures vitamin-mineral concentrates that major food processors use in such things as cereals and infant food. Since each mixture is custom made, Fortitech was doing all the formulating and batch mixing by hand. That tied up expensive labor on essentially mundane tasks. "We needed a computer system for that work," says Borisenok.

So Fortitech turned to the Northeast Manufacturing Technology Center for help. Within six months, NEMTC professionals "wrote the program for us, trained our personnel, and got us up and running," says Borisenok. "Now we make and ship each order faster, by as much as a week."

The cost of this help varies and may depend on how long the local program has been operating. Because MTCs receive federal start-up money but must be self-supporting by year six, help is often free for the first year or two. After that, small manufacturers pay up to two-thirds of costs.

High Fives at Highland   Highland Manufacturing, Inc., is another of more than one thousand small companies that have sought help from the Northeast MTC. Dominick Martorana owns this twenty-five-year-old firm with fifteen employees in Highland, New York. Highland makes components for electronic devices such as printing press ink regulators and food packaging systems.

Martorana discovered the technology center when he began searching for computer-aided design and manufacturing (CAD/CAM) techniques. "As a small business owner, I don't have time to research all the hardware and software myself," he says. So NEMTC did it—at no cost to Martorana. Program experts studied the company and supplied evaluations of software choices.

Painting Profits AccuSpray and Bessam-Aire, family-owned companies that share facilities in the Cleveland suburb of Bedford Heights, invested $15,000 in the Great Lakes MTC (GLMTC) and realized cost savings and other profit increases that by now measure in the millions. The MTC showed Accu-Spray how it could use its plant more efficiently and avoid spending $500,000 on a new facility.

Bessam-Aire was designing its large air-handling ductwork by hand; the MTC introduced it to computer design and saved tens of thousands per year. AccuSpray was tapping into a booming market in more efficient, less polluting low-pressure paint sprayers, mandated by strict air quality laws in many states. GLMTC helped design a 50% more efficient compressor.

A CAD for Profits At Steris Corp., a fast-growing manufacturer of sterilizing equipment for surgical tools, based in Mentor, Ohio, the biggest manufacturing challenge has been designing new custom-fit instrument trays for an ever-changing array of medical instruments in complex shapes. A single tray prototype costs about $20,000 to design.

Computer-aided design (CAD) was the solution. GLMTC helped Steris test and select the best hardware and software for the job, putting the company on the track to estimated annual labor savings of over $100,000. The cost to Steris for the expert help: $1,200.

So far, companies have been locating MTCs mostly through word of mouth. Some firms that have been helped are one-person operations; others have over a hundred employees. The main requirements are that you manufacture something and you need a technology boost. Available areas of help include

- Computer-aided design and computer-aided manufacturing;
- Quality and inspection improvement;
- Plant layout;
- Equipment upgrade;
- Production planning and control; and
- Special projects.

The centers also conduct manufacturing workshops and have facilities equipped with millions of dollars in hardware and software that you can test drive. See the Follow-up File for MTC locations.

TACTIC #80
Pare Your Product Packaging

Eliminate redundant or unnecessary packaging to cut costs. Gus Blythe, owner of SecondWind Co., in Paso Robles, California, blew out excess packaging and saved a small fortune for his company. SecondWind is a fifteen-employee firm that makes athletic shoe and foot-care products and accessories— deodorizers, replacement insoles, cleaners, and creams that extend shoe life. Blythe estimated that 25% to 35% of his costs (SecondWind's products mostly sell for under $10) were due to packaging.

During its first eight years in business, SecondWind packaged all ten of its products in individual boxes. Now only one product is boxed. The result is a dramatic reduction in materials costs—SecondWind eliminated twenty-eight tons of paper and cardboard annually, saving the company $68,750 to start. Blythe went further, axing the plastic caps and applicator sponges that came with some product packaging, producing another $12,000 annual savings. Even the little cardboard strips that SecondWind's shoelaces come wrapped around were downsized to trim costs.

Blythe says the packaging reductions proved so efficient that he was also able to cut his prices and move more products.

TACTIC #81
Join a "Flexible Manufacturing Network"

"Flexible manufacturing networks" are one of the hottest cost-cutting moves of the decade for small manufacturers. Dozens of local networks—from Chicago's Metalworking Consortium to the Kentucky Wood Manufacturers Network, Indiana's FlexCell Group, and the Tri-State Manufacturers Association (Minnesota and North and South Dakota)—have sprouted since 1990, enabling smaller firms to cut costs and become more competitive through strength in numbers. They offer group members more efficient purchasing, lower-cost worker training, shared access to production expertise, and more marketing muscle both in the United States and abroad.

At the Pacific Wood Products Cooperative—a 190-member manufacturing network in Washington State—joint purchasing has helped member companies cut supply expenses by as much as 80% in some cases. Check with your manufacturing industry peers as well as local, state, and national industry associations to locate a network in your area.

TACTIC #82
Get Out of the Warehouse Business

Sure you need warehousing. But do you really need to own or lease your own exclusive space? For thousands of companies, the answer is no. They'd rather focus on their core manufacturing business, not the storage/warehousing business.

If you own or lease a warehouse, consider what it's costing you in overhead that may be hidden in your overall costs of doing business:

- Hiring, training, and paying employees to conduct warehouse and distribution activities. Include benefits and sundry administrative costs.
- Cash that's tied up in your building.
- Maintenance and taxes.
- Equipment—forklifts, trucks, trailers, and the like.
- Insurance.
- Utilities. Are you paying to heat or cool a half-empty space?

Public warehousing can help you cut costs and free up cash for more productive investment. Public warehousing can work especially well for manufacturers, import-export firms, mail-order companies, and distributors of various types. You pay only for what you use. When your inventory drops, *so should your warehousing costs.* No matter what your product, you gain access to storage, inventory, labeling, packaging, and other services that you pay for as needed. Some cost-conscious considerations:

- *Seasonal products:* Pay for space only when your products are ready to be stored or shipped.
- *Room for all types and sizes*, from candy bars and paper goods, to autos and electronics. Whether you need warm, cool, or freezer space, it's available.

- *Pick and pack:* Individual orders can be repackaged and fulfilled to be sent to your customers.
- *Advance cost analysis:* The warehousing folks can help inventory your goods, provide activity reports, predict labor hours, and anticipate your overall warehousing and distribution costs. They can generate shipping orders and invoices too. Some businesses are linking computer-to-computer with their warehousing firm through an electronic data interchange system. That eliminates paper and speeds everything.
- *Freight consolidation:* Warehousing firms can combine goods from several manufacturers for shipping to the same location, thus saving on trucking costs.

A switch to public warehousing might even gain your company an approving nod from the bank. "Public warehousing reduces fixed costs," says George Contarsy, head of commercial lending at Manufacturers Bank in Chicago. "If you take a fixed cost like real estate and convert it to a variable cost like public warehousing, it can make all the difference in the world to a company's bottom line."

Animal Crackers Goes Public Stauffer Biscuits, the York, Pennsylvania–based maker of Animal Crackers and other cookies, uses public warehousing to streamline production and cut costs. In the late 1980s, this growing company considered building its own warehouses. A decision to "go public" instead is now credited with helping the firm grow at a 15% annual clip.

"If we built our own warehouses, they'd need to be large enough to support our business during peak periods," says Carlous Sutton, operations VP at Stauffer. But a warehouse big enough to do that would be *too* big during much of the year when business is slower. Sutton estimates that the idle warehouse space would be costing Stauffer an extra $100,000 annually.

The cookie baker also reckons that freight savings due to

combined shipping comes to another $100,000 annually for the firm. Stauffer ships about two million cases of products per year and uses about thirty thousand square feet of storage.

Other "name" firms big on public warehousing, according to the American Warehouse Association, include General Electric, Molson Breweries, Scott Paper, Bumble Bee Seafoods, Weyerhaeuser Lumber, John Deere, and Tropicana.

Comparison Shop for Warehousing Space Inspect any facility you are considering. If it doesn't look well run, it probably isn't. Ask if you're allowed to pick up and deliver items yourself to lower your costs. Investigate the warehousing firm's insurance coverage and check with your own insurance carrier to see what coverage you have or need. Get references and talk to some of the firm's other customers. See the Follow-up File for more.

TACTIC #83
Cut Your Materials Costs

Operations account for 20% to 40% of all manufacturing costs, while materials account for 60% to 80%. So why do most manufacturers look first to the operations side for cuts?

Good question, says A. T. Kearney, Inc., a global management consulting firm based in Chicago. To find some answers, Kearney studied cost-cutting efforts at twenty major manufacturers, including Ford, Xerox, GE, Rockwell, Dow Chemical, DuPont, Hewlett-Packard, Motorola, Black & Decker, 3M, NCR, TRW, Emerson Electric, and others. According to Kearney, the average company that tries to reduce materials costs achieves savings of about 12%. Over a three-year period, the twenty manufacturers studied zapped an estimated $24 *billion* in materials costs from their budgets. Gadzooks! Kearney fingered three basic techniques that the best cost cutters used:

1. *A broader supply base.* The best deals on materials aren't necessarily available in your state, region, or even the United States. The big guys now consider the entire world their supply base. They go where they get the best deal.
2. *Consolidation.* You know the drill. The more you buy from one supplier, the better deal you'll get. If your company has more than one location, product line, or division, make sure they buy in unison.
3. *Aggressive, long-term agreements.* When you do find a bargain, *lock it in.* Three- to five-year supply deals are common. "While many U.S. manufacturers stress long-term agreements with their suppliers, the leaders are more demanding of their supplier partners," says James Kuhn, who conducted the cost-cutting study at A. T. Kearney. "They typically build in tough clauses to agreements that require suppliers to achieve a preestablished schedule of improvements in cost, quality, delivery, and lead time."

It's not just big companies that save. Scott Fisher, owner of Topflight Products, Inc., in Franklin, Wisconsin, manufactures kites and aviation novelties. After more than ten years of growth, which brought his business to $1 million in revenues and twenty-two employees by the beginning of the 1990s, Fisher figured it was time to trim his company's costs. One of Fisher's first moves was to consolidate raw material purchases at fewer vendors in return for a 5% discount.

TACTIC #84
Get the *Right* Information

When bumbling Inspector Clouseau (Peter Sellers) arrives at a quaint village hotel in Germany in *The Pink Panther Strikes Again*, he spots a sleeping dog near the front desk.

"Does your dog bite?" Clouseau asks the disinterested inn-keeper.

"No," says he, nose buried in a newspaper.

Thus assured, Clouseau tries to pet the pooch, which promptly provides a vicious bite.

"I thought you said your dog didn't bite," barks an indignant Clouseau at the innkeeper, who still hasn't looked up.

"I did," says the innkeeper, pausing a beat for the finisher. *"That's not my dog."*

Clouseau learned a lesson of modern business management: Information—even the kind you explicitly seek—doesn't always mean what you thought when applied to the real world.

The same goes for information you *think* you have on your manufacturing costs. There may be hidden meanings; hidden costs. Labor costs, for example, are usually shown as a single number. But according to a couple of CPAs with the Northbrook, Illinois, firm of Miller, Cooper & Co., that kind of conventional thinking may be bankrupting American industry. In fact, say William Wiersema and Robert LeFevre, labor costs aren't so simple.

An aggregated labor expense figure hides costs of downtime, overtime, setup, rework, use of old equipment, and needlessly manual operations. Poor product design also ups labor costs and so do small orders that take a disproportionate share of setup time and thus result in less profit. "Some companies engage in the dangerous practice of labeling certain overhead items as 'fixed' and then totally disregard them when attempting to control costs," say Wiersema and LeFevre.

The solution: *Identify the root cause of each cost.* Only then can you control that cost. Here's what the two CPAs say you can do to get better info on your real manufacturing costs:

- Split the cost of scrap, downtime, and idle facilities from other production costs. For example, scrap is often a large, *controllable* cost that shouldn't be disguised as materials or overhead. Here's the problem. Consider a company that cuts sheet metal into squares and circles. Assuming the same amount of work is required for each shape, the company applies the same scrap cost to the square as the circle. But any grade schooler with a scissors knows that ain't so; the circle generates more scrap.

By lumping it all together, there's no incentive to find efficiencies in the less efficient operation. Say the CPAs: "Scrap cost can be controlled by changing sheet size to one just large enough for the shapes; by rearranging the pattern, which determines the shapes cut from the original sheet; or by modifying the size of shapes fabricated."

- Don't simply count idle time; look for causes that you can correct. Say, for example, you must stop assembling flashlights because one of the parts is late or faulty. The cost of that downtime gets charged to the purchasing area, and it should be considered when you decide what to pay the vendor for that item.

- Determine your costs by *customer*. If one customer orders a thousand flashlights built to certain specs, needs them shipped a thousand miles, and pays you in ninety days, while another orders ten thousand, is located fifty miles away, and pays in thirty days, your overhead costs by customer are different. Unless you know what those costs are, you can't accurately calculate minimum order levels or volume discounts.

SAVE-A-BUNDLE FOLLOW-UP FILE

I Want My MTC!

- Northeast MTC, 385 Jordan Road, Troy, NY 12180-8347; (518) 283-1010; fax (518) 283-1112.
- Southeast MTC, P.O. Box 1149, Columbia, SC 29202; (803) 252-6976; fax (803) 252-0056.

• Great Lakes MTC, 2415 Woodland Avenue, Cleveland, OH 44115; (216) 987-3202; fax (216) 361-2900.

• Midwest MTC, P.O. Box 1485, Ann Arbor, MI 48106; (313) 769-4377; fax (313) 769-4064.

• Mid-America MTC, 10561 Barkley, #602, Overland Park, KS 66212; (913) 649-4333; fax (913) 649-4498.

• Upper Midwest MTC, 111 Third Avenue South, #400, Minneapolis, MN 55401; (612) 338-7722; fax (612) 339-5214.

• California MTC, 13430 Hawthorne Boulevard, Hawthorne, CA 90250; (310) 355-3060; fax (310) 676-8630.

• National Institute of Standards and Technology (NIST), Manufacturing Technology Centers Program, Kevin Carr, Deputy Director, Building 224, Room B115, Gaithersburg, MD 20899; (301) 975-5020; fax (301) 963-6556. NIST is the U.S. Commerce Department division that oversees the MTCs. Plans call for expanding the program to thirty centers.

• The National Technology Transfer Center (NTTC) was created by NASA and the U.S. Congress to accelerate technology transfer from federal labs to commercial companies. NTTC acts as a corporate advocate inside the maze of seven-hundred-plus federal laboratories (including a hundred thousand researchers and $22 billion in annual funds), helping U.S. businesses of all sizes tap a vast pool of developed and evolving technologies. NTTC uses a sophisticated data base to scan tens of thousands of government research projects for information that might be helpful. It then arranges introductions between the company and the researchers, and monitors those contacts to make certain something happens. The program's still new and unproven. But if it works as planned, it could be a good way to leverage your R&D dollars or establish first-time R&D at little cost. Call NTTC (based at Wheeling Jesuit College in Wheeling, West Virginia) at (800) 678-NTTC; fax (304) 243-2463.

• Some federal research labs are establishing their own programs to help small and midsize companies solve manufacturing problems and cut costs. Problems that can be resolved in a few days are often handled for free; tougher issues may involve a charge. Agencies that have launched such programs include Oak Ridge National Laboratory, Oak Ridge, Tennessee, and Sandia National Laboratories, Albuquerque, New Mexico. Free advice from Oak Ridge experts has helped scores of small Tennessee manufacturers save tens of thousands of dollars. For example, Star Manufacturing Co., which makes popcorn poppers and hotdog cookers in Smithville, reduced costs by $10,000 per year when Oak Ridge suggested a way to eliminate a welding-caused blemish on the front of its griddles.

• New York State's Industrial Effectiveness Program (IEP) is a highly regarded effort that has helped hundreds of small manufacturers since 1988. Run by the state's Department of Economic Development, the IEP finds consultants, shares costs, and helps small New York manufacturers implement new high-tech procedures. Call (518) 474-1131. Check your state agencies to see what's available. Pennsylvania, for example, has set up eight not-for-profit corporations to offer hands-on services for small and midsize manufacturers that can't afford expensive consultants. Other states with active field programs include Georgia, Indiana, Iowa, Maryland, New Jersey, North Carolina, Ohio, South Carolina, Tennessee, and Virginia.

• *Technology Access Report* ($447/year) is a San Rafael, California–based newsletter that covers technology issues. Call (800) 733-1516; fax (415) 507-0661. Free sample available.

• For information on using a public warehousing firm, contact the American Warehouse Association, 1300 West Higgins Road, Suite 111, Park Ridge, IL 60068; (708) 292-1891; fax (708) 292-1896.

• Gearing Up, which bills itself as a shopping mall of advanced research and resources for manufacturers, hopes to be a yearly event that brings together the best new manufacturing ideas from corporate America, government, and academia. The first Gearing Up, in 1992, was sponsored by heavy manufacturing hitters, including Whirlpool Corp., General Motors, Dow Chemical, and Dow Corning. It offered participants help with eliminating scrap, getting better results without buying new equipment, and reducing downtime. Though its future is uncertain, it's worth a call to Donald Schutt, AMPM Marketing & Advertising, in Midland, Michigan, at (800) 530-9100; fax (517) 832-0781. Attendance at the nonprofit event is also priced right: about $35.

CHAPTER 7

Terrific T&E for Less

TACTIC #85
Write a Company Travel Policy

You need one to stipulate what level of travel the company is willing to pay for and what procedures employees are expected to follow. Will the company pay for a nonstop flight when a cheaper one-stop fare is available? What class of hotel fits your budget? How are expenses reimbursed? What documentation is required? James Firestone, executive vice-president with American Express Small Business and Corporate Services in New York, says that a written policy alone can save your business as much as 35% on total T&E costs.

Make the policy unambiguous, easy to understand and enforce. Consider taking these cost-control positions in your travel policy:

- The biggest travel savings of all come from *not traveling*. Set guidelines on when travel is permitted, and when a conference call will do. Review "automatic" attendance at trade shows, seminars, and other meetings. Are too many people going to unproductive gigs?
- Require that travelers take the lowest airfare offered within a reasonable schedule.
- All T&E buying must be done through the company's travel agency or in-house travel coordinator. That helps with record keeping and lets the agent bargain for volume discounts.
- Moderately priced hotels are a must. No top-of-the-line palaces of pampering. The travel agent can pick 'em and book the best corporate rates. Larger companies, or firms that deal with large agencies, may have access to lower

negotiated rates at certain hotels where travelers should be required to stay. No in-room movies.
- Travelers must account for all expenses that the company will reimburse.
- Book midsize cars or smaller and inquire about any free upgrades when checking in. If other insurance is in force, make sure employees decline the optional (and expensive) insurance coverage.
- Require that gas tanks on rental cars be filled before the car is returned.

A travel management firm with strong business ties can help you establish a company travel policy. USTravel, for example, with nearly five hundred locations, provides its clients with a detailed manual called the *Corporate Travel Cost Control Guide*. And Rosenbluth Travel, an industry giant, often helps companies customize their travel policies. Once you have a travel policy, *follow it!*

TACTIC #86
Abolish Last-Minute Bookings

Procrastination is the mother of all travel money wasters. It can pump your T&E payouts to Arnold Schwarzenegger proportions. Conditions change constantly, but in general, the earlier you book, the more you stand to save. Booking your travel one to three weeks or more in advance with a Saturday night stay can cut costs 50% or more. Even without the Saturday stay, advance bookings often produce savings.

Problem: Traveling employees usually don't *want* to stay a Saturday night.

Solution: An incentive plan that shares savings with the inconvenienced employee can be a win-win deal. Also, by inviting employees to use their personal frequent flyer awards for company travel, then reimbursing them for, say, half of what the ticket would cost, you are giving employees a way to turn flyer coupons into cash, and the company saves money too.

TACTIC #87
Nix Cash Advances

Cash advances are a costly way to pay for T&E. They can create a paperwork nightmare for the company. Someone has to keep track of the money going out and the receipts coming back in, as well as collect any unused cash. A reimbursement system is incentive for employees to submit expense reports quickly, thus helping streamline your accounting.

TACTIC #88
Big or Small, You Can Save with Negotiated Rates

Big companies usually have enough leverage to negotiate special rates with airlines, hotels, and rental car firms, while small businesses can tap into negotiated savings through travel agencies or affinity groups. Larger agencies—such as American Express Travel Services Group, Carlson Travel, Rosenbluth, USTravel, and Thomas Cook—can provide bargaining muscle that small firms don't have on their own. Even local travel agencies can now pass along discounts they tap into by joining a travel consortium. The result has been a cost-reduction windfall for small businesses that plug into the agency system for their travel needs.

Rosenbluth International has a terrific money-saving travel program specifically for smaller, growing businesses, called BusinessChoice. Members of BusinessChoice (no cost or obligation to join) can book travel on a 24-hour, toll-free line, get guaranteed lowest air fares, specially negotiated hotel and car rental rates, regular reports that detail travel spending, and other perks. Call (800) 332-4642.

Most corporate travel managers negotiate some form of hotel rate concessions for their business travelers, according to a survey by Runzheimer International, a travel consulting and research firm in Rochester, Wisconsin. Typical room rate discounts range from 10% to 29%, with a few going as high as 39%. In return, travel managers guarantee volume, measured in number of "room nights." Typically, companies guarantee below 130 room nights per year with individual hotels, and over 130 when dealing with hotel chains. At a rate of $100 per night, the 130-room-night level means spending $13,000 per year at the individual hotel or chain.

Some companies negotiate with individual locations of national chains for extra room discounts. Even individual travelers can sometimes snag a better rate just by asking. If the person checking in next to you is getting a better deal, for example, request the same yourself. Hotel rates, deals, and discounts have become as convoluted as airfares. The same room might have a dozen or more different rates. Left up to the hotel, it's a crapshoot as to which one you get.

TACTIC #89
Take These Negotiating Tips to the Bank

Hotels In the grim hotel market of the nineties, even highfalutin hostelries have had to hunker down on rates and take what they can get. To bed down bargains, business travelers should know about three basic hotel rates. First there's the rack rate, the posted rate that each hotel *hopes* to get but rarely can. Next is the corporate rate, a modest 10% to 20% reduction from the rack rate. Then there's the negotiated rate, which can reduce it another 20% to 30% or more. Here are some strategies to follow:

- Target specific hotels and chains where you are likely to stay. The best person to approach is often the local sales manager of individual hotels, not the national sales manager. The latest trend, however, is for national sales offices to arrange local-site discounts. Most of the major chains have new programs to do this, offering breaks of 5% to 30%, some with no minimum stay guarantee required. Examples:

Best Western International: Corporate ID Program
Days Inns: Corpo Rate Program
Forte Travelodge: Business Break Club
Four Seasons: Private Reserve
Hilton: Worldwide Corporate Rate
Holiday Inn: Worldwide Corporate Account
Hyatt: Preferred Rate Program
ITT Sheraton: Corporate Rate Program
Marriott: Corporate Business Rates
Omni: Executive Service Plan
Radisson: Worldwide Hospitality Program
Ramada: Business Card Program
Red Lion: Frequent Guest Dividends
Stouffer: Guaranteed Corporate Rate Program
Westin: Guaranteed Corporate Rate

- Be prepared to guarantee a certain annual volume (room nights per year) or to protect current volume. The higher your guarantee, the bigger your discount. The best discounts come with room night guarantees over 130 per year, but good discounts can still be had for guarantees of as little as 30.
- Make sure your people stay at the hotel where you've negotiated the discounts.

Airlines It's not just big companies that can get airfare deals. According to the industry newsletter *Runzheimer Reports on Travel Management,* if ten or more people are traveling to the same destination within a given week—regardless of where they are coming from—you may be able to cut a group deal for travel. The size of discounts varies widely; the most typical cases range between 20% and 45%. Follow these steps:

- Compile numbers on your past airline travel, including frequency and destinations. Ask your travel agent for help, but do the negotiating yourself.
- Prepare a specific proposal to present to an airline with flights to your most frequent destinations.
- Be flexible in your travel schedules and be prepared to channel all your air travel to the airline.
- If you have something to barter, consider that in your approach. Airlines are more likely to grab a barter deal that involves no cash.

Car Rentals Again, do your homework. Add up your annual spending on car rentals, including the number of rental days, and attach future projections. The more numbers you show, the stronger your case. Be prepared to guarantee a set volume of business. Here are some negotiating tips:

- Typical negotiated corporate car rental discounts run 10% to 20% off published rates. Many businesses negotiate a flat daily rate for all times and locations.
- The best contact is usually the rental firm's national sales manager. If your rentals all come in one or two locations, however, the local manager can be your target.
- If deep discounts are difficult to get, try to have various add-ons, such as drop-off charges or local taxes, waived.

TACTIC #90
Grab Great Hotel Deals in New York and L.A.

If you travel to New York or Los Angeles—America's two largest and most expensive business travel destinations—you can save on hotels and perhaps airfare too by booking through a third-party firm that negotiates the discounts, books the rooms, passes along the savings, *and* provides outstanding customer service.

Boulder, Colorado–based Express Hotel Reservations (EHR) pools the buying power of over five thousand companies to negotiate lower rates at about thirty hotels in New York and Los Angeles as well as airfare deals to and from those two cities from almost anywhere in the United States. EHR can save you 20% or more *on top of* a hotel's normal corporate rate. The combo of cost-cutting, convenience, and customer service makes this a powerful deal for small business—but largely undiscovered since EHR doesn't advertise the service. Even big companies are tapping EHR's rate-cutting service, including Cole-Haan shoes, The Gap, Hallmark Cards, L.A. Gear, Mattel, and Turner Broadcasting. *The service is free to any business traveler.* EHR makes its money in hotel commissions.

The firm has about twenty booking agents and is a stickler on service. Says EHR founder James Dick: "We sleep in our hotels and can tell you everything about them—from location to decor to special amenities." EHR, at (800) 356-1123, is one of several discount hotel reservation services that are catching on with independent business travelers and small companies. See the Follow-up File for the names and numbers of others that can put you on the road to big hotel savings.

TACTIC #91
Use Alternative Ground Transportation

To zap rental car costs, use other ground transportation if all you need to do is get from an airport to your hotel and/or downtown and back again. Renting a car for that alone is a waste. Many hotels will provide a gratis ride to and from the airport with a courtesy van or limo. Not quite as convenient as jumping in a waiting taxi, but a huge cost savings multiplied by many trips and travelers. Head for the courtesy phones before picking up your luggage to call for a free ride.

Travel management firm Rosenbluth surveyed the cost of ground transportation options in a sampling of cities and came up with these cost-saving comparisons. Spreads are similar in other major cities.

ATLANTA
Airport:	Hartsfield
Distance downtown:	10 miles
Taxi:	$25–30
Shuttle:	$7.50–9.50
Rail/Bus:	85¢

BOSTON
Airport:	Logan
Distance downtown:	3 miles
Taxi:	$9–15
Water shuttle:	$7
Airport limo:	$4
Rapid transit:	85¢

CHICAGO
Airport:	O'Hare
Distance downtown:	18 miles
Taxi:	$22
Airport bus:	$9
Bus:	$1

DALLAS
Airport:	DFW
Distance downtown:	20 miles
Taxi:	$20–25
Airport limo:	$9
Bus:	$6

HOUSTON

Airport:	Intercontinental
Distance downtown:	22 miles
Taxi:	$24–26
Limo:	$45
Shuttle:	$8.50–10

PHILADELPHIA

Airport:	International
Distance downtown:	8 miles
Taxi:	$16–18
Airport limo:	$6–8
Rail:	$4.75
Bus:	$1.50

SAN FRANCISCO

Airport:	International
Distance downtown:	14 miles
Taxi:	$20–25
Shuttle:	$10
Bus:	$6

TACTIC #92
Get Receipts for *Everything*
(But Don't Become
an Expense Audit Fanatic)

The IRS requires receipts for any outlays over $25. Some companies follow that standard, shunning the extra paperwork spawned by a lower level. "That's a big mistake," says James Firestone of American Express. "You can save yourself a lot of money by lowering your requirement for receipts to an in-house standard of ten dollars. If no receipt is required, employees tend to estimate or round off the amount." As a result, companies consistently overpay. "Studies on the use of tear-tab receipts show that 73% of the time they came from restaurants that would have accepted the organization's business charge card. That means the employee made a conscious decision to use cash instead of charging the meal. But because the employees fill out the stubs themselves, usually much later, the amount is often an estimate. As a result, the average tear-stub meal charge is 25% *higher* than the average documented meal charge in the same price range."

But don't be fanatic about rooting out errors. Better to focus the big guns on travel *usage* rather than billing errors. Says Firestone, "One mistake many companies make is to spend all their time and energy auditing expense reports. When you do that you are saying that the area of greatest value is either employee mistakes or employee cheating. We find that the area of greatest value is determining what hotels and airlines you should use and making sure that everybody uses them. . . . You want to track what percentage of your employees actually use the hotels you've identified as most advantageous, and you should require specific explanations for any exceptions."

TACTIC #93
Trim the VAT Fat

Doing business in Europe? If so, and if it involves traveling there, you're probably paying a bundle in value-added taxes (VATs)—the European equivalent of sales taxes. But here's a bundle-saving secret: European governments grant at least partial refunds on many VATs. All ya gotta do is apply. Depending on the country, you may be able to recover taxes of as much as 18.5% on hotel rooms, rental cars, gasoline, professional fees, trade shows, training courses, and meals.

"Companies that do business abroad, even occasionally, should realize how VATs add up," says Martin Hockey, an international tax partner with the Chicago-based accounting firm Grant Thornton. "Consider London, where the value-added tax on a hotel room is 17.5%," says Hockey. "That comes to $35 a day on a typically priced room. So, a company sending ten employees to London for ten days annually could incur $3,500 in hotel value-added taxes alone."

You'll need documentation to get back your dough. Start by asking hotels and other suppliers for a VAT invoice showing the name and address of the traveler's U.S. firm, the hotel or supplier's VAT number, the amount excluding VAT, the VAT rate and amount, and the total including VAT. The invoice should also include date, name and address of supplier, and a description of services. Most European suppliers already know the drill since domestic businesses must run the same gauntlet to reclaim VAT sums. Naturally, procedures differ country to country. According to Hockey, hotel VATs can be reclaimed only in Germany, Luxembourg, the Netherlands, Sweden, and Britain.

Says Hockey, "Setting up procedures to gain refunds can pay off handsomely."

TACTIC #94
Focus Travel Buying with One Agency

Most small companies already use a single travel agency. Now more large companies—right up to giants like General Electric and AT&T—are consolidating for greater discounts and beefed-up enforcement of company travel policies. A decade ago, AT&T used over three hundred travel agencies. Now it uses three. That also makes it easier for Ma Bell to nab miscreants who violate the company's cost-control policies. Travel agencies have no qualms about ratting on employees who spend more than they need to. GE, with an annual T&E tab of some $600 million, agreed in 1992 to focus all of its travel buying through Carlson Travel Network for estimated annual savings of a whopping $50 million or more. About half of all

Fortune 500 firms have made similar moves in the past ten years, cashing in on average savings of 10% to 20%.

TACTIC #95
Charge More for Personal Use of Company Cars

If your company provides cars for salespeople or other employees, you probably allow unlimited personal use of the car as long as the employee pays for gas plus the IRS rate (recently 5.5 cents) for personal miles driven. As a result, employees are probably taking advantage of this generous deal. Your cars are wearing out earlier than they should. And the company is forced to buy new ones sooner.

Many large companies with fleets are changing their tune. Wisconsin-based Johnson Wax, for example, raised the charge for personal use of the company car to a more reasonable (from the company's point of view) twenty cents per mile. That's still well below the official IRS mileage rate, so employees are getting a deal. But the higher rate should reduce mileage and keep the company's fleet rolling longer between replacements.

TACTIC #96
Outsource Your T&E Reimbursements

It costs the average business around $10 to process an employee's expense account statement and reimbursement. That includes handling the paper, punching information into a computer, verifying the numbers, and issuing a check. But there are alternatives. For example, Gelco Payment Systems, Inc., in Minneapolis, has an automated expense reimbursement plan for business called the Traveletter System. Employees can punch in expense totals by phone (hard copies are filed later) and have funds electronically deposited in their account. You save on check production and get detailed reports for cost control. Average cost: under $2 per transaction. Call (800) 444-6588 or write to Gelco at 7301 Ohms Lane, Minneapolis, MN 55439; fax (612) 832-3600.

TACTIC #97
Don't Forget Those *Other* Frequent Flyer Bonuses

Racking up frequent flyer miles gets you more than free plane tickets or upgrades. Many plans, including United Mileage Plus and American Airlines AAdvantage, dish out discount hotel and car rental coupons (up to 50% off) on top of the airfare deals. Some frequent flyer participants, interested only in the airfare goodies, stash these valuable bonus coupons away and forget about 'em. Don't.

TACTIC #98
Grab These Golden T&E Nuggets

- *Eat more business breakfasts.* They're a lot cheaper than business lunches, and a whole lot less than business dinners. But don't eat 'em at hotels. Ask for a nearby restaurant recommendation for breakfast when traveling.
- *If you have an American Express Corporate Card,* you are guaranteed at least 10% off the corporate rate at over twenty-five hundred hotels through the Privileged Rates Hotel Program and 15% off car rentals through the Privileged Rates Car Rental Program. Participating hotel

chains, at this writing, include Stouffer, at (800) HOTELS-1; Hilton, at (800) HILTONS; and Choice Hotels International, at (800) CLUB-VIP. Rental participants are Avis, Budget, National, and Thrifty. Call Amex at (800) 492-3344 for details.

- *Try the train.* Amtrak's northeast corridor Metroliner service between Washington, D.C., New York, and Boston is a less costly alternative to flying the shuttle, and you avoid expensive airport cab rides.

- *Ask your agent for a fare code analysis.* This will tell you the kinds of tickets your business is buying and how they compare to other fare classifications. In short, you can see if travelers are blowing money on special-request tickets, extra perks, or poor planning.

- *Avoid the high cost of hotel extras.* When you order hotel room service food (which in some cases may already be priced 20% higher than the same items in the restaurant), most hotels include a 15% to 17% tip on the bill. If you intend to boost that for extra good service, fine. But ask or check the bill first before shelling out a gratuity that duplicates what you're already paying. Mini bar prices are often outrageous; and sending a fax from a hotel can cost $4 or more per page. Avoid both.

- *Check out the travel discount clubs.* For modest annual dues in the $50 to $100 range, you can tap discounts of up to 50%. A few choices: Encore ($49 per year); call (800) 638-8976. Great American Traveler is $49.95 per year; call (800) 548-2812. World Hotel Express ($49.95 per year) can be reached at (800) 634-6526.

- *Use off-the-beaten-path car rental firms.* Small regional or local firms that can't afford front-row counters at airports may still have nearby locations (reachable by shuttle bus) that can save your business major car rental dollars. Your travel agent can be helpful tracking down low-cost firms in any particular location.

- *Use # to save money on phone calls.* Some hotels still levy a small (usually seventy-five cents to a dollar) surcharge for each long-distance call you make with your own calling card. Responding to customer complaints about this practice, Stouffer and Hilton were two of the first chains to end such calling card fees. Other major chains will probably follow. Before you start calling, ask the hotel its policy. To avoid the charge on multiple calls, press the # key after each call, then dial the next number without hanging up. You'll pay the surcharge only once.

SAVE-A-BUNDLE FOLLOW-UP FILE

- Discount hotel reservation services: Capitol Reservations, (800) 554-6750; Express Hotel Reservations, (800) 356-1123; Hotel Reservations Network, (800) 964-6835; Quikbook, (800) 221-3531; San Francisco Reservations, (800) 677-1550; Washington, D.C., Accommodations, (800) 554-2220.
- The Travel Management Division of Runzheimer International, a travel research and consulting organization, publishes the monthly newsletter *Runzheimer Reports on Travel Management* ($295/year); call (800) 942-9949; fax (414) 767-2476. Good insider advice and cost-saving ideas. Also offers occasional seminars on such topics as negotiating rates and travel expense accounting.
- *Business Travel Management* magazine, published by Coastal Communications Corp., 488 Madison Avenue, New York, NY 10022, is a monthly aimed at business travel managers. Call (212) 888-1500; fax (212) 888-8008. This is a controlled circulation magazine, which means you may be able to get it free if you "qualify" (to qualify you must be involved with managing travel for your company).
- *Corporate Travel* magazine (monthly, $65/year) from Miller Freeman Publications, New York City. Call (800) 964-9494 to order. News/ideas for business travel management.
- *Business Travel News* offers tips on organizing business travel. Published twice monthly by CMP Publications, 600 Community Drive, Manhasset, NY 11030; (800) 645-6278, ext. 5882. Circulated free to individuals involved in the business travel industry; others pay $95 per year.

- *Business Traveler International* is a monthly ($30/year) that offers tips and cost-saving information to the international traveler. From Perry Publications, 51 East 42nd Street, #1806, New York, NY 10017; (800) 726-1243.
- *Best Fares Discount Travel Magazine* (monthly, $58/year), 111 West Arkansas Lane, Suite C, Arlington, TX 76003; (800) 635-3033; fax (817) 548-9531.
- *Consumer Reports Travel Letter* (monthly, $37/year) offers a steady diet of cost-cutting T&E tactics with a money-back guarantee. Write to Subscription Dept., Box 53615, Boulder, CO 80321-3615.
- *Fly There for Less: How to Slash the Cost of Air Travel Worldwide* (TeakWood Press, $18.95) by Bob Martin details the ins and outs of cutting costs with better travel planning, low-fare searches, business air passes, air taxis, and no-frills travel agencies. Call (800) 654-0403.
- The National Business Travel Association, 1650 King Street, #301, Alexandria, VA 22314, holds an annual convention and exposition for business travel managers. Educational seminars deal with cost-cutting travel tactics. Call (703) 684-0836; fax (703) 684-0263.
- If you don't mind bare-bones service and paying by check instead of credit card, consider buying airline tickets from travel "consolidators," or "rebaters." For example, Travel Avenue, at (312) 876-1116, a Chicago rebater, offers 7% cash rebates on tickets. San Francisco–based C. L. Thomson Express International, at (415) 398-2535, is one of the nation's largest airline ticket consolidators.
- Here's an excellent accounting firm freebie that can help you save a bundle by keeping your T&E deductions in line. Price Waterhouse offers a booklet called *Meal, Entertainment and Travel Deductions* that does a good job explaining the complex rules on T&E deductions. Get it from any local Price Waterhouse office.

CHAPTER 8

Make Wise Cost-Cutting Choices with Technology

TACTIC #99
Add E-mail for a Cost-Cutting Punch

E-mail is one of those superpromising technologies that's been around for years but hasn't yet reached its full potential. That's changing, and E-mail will be a vital part of the business landscape by decade's end.

Basically, E-mail is a way for me to send written messages that I create on my computer directly to your computer's electronic "mailbox." I write it, send it; you read it and possibly send it along, with no paper changing hands. It's fast, cheap, accurate—and growing quickly.

The number of electronic mailboxes has been increasing about 50% per year in the 1990s. Helping spark E-mail is the Electronic Mail Association (EMA), an Arlington, Virginia–based industry group that has over 350 members. EMA has compiled case histories of how E-mail is saving money for companies in a variety of industries. Two examples:

- A truck manufacturer switched to an E-mail system for sending price quotes on customized truck features. Before E-mail, dealers would look up features in a manual and request a quote. The manufacturer would analyze the request and send a quote back to the dealer, who then called the customer. It took about a week and cost an average of $9 per quote. Now the manufacturer turns around the price quotes in a day or two electronically at an average cost of $1.
- A doctor who submitted claim forms manually to insurance companies switched to a "value-added" E-mail service and dramatically reduced errors and accelerated payments. Due in part to errors on the forms and misread-

ing of the original numbers, payments under the manual system took at least three weeks. Missing or incorrect coding delayed one in five payments even longer. The doctor now receives 95% of payments within ten days.

The legal biz is an area ripe for E-mail savings. Companies have been clamoring for E-mail links with their law firms as a way to cut their costs by sheer speed if nothing else. Xerox is one corporate giant that's grabbed for the E-mail gold—and found it—by linking up to outside law firms via E-mail. As a means of communicating with lawyers in particular, companies love E-mail. If you figure a lawyer's gonna bill your company each time she calls, E-mail offers immediate savings on that count alone.

Electronic mail is more efficient than faxing—you can send a fifty-page document in seconds. And it's cheaper than any other transmission system. In addition to lowering fax costs, you also lower your company's secretarial and administrative costs since the same person who creates the document can also send it—without holding a Ph.D.

E-mail *is* the future of business communications. See the Follow-up File for a list of E-mail services. For more examples of E-mail savings, request a free copy of *The Electronic Mail Advantage: Applications and Benefits* from EMA at 1655 North Fort Myer Drive, Suite 850, Arlington, VA 22209; (703) 524-5550; fax (703) 524-5558.

The latest phenomenon in the E-mail arena is Internet—a kind of super database and E-mail network linking some 12,000 smaller networks worldwide. Once the exclusive turf of academics, bureaucrats, and hackers, this network of networks has suddenly become the darling of corporate America. Despite its user-hostile complexity and ongoing security concerns for some companies, businesses are plugging into Internet at a breathtaking pace. In short, Internet has become the latest gotta-have corporate status symbol. It's the closest thing there is to an advanced public data network.

To learn more, your first move is to contact Internic, a group formed in 1993 to help funnel information about Internet to nontechies. California-based Internic is jointly sponsored by General Atomics of San Diego, AT&T Bell Laboratories in New Jersey, and Network Solutions of Herndon, Virginia. Call (800) 444-4345 or fax an information request to (619) 455-4640.

Dozens of private firms sell commercial access to Internet. Two examples: Falls Church, Virginia–based UUNET Technologies, Inc., at (800) 488-6383; and Reston, Virginia-based PSI at (800) 827-7482.

TACTIC #100
Use Voice Mail the *Right* Way!

Voice mail can cut your costs. It can also piss off your public. Blame David Ladd, the executive at VMX, Inc., in San Jose, California, who invented it. There's good reason that companies everywhere are adopting voice mail with relish: money. As in saving lots of it. You can sign up with an outside voice mail service or buy your own. A system that can handle a twenty-employee company goes for under $8,000 these days, down from six-figure territory in the 1980s. That figure alone hints at the savings: Try hiring a full-time receptionist or two for $8,000 (including benefits) these days. The trick is to use this money-saving technology the *right* way; avoid sending innocent callers to voice mail jail.

Properly handled, voice mail can be a dream time saver. Half of all business calls are best handled with voice mail rather than a real-time conversation. Messages can be kept private (accessed by personal ID code), they can be forwarded, and they can be picked up from anywhere. Calls are answered fast; no customers waiting endlessly on hold or receptionist trying to juggle four calls at once.

Some Voice Mail Tips:

- Remember: you are installing voice mail to *enhance* service, not replace it.
- Change individual outgoing messages frequently; if you're out for the day or longer, let callers know your whereabouts. It'll make 'em feel better about their chances you'll call back, and when.
- Check messages often, and return calls promptly.
- Install a system that allows callers to quickly reach a human (by hitting "0," for example).
- Keep the number of choices callers are given to a minimum. One of the most maddening things about voice mail is having to wait through a laundry list of options before hearing the one you want.
- Make it easy for callers to correct their mistake if they punch the wrong button. *"Press the pound sign (#) if you make a mistake."*

Two resources can help you find the best system for your company:

- *What to Buy for Business*—an independent publication that analyzes business equipment and accepts no advertising—offers a guide to voice mail products and automatic attendants that can be added to an existing phone system. The guide profiles over fifty vendors and covers systems for small, medium, and larger offices. Subscription is $112/year for ten issues. The *Voice Messaging Guide* single-issue cost is $24. Call (800) 247-2185; fax (914) 741-1367.
- *Voice Processing* magazine. Subscription is $24/year. The *Buyers Guide* single-issue cost is $45. Advanstar, 131 West First Street, Duluth, MN 55802; (800) 346-0085.

TACTIC #101
Expand on the Cheap with Budget-Priced Interactive Answering

Interactive telephone answering systems—the kind that provide callers with various items of information they select from a menu—are now available in a price range that makes sense even for tiny companies. For a few hundred dollars, you can now buy a system that hooks to your personal computer and will give your business capabilities that big companies were paying hundreds of thousands of dollars for a few years ago. This can allow your business to grow without hiring new workers. See the Follow-up File for vendor leads.

TACTIC #102
Save Money with Tele- and Videoconferencing

This tactic could also be in the T&E chapter as the ultimate travel cost saver: *Don't go!*

That's exactly what heaps of companies are doing. Instead of hopping a plane, they're hopping onto the bandwagon for two cost-cutting technologies that are now hitting their stride—teleconferencing and videoconferencing.

Teleconferencing The teleconference is one of the most cost-effective ways for business folk to communicate these days. As long as the parties are within reach of a phone—and in these cellular days, that's *anywhere*—a teleconference is possible. Here's a bit of what's going on:

- Companies of all sizes are substituting teleconferences for costly face-to-face meetings. They're using teleconferencing to powwow with sales reps and brief staff on new product introductions.

- Marketing research firms are using teleconferences as a cheap and convenient way to sample customer preferences.
- Public companies are conducting meetings with hundreds of investment analysts via teleconferences. (Today you're apt to find as many as twelve hundred people participating in a single teleconference.)
- Managers are talking to widely disbursed employees through teleconferences instead of miring themselves in memos.

The cost-control capabilities of teleconferencing have sparked an industry explosion. The Washington, D.C.–based International Teleconferencing Association reports year-to-year revenue growth of more than 40%; business is now spending over $2 billion per year on teleconferencing and saving big time on travel costs.

How much? The average business trip now costs $1,023 per person. By contrast, the average teleconference meeting— ten participants convening for fifty minutes—costs $170. That's $17 per person; less than the typical catered business lunch. Savings go even higher when you substitute teleconferencing for *international* travel.

When Boston-based Krupp Securities wanted to trim the cost of holding regular meetings with its national sales force, it turned to the teleconference. Now Krupp conducts weekly teleconferences involving about two dozen people, saving money on travel and keeping the salespeople in the field where they belong. When the group does meet face-to-face in Boston, the meetings generally cost about $15,000, while the average teleconference cost is $150. Each weekly conference runs about an hour and is arranged through Darome Teleconferencing. Next to AT&T, the industry leader, Chicago-based Darome has moved up to a strong number two in the field by pushing teleconferencing's potent cost-saving pitch. Call Darome at (800) 334-5029.

Videoconferencing Videoconferencing, which adds a television picture to this story, has also blasted off. Small business owners who wouldn't think of *traveling* to attend a business seminar are flocking to videoconference seminars at universities, community colleges, and other locations across the country. No long absences from the business; no costly plane tickets or lumpy hotel beds.

Big companies are going solo. One reason is plunging prices for videoconferencing systems. A system that cost a quarter-million clams five years ago now costs under $40,000. And the cost of transmitting the signal over phone lines has dropped dramatically thanks to "bandwidth on demand service." High-speed circuits have reduced transmission costs in some cases by up to 70%. And a dial-up capability means that companies no longer have to make a special call to the carrier to set up the videoconferencing call. Now it works just like making a regular telephone call. A user can dial direct to another installation and connect customers, vendors, and corporate partners on the network as needed. See the Follow-up File for resources.

TACTIC #103
Capture Your Cash Electronically, *Now!*

Electronic payments have long had a Jekyll and Hyde personality. They're fantastic for the party receiving the instant cash; less great for the party giving it up.

As America becomes more comfortable with electronic money, however, consumer acceptance of direct debits has been rising. Health clubs, insurance companies, and utilities are having great success collecting consumer payments electronically. What's more—and this is the big surprise—increasing numbers of businesses are successfully coaxing their corporate customers to pay electronically. Recipients of electronic funds transfer (EFT) payments save on bill preparation, mailing, processing. And the faster the money's in the bank, the faster it starts making *more* money.

Payers like the convenience of EFT. They, too, lower their processing costs—no checks to write, mail, and reconcile. Electronic payments also ensure that quick payers can earn early payment discounts right up to the deadline, without having to mail checks several days ahead of time. And there are no delayed shipments as vendors wait for their checks.

The National Automated Clearing House Association (NACHA), at 607 Herndon Parkway, Suite 200, Herndon, VA 22070—(703) 742-9190; fax (703) 787-0996—can provide general information on the benefits of direct payments and can refer you to an affiliate in your area who will help you set up a program to save your company money. For example, Calwestern Automated Clearing House Association, based in South San Francisco, works with companies in the western United States. Call (415) 871-8762; fax (415) 871-9326.

TACTIC #104
Make Dividend and Pension Payments Electronically

Met Life, Procter & Gamble, 3M, Northern States Power, Hormel, and Martin Marietta Energy Systems are a few corporate biggies that are saving an estimated sixty-two cents on every stock dividend and pension payment they make. They're all using an automated clearing house (ACH) to make those payments electronically. No checks. No postage. With millions of shareholders and retirees involved, the savings are huge.

Martin Marietta Energy Systems offers electronic pension payments to its more than 128,000 retirees, and the 65% who've signed up receive about $84 million per month. The system has helped the company crack a recurring cash flow crunch since deposits to the disbursement account can be precisely timed for the payment due date.

TACTIC #105
Dig into Desktop Publishing

Desktop publishing is one of the biggest small business money savers of the 1990s. Basically, desktop publishing describes a combination of computer, software, and printer that lets you design and prepare your own published materials for printing. That might include marketing brochures, catalogs, newsletters, reports, newspaper ads, direct-mail pieces, restaurant menus, flyers, or any other printed item you can think of.

If you already have a computer and laser printer, you're two-thirds of the way there. Just add desktop publishing software (and maybe a sense of adventure). There are several terrific programs available. And the latest version of popular word processing packages such as Microsoft Word and Word-Perfect have desktop publishing capabilities built in. Prices start at under $100, though the more powerful programs will run $500 to $800.

Firms that once spent tens of thousands of dollars to have their marketing and other materials produced by outside firms now do them in-house at a fraction of the cost. If your company spends significant money on preparing materials for print and hasn't looked into desktop publishing, you're missing a major opportunity. Even if you need to buy equipment, you'll probably save enough to pay for it the first year or two.

Books on desktop publishing abound. Check the computing department at your local bookstore. Other resources:

- *Publish*, a monthly magazine about desktop publishing, carries helpful articles on getting the most from your equipment. A subscription is $29.95 from Integrated Media, Inc., 501 Second Street, San Francisco, CA 94107; (800) 685-3435. Also a good source for vendor information.
- To get a low-cost feel for how it all works, try test-driving a desktop publishing system at a local print shop. National chains such as Kinko's, Alpha Graphics, Sir Speedy, and

PIP offer self-serve desktop systems in many of their locations. Some also conduct training sessions on using desktop systems (they hope that once you design your materials, you'll bring it to them for printing).

- There are three ways to go on software:

1. *Basic:* The word processing program you already use may have some basic desktop publishing features.
2. *Midrange:* Low-cost programs in the $100 to $200 range have more features and are suitable for the non-professional design needs of most small businesses. Choices include Timeworks' Publish-It, Microsoft Publisher, and Publish-It Easy.
3. *Sophisticated:* The Cadillacs of the business—the software that design professionals use—are QuarkXPress (the software of choice for magazine designers), Ventura Publisher, and Aldus PageMaker. Suggested retail prices are in the $700 to $800 range, but you can find them at software discounters for more like $500 or less.

TACTIC #106
Upgrade Quickly for Cost Savings and Growth

Rapid growth can quickly overwhelm a business as costs soar, efficiency tumbles, and current computers can't keep up. American Inventors Corp. (AIC), a sixty-employee firm based in Westfield, Massachusetts, beat the problem by upgrading its computer system *before* things got out of hand, installing a productivity software package and thereby boosting the firm's capacity *without having to hire more workers.*

AIC *needs* a good computer. The company must navigate a choppy sea of red tape, research reports, patent attorneys, government guidelines, and manufacturing contacts in helping inventors bring new ideas to market. But the PCs the firm had were maxed out. So AIC president Steve DiGiro went to a minicomputer to cure his rapid-growth dilemma.

DiGiro installed an IBM AS/400, a popular midrange computer for smaller companies and billed as a supersimple machine that you can plug in and be using in ten minutes. This particular machine, starting in the $12,000 range, comes factory loaded with a bevy of special software. Industry-specific applications for contractors, retailers, CPAs, health-care facilities, mortgage companies, and others are available. For information on this machine call (800) IBM-6676.

TACTIC #107
Equip Your Office with Fax Modems

These babies are great time and money savers. Instead of writing a price quote, order inquiry, memo, letter—you name it—printing it out, walking to the printer, taking the piece of paper, walking to the fax machine, punching the buttons, and waiting for the fax to flow, a fax modem makes it a one-step deal. The fax modem (with the accompanying software) lets you send your correspondence directly from your computer, via modem, to the recipient's fax machine.

Not only is this quick and cheap (the phone call is faster, and therefore cheaper), but the quality of the fax on the other end is a great deal better and could save you from having to resend garbled faxes. If you're getting a modem for the first time, select one that comes with this feature for only a little more money.

TACTIC #108
Get High-Tech Help to Follow Your Fleet

If your business puts vehicles on the road daily—even a few of 'em—you know the costs and headaches of moving them around efficiently. A new high-tech fleet management system developed by PacTel Teletrac is helping many companies save money by staying in closer touch with their vehicles. It's called PacTel Teletrac Fleet Director, and it's available in Chicago, Dallas/Fort Worth, Detroit, Houston, Los Angeles, Miami, and a few other major cities.

Fleet Director is a nifty marriage of wireless vehicle-tracking technology and data communications services. It offers instant, real-time information for local and regional fleets, and does it more efficiently than traditional two-way communications systems and more affordably than satellite systems.

Mike Cattaneo, of Greater Detroit Heating and Cooling, says that Fleet Director immediately slashed his fleet's monthly mileage from 9,000 to 5,000, saving him $300 a month in fuel costs alone, plus more on insurance and other items. "It only took us a month to recover the cost of the dispatcher's PC, which runs the software," he says. It works like this:

To check the location, direction, and speed of any of your vehicles, you log on to the PacTel Teletrac network on your computer, using Fleet Director software. In seconds it tracks your trucks (or whatever) to within 150 feet. A dispatcher can quickly decide which vehicle is closest to an address and figure an arrival time. Other goodies include a sensor alert to protect untended vehicles from thieves and an in-vehicle message display terminal. The onboard hardware costs about $595 per vehicle. Once you're on-line, it costs only two to three cents to locate a vehicle. PacTel Teletrac is based in Inglewood, California. For information call (800) 800-7501.

TACTIC #109
Keep Your Software Simple

It sure is tempting for companies to equip themselves with each sexy software selection that passes by. But unless you've got a bunch of computer nerds working for you, a good way to save some money and keep productivity up is to stick to the basics. Software bloat will only slow you, your computers, your employees, and your company down. If you don't need the bells and whistles, don't buy 'em.

For many small businesses, the ideal approach is bundled software that provides the four basic computing necessities—word processing, data base, spreadsheet, and communications—in one easy-to-use and low-cost package. A good example is Microsoft Works, which first processed the words you see here and also comes with data base, spreadsheet, and communications modules, available for both IBM and Apple. For under $200 you can get all the basic computing power your small business needs.

TACTIC #110
Save Big with Highly Specialized Software

The flip side to saving with simplified software is to look for ways that *highly specialized* software can save your business money in one particular department. Take product distribution, an area in which Columbus, Georgia–based Tom's Foods, Inc., reckons it is saving itself hundreds of thousands of dollars per year with a specialized "logistics" software package that cost Tom's about $60,000.

Tom's manufactures and distributes snack foods in forty-two states from five manufacturing locations—a distribution-intensive business that can benefit greatly from well-planned schedules. That happens to be a specialty of CAPS LOGIS-

TICS, Inc., an Atlanta-based logistics software developer. Its software products focus on the specialized business science of getting the right product to the right place at the right time for the lowest cost.

To help cut costs, Tom's went looking for a system powerful enough to adjust master routes based on the quantity of daily orders, add backhauls to current routes, and generate tailored management reports and answer "what if" questions, all at the same time. It found the answer in the CAPS LOGISTICS TOOLKIT package for day-to-day dispatching (priced between $40,000 and $80,000), which streamlines the distribution planning process and makes last-minute changes possible. Before TOOLKIT, Tom's was making daily changes manually. After TOOLKIT was installed, Tom's discovered that several routes could be eliminated entirely, resulting in six-figure savings.

For help locating specialized, industry-specific software, World Class Software, of West Palm Beach, Florida, is a good resource. See the Follow-up File for details.

TACTIC #111
Tap Free (or Low-Cost) Info from State-Run Data Bases

At least thirty-one state governments operate electronic information systems that companies can tap for little or no cost with a desktop PC and a modem. These data bases are little known since state governments rarely publicize them. But they can be a great low-cost source of business leads (new incorporations, expansion permits, for example), sales tax records, economic statistics, demographics, or other info. At last count, these states were operating data bases open to the public: Alaska, Colorado, Delaware, Florida, Hawaii, Indiana, Iowa, Kentucky, Louisiana, Maine, Maryland, Massachusetts, Michigan, Minnesota, Missouri, Montana, Nebraska, Nevada,

New Jersey, New Mexico, New York, North Carolina, Ohio, Oklahoma, Pennsylvania, Texas, Virginia, Washington, West Virginia, and Wisconsin. Call your state's commerce department for the phone number of the data base in your area.

TACTIC #112
Check Out Small Biz Shareware

Shareware is a fantastic way for almost any business to pick up handy programs and save a bundle. Basically, as computing guru Alfred Glossbrenner puts it, shareware is "software on the honor system." Shareware is business software you can obtain for nothing, try out, and then—if you like it and decide to keep using it—send in a small registration fee to the software's copyright owner, on your *honor*. This is not the same as public domain software, which is available to all for the taking at no cost. Shareware registration fees are generally under $100. By outfitting your business with shareware products, you can save thousands over the comparable commercial software products, whose makers spend millions every year on advertising.

Shareware covers all major business needs. And many of the programs are considered top-shelf. Just because it's shareware doesn't mean it's a clunker. Cost is low but quality can be high. Glossbrenner himself uses shareware programs to operate his small business, including PC-Write (for word processing), File Express (to track sales), ProComm (for communications), and As-Easy-As (a Lotus 1-2-3 spreadsheet clone). Other top shareware includes Pony Express, for managing mailings, and the Medlin Accounting series.

According to Glossbrenner, most businesses can get all the computing power they need, and then some, from inexpensive shareware. The programs are widely available through local computer user groups (check for listings in your area), mail-order houses, and on-line vendors.

A terrific source of info in this area is *Glossbrenner's Guide to Shareware for Small Businesses,* $37.95, published by Windcrest/McGraw-Hill, 13311 Monteray Lane, Blue Ridge Summit, PA 17294-0850; (800) 822-8138. This four-hundred-page book, first published in 1992, has it all. Glossbrenner's favorite shareware programs are also available through Glossbrenner's Choice for $5 (5¼″ disk) or $6 (3½″ disk) each plus $3 shipping. A special eleven-disk Business-Pak is available at a 35% savings. For a free catalog, write 699 River Road, Yardley, PA 19067-1965.

For $7.50 (postage paid) you can get a computer disk listing over one thousand shareware programs from the Association of Shareware Professionals, 545 Grover Road, Muskegon, MI 49442; (616) 788-5131; fax (616) 788-2765.

SAVE-A-BUNDLE FOLLOW-UP FILE

• A few simple software picks: Microsoft Works from Microsoft Corp., (800) 426-9400; Alpha 4 from Alpha Software Corp., (800) 451-1018; Smartware from Informix Software, Inc., (800) 438-7627.

• Computer Associates (CA), based in Islandia, New York, has created a special small business package that it calls CA-Simply Business. Includes accounting, word processing, spreadsheets, scheduling, and graphics software all for a package price of under $600. Call (800) 225-5224 for the name of a dealer near you.

• SoftFind, from World Class Software, of West Palm Beach, Florida, is a computer disk listing over four thousand business software applications. Each listing includes a brief description of what the software does, the price, whether there's a demo available, and other information. SoftFind costs $25 plus $3 shipping. Call (407) 585-7354; fax (407) 547-1703.

• *Directory of Software,* available from New England Business Service, Inc., lists over eight hundred software packages for business. It's free. Call (800) 225-9540.

- Major E-mail services:

    AT&T Mail: (800) 367-7225
    MCI Mail: (800) 444-6245
    SprintMail: (800) 736-1130

    On-line services with E-mail feature:

    CompuServe, Inc.: (800) 848-8199
    Dialog: (800) 334-2564
    GEnie: (800) 638-9636
    America Online: (800) 227-6364

- The International Teleconferencing Association (ITCA) is a nonprofit professional trade association that promotes teleconferencing and videoconferencing. Write to ITCA, 1150 Connecticut Avenue, N.W., Suite 1050, Washington, DC 20036; (202) 833-2549; fax (202) 833-1308. *The International Video Teleconferencing Source Book,* published jointly by AT&T Global Business Video Services and the ITCA, is $7.95 (payable to AT&T Directories). Order from P.O. Box 9006, Paterson, NJ 07509; or call (800) 426-8686. For information on listings call (800) 562-2255.

- The Education Satellite Network, in Columbia, Maryland, publishes a monthly tele- and videoconferencing program guide called *Education SATLINK Magazine and Satellite Program Guide* ($90/year). Call (800) 243-3376.

- Three vendors to contact about low-priced interactive answering systems: Talking Technology, (800) 934-4884; The Complete PC, (800) 634-5558; Natural Microsystems, (800) 533-6120.

- Applied Business Telecommunications offers a wide range of valuable help in the teleconferencing area. Publishes *Teleconference* magazine (bimonthly, $60/year); manages the annual Telecon Conference and Trade Show; offers seminars on teleconference training. Call the Oklahoma-based marketing office at (800) 829-3400; fax (405) 743-3426; or the California headquarters at (510) 820-5563; fax (510) 820-5894.

CHAPTER 9

Lower the Cost of Rising Crime

Crack Down on Telecrooks

A scary outlook from former U.S. Secret Service operative James Snyder (the Secret Service and FBI have jurisdiction over long-distance toll fraud): "There are two kinds of [telephone] customers: those who've been victims of toll fraud, and those who *will* be." Snyder now heads fraud investigations for MCI.

For U.S. business, toll fraud—the theft of long-distance telephone service billed to *your* lines—may be the most costly high-tech crime of the nineties. "Hackers" figure out how to hook into a company's lines and roll up thousands, maybe tens of thousands, of dollars in charges before anybody catches on. The crime costs business an estimated *$1.2 billion* per year. Count the public at large and the fraud figure soars to *$4 billion*. Government agencies are big victims too—NASA got nailed for an estimated $12 million from one toll fraud scheme.

Rapid technological change fuels the problem—each advance creates new telecrook opportunities. Sure, the phone company can block the thieves quickly once someone catches wind. But the crooks need only a day or two to rack up huge charges, either themselves or from selling entry to your system to others. According to *Forbes*, a working credit card number sells for $50 to $100 on the street these days, while a remote access code—harder to track and with a much longer "shelf life"—can sell for up to $10,000.

Cellular phones are especially vulnerable; high-tech crooks can snatch vital information literally out of thin air and use it to ring up charges on your bill. Your company's trash can also yield information on phone access codes to Dumpster divers. Crooks with telephoto video cameras or other viewing devices peer over your employees' shoulders ("shoulder surfers") in airline terminals as they punch in company credit card numbers.

A $6 million firm called Interplex Electronics, Inc., in New Haven, Connecticut, got zapped for about $17,000 in fraudulent charges and perhaps much more in lost business when the company's lines were jammed with crooked callers and real customers couldn't get through.

Your phone system is most vulnerable if it's the kind that allows employees to call up (via a remote access feature), punch in a code, and make long-distance calls as if they were in the office. Anyone with the code can do it. External call forwarding is another feature that's vulnerable to fraud.

Find out if your phone system has these features. If it does, switch to something more secure. Ask the phone company what's available. And put restrictions on international calling—if you don't need it, have your lines blocked. Change your access codes periodically. Also, talk to your long-distance representative about what the phone company can do to monitor your call usage more closely to detect any sudden surge in calls.

If your phones are victimized, you'll be expected to pay up. Phone companies want their money, but may offer a partial discount. MCI, for example, grants first-time victims a 30% break. The average hit: about $90,000.

In response to an explosion in toll fraud, long-distance companies are offering a new product—telefraud insurance—that will limit your liability. But such insurance is prohibitively expensive for all but the biggest companies. Smaller firms have a better choice—use telephone calling cards, which limit your liability to $50 if the numbers are stolen and abused.

Other fraud prevention tips from Randy Plimpton, director of network operations for Burlington, Vermont–based Long Distance North:

- Detailed call records on your monthly bill are your best friend in fighting toll fraud. Monitor them monthly.
- Block international calling from your phones. Use calling cards instead.

- Block any area codes your company never calls.
- Block voice mail access to outside lines.
- Deactivate the codes that came with your phone system and install your own, using the longest codes possible. Change the codes frequently.
- Educate your employees about the risks of toll fraud.
- Shred proprietary documents to thwart Dumpster divers.
- Hide your calling card number from shoulder surfers in public places.

TACTIC #114
Collect Civil Fines from Shoplifters

Jack Eckerd Corp., a large Clearwater, Florida–based drugstore chain with stores in Florida, Alabama, and South Carolina, is pocketing an estimated $1 million per year or more in savings through a new antishoplifting tactic—civil fines, imposed and collected by the business involved, following state-set guidelines. There's a dual benefit: (1) Civil fines eliminate costly criminal prosecution. (2) Fines that are collected can partially compensate businesses for shoplifting losses.

Civil fines for shoplifting, authorized state by state, are a relatively new business weapon in the war against shoplifting. At this writing, the tactic is available in forty-four states, pending in all others. Twelve states allow companies to apply the same rules to employee theft. Generally, the laws permit retailers to collect civil fines from shoplifters of anywhere from two to five times the value of the merchandise when goods are returned. New York, for example, permits fines of five times the value of the goods, up to $500. The Texas fine is actual damages (cost of the goods, cost of employee wages for pursuing the case, etc.) plus a maximum penalty of up to $1,000. Indiana fines run three times actual damages. Each state is different, and most impose a minimum fine of $50 to $200.

It works like this. Your store catches a shoplifter. Instead of calling the cops and pressing a criminal action—though you retain the right to do so later—you fill out a store report to document the incident, making certain to verify the individual's name, address, and phone number. If the individual won't cooperate, you may have no choice but to phone the police. Most thieves prefer to cooperate, however, since the alternative is a criminal action.

You then inform the individual, perhaps with a written notice, that under state law the business may decide to take further action. No formal arrest is made; no immediate action is taken by store personnel. The shoplifter leaves, and you turn the information over to a collection agency or attorney to press for payment and fines as a civil rather than criminal action, following state guidelines. If the thief is a minor, many states permit stores to demand payment from parents.

Loss Prevention Specialists, Inc., a theft-prevention consulting firm based in Winter Park, Florida, works with both large and small retailers in all states that permit civil shoplifting fines. The stores turn over the documentation to Loss Prevention's attorneys, who try to collect. The firm keeps a percentage of what it collects, so the action costs the store nothing out of pocket. For information call Loss Prevention Specialists at (800) 366-5774.

TACTIC #115
Stop Shoplifting *before* It Happens

The best defense against shoplifting losses is a good offense. Here are some things your business can do:

- Training employees to spot shoplifters and be attentive to shoplifting potential is a big help. Shoplifters often display telltale signs: They glance around and seem nervous. They wear oversized, loose-fitting clothing and carry large packages. They are indecisive and handle lots of merchandise.

Shoplifters don't *want* a salesperson's help and they don't seem to have any particular shopping purpose. When salespeople are busy, a simple acknowledgment to waiting customers that they'll be helped in a minute is a deterrent. Tell employees to be alert to groups of "shoppers" who enter together and then split up, or to a particularly insistent customer who monopolizes a salesperson's time (possibly a diversion). The resources in the Follow-up File can provide training materials. Local police and business groups may offer seminars on shoplifting prevention.

- Arrange your store to deter would-be thieves. Good lighting and unrestricted visibility will send shoplifters elsewhere. For better visibility keep stacks of product displays to no more than three feet in height. Keep merchandise neatly displayed. A cluttered store is an invitation to thieves. Ask local police to do a security check of your store and point out where you may be vulnerable.

- Install security devices such as convex mirrors, electronic alarm tags for merchandise, security cameras, alarms for secondary exits. Hire plainclothes detectives or uniformed guards. You can discourage price tag switching by using tamperproof gummed labels (the kind that can only be removed slowly in itty-bitty pieces), multiple price tags (one hidden), or special pricing codes. A switch to bar codes, scanned at the cash register, can eliminate this age-old form of shoplifting altogether.

TACTIC #116
Burglarproof Your Biz

Businesses in the United States are burgled to the tune of billions in losses every year, and the potential for loss savings is enormous. Adding muscle to your security system can save your business money two ways: (1) fewer theft losses, and (2) lower insurance rates. Money spent on beefed-up security may be returned manyfold in future savings. Here are some things you can do:

- Install or upgrade a security system. Some insurance companies offer discounts for high-tech security—the better the system (motion sensors, central-station alarms), the bigger the savings.
- Upgrade your locks; install dead bolts. If a break-in occurs, the more evidence there is of forced entry, the easier it will be for you to collect from your insurance company. Bar the rear door; that's where the vast majority of break-ins occur.
- Shed some light. Strategically placed (out of reach so it can't be easily disabled) outdoor lighting can help discourage burglars.
- Install solid-core doors. Hollow doors are easily bashed in.
- Even if you have a safe at your business, keep as little cash on hand as possible. Bank the rest every night. Also leave cash register drawers empty and open.

TACTIC #117
Embezzlement Prevention Rx

Embezzlement is tough for most companies to face since, by definition, it involves theft by someone in a position of trust. But according to estimates by the U.S. Chamber of Commerce, this and other forms of white-collar crime are costing companies billions each year. A few basic steps can help:

- Establish internal checks, balances, and general accountability. Make sure no one employee has unsupervised authority over the money. Establish strict separation between the three crucial financial responsibilities: (1) authorizing a transaction; (2) paying or collecting the money; and, (3) record keeping.
- Require two signatures on all purchase orders and examine invoices before signing checks. Don't be rushed into approving invoices or signing checks—an embezzler may try to pass fraudulent paperwork under the crunch of deadlines.
- Any large or unusual orders should require specific authorization by at least two people.
- Have more than one person reconcile the bank statement and review documentation. Examine all canceled checks. Make your own bank deposits, or spot-check those to whom you delegate the responsibility.
- Use prenumbered sales invoices to thwart embezzlers who sell something for cash and simply pocket the dough. Inspect your supply of invoices and checks to make sure supplies at the end of the pack haven't been removed.
- Set a good example. Don't fudge expense accounts, dip into petty cash, or otherwise use company money for personal use, even if you're the owner. Those actions send the wrong signal.
- Have company mail sent to a P.O. box and pick it up yourself. Embezzlers often count on their ability to get to the mail first to cover their tracks.
- Have employees who handle money bonded as a matter of company policy. Bonding is a sign of how seriously your company takes the delegation of financial responsibility and it also puts an outside party on the line if an employee is dishonest.
- Be alert to these ten warning signs, listed by the Council of Better Business Bureaus:

1. Accounting, inventory, and other company books that are not kept up to date by an employee who is responsible for those tasks.
2. Customer invoices being habitually mailed late.
3. Frequent complaints by customers that invoices are inaccurate.
4. Employees who regularly turn down promotions or refuse vacations.
5. Employees who frequently ask for cash advances on paychecks.
6. Employees who are frequently entertained by suppliers or who submit expense accounts that include costly entertainment charges.
7. Employees whose standards of living are much higher than their salaries would indicate.
8. Frequent inventory shortages.
9. Slow collections, which may indicate that payments are being sidetracked on their way to the bank.
10. Unusual bad-debt write-offs by the accounting department.

TACTIC #118
Do Your Employment Due Diligence

The best way to avoid workplace theft is to hire honest employees in the first place. But investigating a potential employee's background can backfire in states (California in particular) that have especially strict privacy laws. Background checks and preemployment screening are best left to licensed pros. Here's where you can get help:

- Pinkerton Investigation Services offers quick and professional background checks on anyone you're considering hiring. "If you don't employ a liar, cheat, or thief, there's a much better chance you won't fall victim to one," says Pinkerton. For a free booklet called *Reference Guide to Investigation Services,* call (800) 232-7465 or fax a request to (704) 554-1806.

- *The Sourcebook of Public Record Providers* lists ninety companies that conduct employment screening. Many services operate on-line and can provide your company with reports quickly via computer and modem. This is a terrific reference book, selling for $18 plus $2 shipping from BRB Publications, Inc., 1200 Lincoln, #306, Denver, CO 80203; (800) 929-3764; fax (800) 929-4981.

- The Credit Managers Association of California (CMAC) has a copyrighted preemployment screening service available to employers nationwide. It provides verification of a job applicant's employment history, including past employee misconduct, criminal convictions, falsification of past employment and reasons for terminations, credit history, and more. CMAC is a consumer reporting agency regulated by federal law and has been providing business information for over one hundred years. Preemployment reports cost about $110 per applicant; "mini-reports" are $60. Call (800) 447-3998. Ask for preemployment division.

- *The Guide to Background Investigations: A Comprehensive Source Directory for Employee Screening* ($124.50), published by Tulsa, Oklahoma–based National Employment Screening Services, offers 936 pages of vital addresses, phone numbers, and procedures. Call (800) 247-8713.

- Chicago-based Reid Psychological Systems provides employee testing services. Call (800) 922-7343. Another firm that provides general employee testing services is the Stanton Pinkerton Services Group, based in Charlotte, North Carolina. Call (800) 438-5959. (Also see Tactic #52 on employee testing.)

TACTIC #119
Guard against Computer Crime

According to the U.S. General Accounting Office, which studied this issue, most computer-related crime is committed by people with limited knowledge of computer technology. In other words, this isn't merely the realm of a few hackers wreaking havoc in corporate computers from the safety of their bedrooms. All businesses are vulnerable. Computers are merely another place for thieves to strike.

Computers have created big opportunities for fraud. "Thieves can transfer proprietary information from a mainframe to a small floppy disk, which can easily be concealed and taken from the premises. Competitors can invade the system over the phone lines or through the use of readily available and relatively inexpensive electronic equipment. Trusted employees can alter computer records to embezzle funds. Vindictive ex-employees can introduce computer viruses," says the Council of Better Business Bureaus in a book called *How to Protect Your Business*. Loss estimates range into the billions of dollars annually—and are climbing.

U.S. firms, from the smallest on up, are paying closer attention to the potential for computer-related crimes. They're more cautious about whom they hire to operate computers, just as they are in hiring people to handle money. They're asking employees who have access to sensitive information stored in the computer to sign confidentiality agreements. And they're implementing formal computer security programs.

Computer files can also be "locked" by using programs that permit access only to key personnel via passwords. The principles of financial internal controls apply here as well. No one employee should have control over the entire computer system, although firms with only a few employees may have no choice. A computer security consultant (ask local dealers for recommendations) can help you design a system that meets your needs.

TACTIC #120
Hang Up on Telemarketing Scams

Companies large and small are also being bilked by telemarketing scams. Phony companies sell bogus products and services of all kinds to unsuspecting businesses, collect the money, and split. Often they entice businesses to buy—anything from imprinted pens to insurance—by offering juicy prizes or deep discounts. Scam operators woo buyers with free trips, electronic equipment, and all kinds of thinly disguised bribes in return for ordering nearly worthless supplies or merchandise.

The Alliance Against Fraud in Telemarketing (AAFT), a Washington, D.C.–based coalition of over seventy groups fighting this type of fraud, has seen it all. These scam artists are masters at making it sound as if they know you, as if they've been doing business with your organization for years. They call to "confirm" an order placed, so they say, by someone else at your company, and in the process dig out valuable information. They brazenly invoice companies for goods never ordered. If they aren't paid, collection action is threatened.

Watch for the warning signs: callers who aren't specific about whom they represent; salespeople who emphasize prizes over the products they're selling; callers who are reluctant to send further information or provide references; callers from "suppliers" whose names you don't recognize.

To avoid being burned, set a policy for your entire company not to make any such purchases by phone. Always ask for further information—names, product literature, addresses, phone numbers—before making a purchasing decision. Don't give out your credit card number *or any other information* about your company to an unknown caller. These scam artists are good at posing as, say, your computer maintenance firm, calling to "verify" (or in their case, obtain) key information such as equipment makes, models, and serial numbers that they can then use to pull off a bogus order and invoice.

SAVE-A-BUNDLE FOLLOW-UP FILE

• *How to Protect Your Business*, published for the Council of Better Business Bureaus by the Benjamin Co., Inc., is a terrific book on crime prevention for businesses of any size. It's thorough, easy to read, and full of specific examples. Covers office supply scams; loan broker and bankruptcy frauds; business opportunity schemes; telemarketing crimes; product counterfeiting; shoplifting; credit card, check, and coupon fraud; industrial espionage; employee theft; insurance fraud; and computer crimes. The paperback is $7.95 in bookstores, or order from the Council of Better Business Bureaus, Publications Department, (703) 247-9310; fax (703) 525-8277.

• SprintGUARD Plus is a phone fraud protection plan that Sprint offers to small businesses and customers of its 800 service. Minimum cost is $100 per month. For information call (800) 877-7330.

• FraudFighter is a software package for PCs that can help fend off toll fraud. It costs $1,995 from Atlanta-based Complementary Solutions, and must be used in conjunction with the call accounting software Telemate, which is included. Call (404) 936-3700.

• A booklet called *Curtailing Crime—Inside and Out*, published by the Small Business Administration, is a brief but valuable collection of crime prevention ideas for small business. Send $2 to SBA Publications, P.O. Box 30, Denver, CO 80201-0030. Specify publication CP2.

• The National Crime Prevention Council (NCPC) offers a small business kit titled *Taking a Stand against Crime and Drugs*, which includes advice on shoplifting prevention. The cost is $24.95. Write to 1700 K Street, N.W., Washington, DC 20006-3817, or call (202) 466-6272 and ask for the distribution center.

• National Loss Prevention Bureau, Ltd., in Smithtown, New York, offers a full line of loss prevention support services, from white-collar crime to product counterfeiting and workers' comp fraud. Call (800) 223-6575. Another firm, Loss

Prevention Specialists, Inc., Winter Park, Florida, specializes in shoplifting losses. Call (800) 366-5774.

• *Crimeproofing Your Business: 301 Low-Cost, No-Cost Ways to Protect Your Office, Store, or Business* by Russell Bintliff (McGraw-Hill, $16.95 in paperback) is a beefy book of specific remedies for crimes that target small and mid-sized businesses. Includes checklists, forms, procedures, and employee training suggestions. Call (800) 277-4726.

• *Preventing Computer Fraud* by Dana Stern (McGraw-Hill, $39.95 in paperback) shows how to combat a problem that's costing American business a fortune in lost time, data, and resources. Call (800) 277-4726.

• BusinessGuardDog ($129 from JIAN Tools for Sales, Inc.) is a theft prevention software program that helps you design and implement policies. It's especially well suited for manufacturing or distribution companies because it covers all aspects of their operations: accounting, data processing, inventory, shipping, and others. The manual is full of graphic detail and specific advice. PC and Mac versions available. Call (800) 346-5426; fax (415) 941-9272.

• The Network, Inc., based in Norcross, Georgia, can help a business set up and manage a loss prevention program. Call (800) 253-0453; fax (404) 441-3634.

• The Alliance Against Fraud in Telemarketing is coordinated by the National Consumers League. Call (800) 876-7060.

• Call For Action (CFA), Inc., based in Washington, D.C., is an international network of more than 600 volunteers who work hotlines at radio and television stations to assist, educate, and solve problems for small businesses that have been victims of scams. It's a free and confidential service. For a booklet of fraud prevention tips and a list of CFA offices across the country call the national office at (202) 537-0585.

• The AT&T Corporate Calling Card guarantees that you won't pay for fraudulent calling card calls made by people you don't know. With the AT&T Card Protect Service you can also place geographic restrictions on calls, establish purchase limits, and install special passwords. Call (800) 448-6060.

• White-Collar Crime 101 is a Vienna, Virginia, financial crime prevention firm that offers several helpful publications and videos. *White-Collar Crime Fighter* is a bimonthly newsletter ($36/year); *White-Collar Crime 101 Prevention Handbook* ($8.95 plus $2.50 postage) offers prevention tips and advice. Call (703) 848-9248; fax (703) 848-4586. *Telemarketing Fraud* and *Embezzlement* are part of a White-Collar Crime 101 video series ($99.95 each plus $3.50 shipping) available through KDN Videoworks of Madison Heights, Michigan. Call (800) 825-4568; fax (313) 546-3749.

• Crime Stoppers International is a program involving police departments, government agencies, business and other organizations all working together. For information and location of the program nearest you, call its headquarters in Albuquerque, New Mexico, at (800) 245-0009.

• Employers Mutual Association/Stores Protective Association, in Simi Valley, California, is a mutual benefit nonprofit association founded in 1929. Provides loss prevention resources for businesses, such as financial transaction approvals; employee background screening; loss prevention training seminars. Call (800) 321-4772; fax (805) 527-3499.

CHAPTER 10

Conserve Energy and Cut Waste for Cool Savings

Tactic #121: Audit and Manage Your Energy Costs
Tactic #122: Take These Simple Energy-Saving Steps
Tactic #123: Get Free Technical Help from NATAS
Tactic #124: Conduct a Waste Audit, Too
Tactic #125: Dicker for Lower Disposal Costs
Tactic #126: Set Up a Recycling Program

Save-a-Bundle Follow-up File

TACTIC #121
Audit and Manage Your Energy Costs

Energy is like cash. The better you manage it, the bigger your profits. Today's cost-saving bias in American business has ignited a powerful round of energy conservation measures. More than half of the U.S. economy's thirst for new energy between now and 2010 will be quenched not by new capacity but by conservation.

Available energy-saving technology can cut consumption in half and costs by a third of what they were in the late 1980s. You don't have to be big to benefit. Witness a Taco Bell franchise in San Diego. The owner asked San Diego Gas and Electric (SDG&E) to conduct a free energy audit, which included a load profile for each energy system (lighting, cooking, etc.) tracked every fifteen minutes for a week. Based on that audit, SDG&E suggested ways to cut monthly energy costs by about 30%, including energy-saving fluorescent lamps and devices to automatically turn off lights. Bottom line: The $440 spent on changes is producing annual savings of at least $655.

Many utility companies offer free or low-cost energy audits, often jointly with the state or a local university. Savings typically range between 25% and 60%. According to the Edison Electric Institute, a utility industry trade association, about two hundred utility companies sponsor over thirteen hundred energy conservation programs—and they're backing those programs with billions of dollars.

One reason they can offer these programs is that utility commissions in nineteen states now let utility companies earn a return on their investments in conservation programs, including energy audits performed for customers and rebates given to customers for investing in energy-saving technology.

Your Energy Management Plan Because gas and electric bills are not itemized, it's tough to perform your own audit. Better to enlist specialists who can provide a breakdown of your bill and show you potential savings.

Your energy management plan should cover these areas:

- Improving the efficiency of lighting, hot water, heating, ventilation, and air-conditioning systems.
- Possible replacement of energy-*in*efficient equipment or machinery your company uses.
- Reorganizing activities to benefit from lower energy rates at different times of the day (off-peak rates can be 30% or more lower) and to use energy more efficiently. For example, light your business areas according to specific needs instead of lighting the entire area brightly.

EG&G Powers Systems, a small manufacturer (with a twenty-five-thousand-square-foot facility) in San Luis Obispo, California, cut its lighting costs 50% after undergoing an energy audit—a bottom-line boost of more than $11,000 per year. Light fixtures were retrofitted with optical reflectors (they increase efficiency with less power) and high-efficiency electronic ballasts. Only half of the original lamps were reinstalled.

Likewise, Fox River Mills, a small manufacturer of socks and gloves in Osage, Iowa, invested about $40,000 in energy-saving measures (new lights, better insulation, etc.)—a move that netted the company monthly savings of about $3,000. Money spent on energy-saving measures usually is recovered within ten to fourteen months.

TACTIC #122
Take These Simple Energy-Saving Steps

For most companies, saving energy requires a series of small steps. A nudge from Mr. Big at your company will help.

When Stan Gault became chairman and CEO of an ailing Goodyear Tire & Rubber in 1991, one of his first actions was to remove two dozen light bulbs from lamps and various other fixtures in his office. The move was intended to be symbolic for the company's ninety-seven thousand employees, but Gault figured he'd just saved his company $230 per year.

Here are some things you can do:

- Install cheap devices that douse lights automatically. These "occupancy sensors" can be installed in storage rooms, rest rooms, hallways, and stairwells. One manufacturer of such devices is RAB Electric Manufacturing, Inc., in Northvale, New Jersey, at (201) 784-8600. RAB claims that its LIGHTAlert occupancy sensor can cut some lighting costs by 50%. It's a passive infrared sensor that turns lights on when a person enters and douses lights after the room is vacated.
- Replace standard lamps with compact fluorescent bulbs— the latest advance in energy-efficient lighting. These babies last up to ten years, or an average of ten to thirteen times longer than standard incandescent bulbs. They cost more than incandescents (about $15 to $25 per bulb), but they use as much as 75% less energy over their lifetime. Other advantages: They start immediately (no annoying flickering), burn cool, and give off an incandescent-like glow.
- Review your lighting locations. Many fixtures are ill-placed. By moving fixtures closer to where the light is needed (called "task lighting"), many companies are finding that they need far fewer lights.
- Install fluorescent light reflectors. These inexpensive devices will boost lighting efficiency and allow you to use less energy. Some manufacturers include Reflect-a-Light of Palatka, Florida, at (800) 537-1629; and Mirrorlight, Inc., in New York, at (800) 348-8673.
- Rev up your air-conditioning "economizer." Making your old cooling system work more efficiently is one way to

save money with little investment. Many existing systems are already equipped with a device called an economizer, though it may not be working properly. The economizer is a control that measures outside temperature and humidity. When it's cool and dry enough, the economizer kicks in and tells the system to begin drawing fresh (and free) outside air into the building, rather than spending money cooling the warmer inside air. Have a qualified mechanic check your system to see if it's working properly.

- Turn office machines off at night. Consider installing a timer that will shut them down.

Do the measures work? LSI Logic Corp., a maker of semiconductors in Milpitas, California, computed annual savings of $88,000 by switching to low-energy fluorescent lighting, motion sensors, and computerized climate control systems.

TACTIC #123
Get Free Technical Help from NATAS

Need technical help to design and implement a unique energy conservation program at your small business? An obscure U.S. Department of Energy office cloistered in Butte, Montana, might be able to help, gratis. This government-sponsored program, called the National Appropriate Technology Assistance Service (NATAS), bills itself as "a one-stop resource for small businesses, entrepreneurs, non-profit organizations, utilities, investment bankers—anyone who needs energy-related business assistance." Call (800) 428-2525; in Montana call (800) 428-1718.

TACTIC #124
Conduct a Waste Audit, Too

Waste costs you money two key ways: in disposal costs and in raw materials. LSI Logic, the semiconductor maker, cut 78% of the hazardous waste from its chip-making process by substituting nonhazardous chemicals for hazardous ones. One-year savings from reduced disposal and purchasing costs were over $300,000.

Quad Graphics, Inc., a Wisconsin-based printing company with over five thousand employees, $500 million in sales, and plants or offices in seventeen cities, has been a waste management and energy reduction innovator. In 1989, Quad calculated that waste disposal was costing the company $168,000 per year and that wasted materials were costing even more. By conserving manufacturing materials, such as paper, Quad Graphics is now netting seven-figure savings annually.

Some ways this company has cut waste and related costs:

- Quad now separates its waste paper into 23 grades and sells it to 170 different mills for recycling. The company recycles about 90,000 *tons* of paper per year.
- An aggressive energy management program slashed Quad's net energy use per page printed by 24%.
- Wooden pallets—an increasingly expensive item for manufacturers—get loving attention at Quad. Two employees repair an estimated 200 to 300 broken pallets per day at Quad's Pewaukee, Wisconsin, plant, saving the company thousands of dollars per year.

Furniture Maker's Impressive Savings Herman Miller, Inc., a $900 million office furniture maker in Zeeland, Michigan, has posted impressive savings by reducing waste, conserving energy, and recycling materials.

- Styrofoam and cardboard packaging used to ship office partitions was cut by more than two-thirds. Annual savings: $250,000.

- Shipping containers for office chairs were made reusable. Annual savings: about $300,000.
- A North Carolina company now takes Miller's fabric scraps and uses them for insulation. Miller previously paid to dump those scraps in landfills. Annual savings: $50,000.
- Other materials, including office paper, lubricating oil, and leather, are swapped or sold as recyclables. Combined annual savings: about $1 million.
- The company invested $11 million in 1982 to build a heating and cooling plant fueled by company waste. That, and other measures, have reduced Herman Miller's waste volume by 90%. Annual savings on fuel and dumping fees: $750,000. The plant paid for itself in less than ten years, pushing today's annual savings directly to the bottom line.
- Total estimated annual savings from reduced packaging: $1.4 million.

A publication called *Waste in the Workplace*, from Keep America Beautiful, Inc. (see the Follow-up File), can help you conduct a companywide waste audit.

TACTIC #125
Dicker for Lower Disposal Costs

The company Dumpster is an overlooked area where you can sniff out savings. "You can avoid a lot of misery and overspending by paying as much attention to your trash service as you do to other suppliers," says trash-reduction consultant Ron Mears of R&M Enterprises in Greensboro, North Carolina. "If your company has used the same hauler for three years or more, shop around. You are probably wasting hundreds, maybe thousands, of dollars."

Landfill fees alone may be costing you $45, $75, even $100 or more per ton, says Mears, not including the trash hauler's service. And considering that even a small business can generate ten to thirty or more tons of trash per month, landfill costs can easily run from $5,000 to almost $40,000 annually.

Mears claims that many businesses overpay for trash removal because they don't understand how charges are levied. Here are some of his cost-reducing tips:

- Never use a Dumpster that's too big for your needs. Reason: The hauler is charged a landfill "tipping" (dumping) fee based on weight. That fee is passed along directly to you. But haulers don't actually weigh a company's trash; most of them estimate the weight *based on the size of your Dumpster or Dumpsters.* The bigger the Dumpster, the more you may be paying, regardless of how much trash you actually deposit. If your Dumpster's only half full, the hauler makes that much more money since you pay the landfill fee anyway. If you aren't filling your current container, get something smaller.
- The fewer pickups you have, the lower the cost. Thus, emptying an eight-yard Dumpster once weekly is cheaper than emptying a four-yard Dumpster twice. If you don't have perishable waste such as food, you can probably get by with less frequent pickups.
- Negotiate a fixed-rate contract if you can. If the hauler won't agree to that, request thirty- or sixty-day notification of any increase and a provision to cancel the contract if an increase is requested. Then dicker for something smaller.

TACTIC #126
Set Up a Recycling Program

Companies that do so generally find cost savings in three key areas:

1. Less waste means lower disposal costs.
2. Materials sold to recyclers can produce cash.

3. A company commitment to recycling spurs employees to look for other conservation measures.

Consider Global Turnkey Systems, Inc. (GTS), a $10 million, ninety-employee Waldwick, New Jersey, firm that produces customized business software. When GTS felt a recessionary pinch, the firm's CFO sidled up to recycling and other waste- and energy-reducing measures. The firm cut its $1,500 per month trash-hauling bill almost in half and netted companywide savings of some $20,000 per year. Global recycles office paper, aluminum, glass, magazines, junk mail, and plastic. The program has been so successful that Global now offers a free recycling guide for business and helps other small companies set up programs. Call Global at (201) 445-5050.

Collins & Aikman Floor Coverings, in Dalton, Georgia, has made similar strides. A recycling program has cut the amount of waste the firm dumps into a local landfill by 47%. In addition to traditional recycling of paper, plastic, cardboard, etc., Collins & Aikman manages and redistributes its office supplies, a move that cuts waste and saves money on purchasing. Scrap yarn (from carpet making) is boxed and sold for reuse. Needles and hooks are collected along with metal strapping and buckles and sold with other scrap iron.

SAVE-A-BUNDLE FOLLOW-UP FILE

• The Energy Efficiency and Environmental Expo, first held in Pittsburgh in 1993, could become the Super Bowl of energy- and waste-reducing expos. It's sponsored by such heavyweights as the National Association of Manufacturers, Edison Electric Institute, U.S. Department of Energy, Arthur Andersen & Co., and the United Nations. Immerse yourself in technology and strategies for minimizing waste, managing energy, and turning savings into profits. Call the Pennsylvania Technology Council at (412) 687-2700 or (800) 388-8820; fax (412) 687-2791; or write to 4516 Henry Street, Pittsburgh, PA 15213.

• The *Green Business Letter* ($97/year) promises to be "the hands-on journal for environmentally conscious companies" and delivers on that promise. The focus is on saving money, with helpful tips on cutting lighting and water use, recycling, securing tax incentives, and more. Published by Tilden Press, Inc., 1526 Connecticut Avenue, N.W., Washington, DC 20036. A free sample is available. Call (800) 955-GREEN.

• Keep America Beautiful (KAB), a nonprofit group formed in 1953, is a good source of how-to information on waste reduction and recycling. Write to KAB, Mill River Plaza, 9 West Broad Street, Stamford, CT 06902, or call (203) 323-8987. One especially helpful publication is *Waste in the Workplace* ($4.50 plus $1.50 shipping), a small business guide for auditing commercial waste, identifying recyclables, reducing waste, and cutting disposal costs.

• *Trash Is Not Just Trash . . . But Big Bucks!* is a fifty-page booklet of advice on how to reduce your trash costs and earn money recycling. It costs $19.95 plus $2 shipping from R&M Enterprises, P.O. Box 38732, Greensboro, NC 27438.

• Energy Analysis and Diagnostic Centers (EADCs) at about two dozen universities across the United States conduct free energy audits for small and midsize manufacturers with up to $75 million in revenues that are based within 150 miles of the center. The audit includes specific cost-saving recommendations. The Western Region is managed for the U.S. Department of Energy by University City Science Center in Philadelphia. Call (215) 387-2255 or fax (215) 387-5540 to locate the EADC nearest to you. The Eastern Region is managed by the Rutgers University Office of Industrial Productivity and Energy Assessments. Call (908) 932-5540; fax (908) 932-0730.

• The American Council for an Energy-Efficient Economy (ACEEE), with offices in Washington, D.C., and Berkeley, California, distributes information on energy-saving tactics. Call for a publications catalog: (202) 429-8873 for the Washington office; (510) 549-9914 for Berkeley.

CHAPTER 11

Collect More of Your Cash

TACTIC #127
Make Smart Credit-Granting Decisions

To save your company from bad debts, check out the customer's credit ahead of time. You can buy credit reports from commercial credit reporting agencies (see the Follow-up File), make inquiries yourself, or combine the two. It's one of the most important decisions a small business can make. Bad credit choices can put you under.

To get information you need for your own credit check, ask credit customers to complete an application that includes the type of business, size, bank and trade references, and authorization for you to conduct a credit check.

For small companies, however, it's hard to beat the deal you get through Dun & Bradstreet Small Business Services—a program designed to help small companies better manage credit and collections. D&B is the leader in business information, with computer files on some nine million U.S. businesses, constantly updated. Small Business Services offers a low-cost, pay-as-you-go plan that lets you tap credit reports with a phone call.

For a flat fee of $50, D&B's Credit Recommendation Service is a bargain. Considering extending credit to a customer? A D&B credit expert will talk you through the firm's recommendation by phone and follow up with a written report by mail or fax. The representative will discuss your situation, your company's needs, the order size, and other relevant items. D&B reps will call credit references, banks, and your customers themselves. Standard turnaround is four business days; a rush one-day investigation costs $75 per company. A simplified credit check, for small orders, is available by phone, twenty-four hours a day, six days a week, for $15 per call. It lets you find out in a few minutes how a company you're planning to do business with pays its bills.

For information on D&B Small Business Services, call (800) 552-DUNS.

TACTIC #128
Become a Better Biller

The appearance of your invoice is a crucial first step toward speedier collections. The invoice should be clear and simple. It should state explicitly, in itemized fashion, what it's for. Fancy colors or cute designs detract from the straightforward purpose—*getting paid.* Make it a *real* invoice, not just stationery with an "amount due" typed in. Make it clear what business name the check should be made out to and include only one address on the invoice—the one where you want the money sent. Include a phone number for questions.

An effective invoice—one that encourages quick and full payment—should clearly state any quick-pay discounts you offer as well as your service charges for late payment. State the customer's obligation to examine goods you've shipped and notify you of any problems within a specified number of days.

A great, low-cost software package for small companies is MyInvoices ($24.95) from Menlo Park, California–based MySoftware Co. It does all your billing and with a keystroke can track your receivables, generate aging reports, and give you sales reports and trend summaries. Call (800) 325-3508.

TACTIC #129
Write Dynamic Dunning Letters

The better your collection letter, the faster the money will flow. Make it a customized, personal letter, *not* a form letter. Letters addressed to no one in particular are worthless. Write to the person in charge, the owner, the one whose reputation stands to be sullied by a bad debt. If you don't have a name, call and get one. An added handwritten note also gains attention.

Before you write, check the latest information on the account. Has the customer disputed the amount? What's the past payment history? Has payment been promised?

Keep the letter simple, direct, and short. Remind the debtor of his or her original *promise* to pay. Ask for *immediate, full* payment. (Somehow, many would-be collection letters forget that obvious item.) Emphasize the seriousness of your dilemma and the need to resolve the balance or take additional collection steps—turning it over to a collection agency, for example.

The right tone is respectful (no insults or threats): an appeal to the customer's "valued reputation," but also a frank demand for the dough. You want action, not excuses.

The package your letter comes in should look like important business correspondence—not like a *bill*, which you know has already failed to shake loose the cash. Think of it as a personalized direct-marketing piece where your sales objective is to collect the overdue cash. Some dunners hand address their envelopes to increase the odds the letter gets opened and read. The first letter can go regular mail. Subsequent letters should be sent certified mail, return receipt requested. Certified mail draws immediate attention. If the recipient refuses to sign, you know you've got a problem.

Still worried? Get the collection specialists at D&B to write your letters for you. The D&B Collection Letters Service prepares customized letters intended to collect your cash while preserving good customer relationships. Two letters cost $25. Call (800) 552-DUNS.

TACTIC #130
Fax Your Letters and Invoices

Don't simply mail your overdue invoices and collection letters; fax them too. The fax adds a little extra urgency to the matter. Also, since other people may see the fax—a fax operator, assistant, or secretary, for example—the debtor might be shamed into action.

TACTIC #131
Make the Call Sooner, Not Later

Most companies wait too long to call. Collections expert Leonard Sklar, of the Sklar Resource Group in Hillsborough, California, says that phoning for money is ten times more effective than writing. The single act of getting on the phone early and often can save your business a bundle—a possible tenfold increase in collections on overdue debt.

Paul Mignini, president of the National Association of Credit Management (NACM), in Columbia, Maryland, says that if you don't have your money by day thirty-one, you or someone at the company should be dialing for those dollars. Get a commitment for payment by a certain date.

Phoning creates a sense of urgency. It also lets you know quickly where you stand with debtors. If there's a problem, they intend to ice your invoice another sixty days, or they don't intend to pay, better you know *now* rather than months from now as your letters go unanswered. On the phone, you can negotiate terms if necessary, convince the customer to pay *you* and let the business that only sent a letter wait, or even suggest that the debtor put the overdue amount on a credit card.

Don't apologize for calling; you have every right to ask for your money. But keep the call short. Clarify the issue and get right to the point: "A review of our records shows an overdue balance on your account of [$AMOUNT]. This amount was due on [DATE] and is now late. We have contacted you several times about resolving this matter, without success." Convince the customer that this matter is serious and needs immediate attention. Tell the customer what must be done to fulfill the obligation. Get a firm commitment that payment will be sent.

Follow up the call with a letter confirming what was said. In all cases, be courteous and professional. Be firm but *never threaten* (intimidation and deception were banned by the federal Fair Debt Collection Practices Act of 1977, although commercial debtors aren't covered by this consumer law).

TACTIC #132
Call In the Collection Cavalry . . . While There's Still Time

---

Each month that passes dramatically reduces your chances of ever getting paid, so don't wait long to call in a collection agency. Only 74% of accounts that reach ninety days past due are ever collected. That figure plunges to 58% at six months and 27% at twelve months. If your profit margin is 6%, you'll have to ring up over $8,000 in sales to offset a single credit loss of $500; a company with a 2% margin must produce $25,000 in sales to make it up.

More and more businesses are finding that bringing in a collection agency more quickly *saves* money even though the agency may take a third of what's collected. John Breneman, a CPA with the St. Louis firm Brandvein, Shapiro, Kossmeyer & Co., recommends that his small business clients move quickly to a collection agency—as early as sixty to ninety days. "Like many small businesses, our own accounting firm was hesitant to bring in an agency. Now we do it and we won't be so slow to do so in the future."

Check out any collection agency before you sign on. Ask for references and current clients you can talk to. The typical agency will be successful at collecting about 22% of your past due accounts and will take 33% to 40% of that amount for its fee. Look for a firm that is a member of the American Collectors Association. One of the biggies in the field is Mid-Continent Agencies, Inc., at 3701 West Algonquin Road, Rolling Meadows, IL 60008; (800) 374-2000.

TACTIC #133
Establish a Credit Policy and Organize Your Receivables System

---

A credit policy? You betcha! Unless your business sells cash-and-carry you'd better establish the creditworthiness of any customer whose promise to pay you intend to accept. Get the materials on how to establish a credit policy published by the National Association of Credit Management (see the Follow-up File).

Monitor receivables monthly. Consider calling some yourself to find out why they haven't paid. A good turnkey workbook is *The Desktop Credit Manager* by Steve Haber, which includes necessary forms, agreements, checklists, strategies, and procedures. It costs $75. Call (510) 736-4649 or write to The Desktop Credit Manager, P.O. Box 2425, Danville, CA 94526.

Mid-Continent Agencies (MCA) offers an Accounts Receivable Management Program geared toward smaller companies that don't have the staff to give collections proper attention. MCA will customize the program for your firm. Nice feature: MCA guarantees that the service will reduce your overall cost of collections and increase your cash flow, and ties the cost to that guarantee. MCA says the service is especially well suited to small distributing companies, professional services firms, and small manufacturers. MCA is based in the Chicago suburb of Rolling Meadows and has offices in Buffalo, Louisville, Atlanta, and Orange County, California. Call (800) 374-2000; fax (708) 797-1575.

TACTIC #134
Offer Carrots for Quick Payment

Discounts of 1% to 3% for paying fast—within ten to fifteen days—work well. By making it more costly for the company *not* to pay early, you can boost your own cash flow. But some customers take the discount even when they aren't paying early. If that happens, rebill for the difference. Or, to lessen the chance that they were honestly confused about which price to pay, make the fast-pay discount offer on a separate coupon enclosed with the invoice, *not on the invoice itself.*

There are other carrots you can dangle, such as coupons good on the next purchase (a great idea that not only speeds payment now, but rings up the next sale as well) and perhaps a chance to win something. For example, Westlake Tennis and Swim Cub, a private club in Westlake Village, California, speeds payments by holding a monthly drawing of all members who pay by the tenth, with the winner getting a month free.

TACTIC #135
Look for Early Warning Signs

Tuning in to early signs of trouble can save you money. By recognizing the signs and taking action, you may be able to stop a credit balance from becoming a delinquent debt. Here are some things to watch for:

- Payments have become increasingly slow.
- There are dramatic changes—up or down—in the customer's purchase patterns. A sudden increase, coupled with other warning signs, could mean the customer has lost credit elsewhere and is forced to buy more from you.
- You receive partial payments or postdated or unsigned checks.

- Checks are returned for insufficient funds.
- Phone calls aren't returned; letters are unanswered.
- You suddenly receive complaints that appear groundless.
- Reports in trade publications or through the industry grapevine suggest financial problems.

If any of these signs appear, be cautious about extending additional credit. Talk to the customer about what's happening. Measured amounts of concern and compassion will likely produce a solution that'll save you money in the long term, and perhaps a customer too.

TACTIC #136
Boot Bum Checks

No matter how much information you write on the back of a check, there's no guarantee it won't turn to rubber. Your best defense against bum checks is to use a check guarantee service, such as TeleCheck, which will guarantee payment of any check the firm has approved. Two national check guarantee firms that can help your business avoid bum checks are:

- Checkcare Enterprises, Inc., based in Columbus, Georgia: (706) 563-3660.
- TeleCheck Services, Inc., in Houston, Texas: (800) 525-8999.

TACTIC #137
Dealing with Unsigned or NSF Checks

Every business that takes checks occasionally receives one unsigned. Can you deposit it? Probably. Here's what will work with smaller checks at many banks:

On the blank signature line, write or type in "over." Then on the back of the check, where the endorsement would go, type in: "Lack of signature guaranteed," then your company's name, account number, and your name and title. Place your signature above your typed name and deposit the check. You are, in effect, guaranteeing that you will take back the check as a charge against your account if the issuer's bank doesn't honor it—something you'd have to do anyhow if the check bounced. With the endorsement, most banks will process the item and remit the funds if they are on deposit in the customer's account.

A check returned as NSF (not sufficient funds) presents a collection challenge. Here's the four-step advice Ohio Bell offers in *Collections: A Guide to Improving Accounts Receivable:*

1. If the check has just been refused for the first time:

   - Redeposit the check and have your bank send you a copy.
   - Call your customer and ask that money be deposited to back the check.
   - Hold further shipments to the customer.
   - Place a copy of the check in your credit file for that customer. You may need information such as the account number for future actions.

2. If the check is returned a second time:

   - Remove the deposit entry from your account.
   - Hold shipment to the customer.
   - Call the customer and request a cashier's check.

3. If no payment is made in one week, call the customer's bank and obtain as much information about the account as you can.

4. Move quickly to start your collection process.

TACTIC #138
Act Early on Aging Accounts

Many companies focus mainly on their worst collection cases—accounts that have gone past 90 or 120 days. But that can be a mistake. Creditors who don't hear from you until 45 days, 60 days, 75 days, or more may assume that it's okay to stretch their payments that long. If a company gets your first dunning notice on day 61, it might start paying all of your invoices on day 59. To prevent that from happening, take action immediately after the first 30 days.

TACTIC #139
Charge Interest

Kathy Thurston, who manages the money for her family-owned business Ideal Construction, in Honolulu, has it right: "We're not bankers," she says. "We're not in the business of financing construction projects. We expect to get paid on time." If your customers are turning you into a banker by stretching payments ever farther, then act like a banker and *charge 'em interest*.

You don't have to *call* it interest—call it a late charge if you prefer. But tack it on, and keep tacking it on until you get paid. Don't get carried away—no Mafia-style rates or antagonistic practices. A simple statement of your policy will do. Later you can offer to waive the charges in return for full payment. Charging interest helps demonstrate your resolve to be paid on time, and the extra money you collect helps dampen your other collection costs.

SAVE-A-BUNDLE FOLLOW-UP FILE

• The National Association of Credit Management is a trade group for business people who deal with credit and collections. NACM has over forty thousand members and produces dozens of publications on collections and standard credit forms. Call or write for a complete list and other information: NACM, 8815 Centre Park Drive, Suite 200, Columbia, MD 21045; (410) 740-5560; fax (410) 740-5574.

• Several Dun & Bradstreet divisions and programs can help:

· Receivable Management Services offers complete collection services, including training. It also gets you access to D&B's huge data base of debtor information—the biggest in the industry. Call (800) 234-3867.

· D&B Receivable Management Services has an international unit that specializes in helping U.S. firms collect overdue accounts overseas. Call (800) 274-6454.

· D&B Small Business Services offers several low-cost ways for small companies to boost their credit and collections. Call (800) 722-DUNS.

• TRW, the biggest of the credit reporting firms, can plug you into both consumer and business credit reports. For consumer, call TRW Resource Center at (800) 831-5614. For business, call TRW Business Credit Services National Hotline, (800) 344-0603. TRW Business Credit Services offers a full line of commercial credit information services, including business profile reports, small business advisory reports, international reports, and an early warning advisory.

• *Debt Collection: Successful Strategies for the Small Business* by Gini Graham Scott is comprehensive, well organized, and available for $17.95 in paperback from PSI Research, Grants Pass, Oregon. Call (800) 228-2275.

• *Credit Collection Manager's Letter* ($143.50/year, twice monthly) contains helpful advice from the Bureau of Business

Practice, a Prentice-Hall division. Call (800) 243-0876, ext. 520.

• *The Check Is Not in the Mail* by Leonard Sklar has loads of great advice on collection techniques for business; $19.95 plus $1.95 postage from Baroque Publishing, 744 Jacaranda Circle, Hillsborough, CA 94010; (415) 348-7071.

• *A Private Eye's Guide to Collecting a Bad Debt* by Fay Faron is published by Creighton-Morgan for $12.95. Call (415) 922-6684; fax (415) 567-5077.

• *Mastering Collections: Business to Business* by Donald Kramer (Kramer & Frank, $39) offers exhaustive advice from an attorney in about 130 pages; call (800) 633-6069.

• Your local phone company may offer advice on how to make effective telephone collection calls. For example, Ohio Bell offers Call Power, business communication workshops for small business. For information call (800) 554-5853.

CHAPTER 12

Tackle Your Telecom Costs

Save-a-Bundle Follow-up File

TACTIC #140
Collect Spoils from the Battle of the Long-Distance Titans

As AT&T, MCI, Sprint, British upstart Cable & Wireless (now wiring into the U.S. business market), and a bevy of smaller firms battle for business customers, money-saving opportunities ring out. The fight is so ferocious that it's worth reviewing your long-distance carrier at least every other year. The big four all offer multiple deals for larger companies. But they've also taken aim squarely at the small business market, where they see most of the growth in years ahead.

AT&T's Partners in Business program, for example, offers discounts of up to 20% on both domestic and international calls for small companies that spend between $25 and $2,000 per month. A business spending $1,000 per month could save $2,400 per year just by signing up for this deal. Put your signature to an eighteen-month contract and AT&T will slice 20% off all calls to the one area code you call most; or gain a 5% break on an 800 line by agreeing to stay put for eighteen months. If your business makes international calls, AT&T has also offered a 30% discount deal on calls to the one country you phone most. The MCI Friends of the Firm program offers small companies big discounts as well, in return for the right to solicit business from the numbers your firm calls.

You may also be able to snag long-distance discounts through business affiliations. Phone firms are striking strategic alliances with big banks, trade associations, and other business groups under which the company or organization offers its customers or members discounted long-distance service (and takes a piece of the action) through the phone firm.

Simplified and consolidated billing offered by the phone combatants can also save you money. For example, Sprint, Cable & Wireless, and others will consolidate billing for all of the different types of business phone service you use—regular outbound calls, incoming 800 lines, conference calls, calling card calls, international calls—on a single invoice. The key feature to look for is "call aggregating," which means that different kinds of calls or calls from different locations are added together to help your company qualify for the best volume discounts. Consolidated billing also makes things easier for law firms, architects, consultants, and other firms that must rebill phone costs to clients.

Deals are constantly changing, so call the carriers for the latest updates. The Follow-up File has contacts.

TACTIC #141
Banish 411

Directory assistance calls were once free. No more. In fact, phone companies are now generating revenues of over *$2 billion* from folks who call for phone numbers instead of looking 'em up.

Have you checked how much your business is paying to have local directory assistance operators find numbers for you? The average call to 411 now costs about sixty-five cents. To reduce or eliminate this cost, make certain that your phone company delivers enough free phone directories to your business to accommodate employees. Then get workers to use the phone books instead of punching 411 and ringing up those charges on your bill.

A good time and money saver is *The National Directory of Addresses and Telephone Numbers* (Omnigraphics, $85)—sixteen hundred pages of names, addresses, phone, fax, and 800 numbers for frequently called corporations, institutions, and organizations. Save money by looking up some of the eleven thousand *toll-free* numbers listed in this directory and calling those instead of the regular numbers. Call (800) 234-1340; fax (800) 875-1340.

TACTIC #142
An Internal 411 Alternative

Large companies or organizations can go to school on Hofstra University's 411 experience at its campus in Hempstead, New York. Hofstra cut its monthly 411 bill in half, to around $10,000, by offering its own in-house directory assistance. Campus callers punching 411—a costly call to the phone company in the past—are now routed instead to *Hofstra's* switchboard, where staffers use a CD-ROM system (a compact disk crammed with directory information) to quickly locate numbers on a computer screen. Such disks are marketed by regional Bell companies, often in conjunction with directory firms such as Reuben H. Donnelley—a Dun & Bradstreet company; call (800) 866-9500—and PhoneDisk USA of Marblehead, Massachusetts: (800) 284-8353. The electronic directory service from NYNEX, for example, is called Fast Track; AT&T has one called Find America.

Because 411 has become such an expense, a major move is afoot to help larger companies and organizations set up internal systems to look up outside numbers—not only to save money but also to generate more complete and accurate information.

If an internal setup isn't for you, but your business still spends big money on 411, ask your regional phone firm if it offers volume discounts on directory lookups. St. Louis–based Southwestern Bell, for example, offers bulk lookups at a reduced price. The $4,000 start-up fee rules out all but the biggest 411 users; but the program slashes the price to fifteen cents per call from forty-five.

TACTIC #143
Avoid Budget-Busting Hotel Phone Charges

Make no long-distance calls that are billed to your room. Since the dawn of phone deregulation over a decade ago, the law of the jungle has applied to the foolhardy who make such hotel calls without knowing what the charges will be. According to Harry Newton, a guru of telephone cost savings and publisher of New York–based *Teleconnect* magazine, you can save money by billing calls to your own credit card. (Also see Tactic #98.)

Better yet, says Newton, get your business an 800 number and use that for all incoming calls back to the office. Rates have been reduced so dramatically on 800 services that they're now among the cheapest calling methods available. *If you and your employees do much traveling, a number dedicated exclusively to this use could pay for itself in short order.* You don't *have* to give the number out to other people! An 800 line can save you money too.

TACTIC #144
Use Money-Saving Hardware

- Cut unauthorized long-distance phoning at your business with a device that hooks to your phones and can block expensive calls to 900, 976, 411, or even an individual long-distance number that's being abused. One such device, Call Controller, costs between $50 and $130 depending on features and also lets you set call time limits from one to fifteen minutes. A key-operated device, Modular Lock-Out ($35), blocks all outgoing calls while allowing incoming. Order from Hello Direct, (800) 444-3556.

- Get triple duty (voice, modem, fax) out of a single-line phone with a voice/data switch or line-sharing device. There are more than seventy varieties available. Manual switches start at about $40; auto switches are $100 and up. Several good ones are available by mail order from Hello Direct, a phone products specialist at (800) 444-3556.

    A few switch options:

  - Fax Director, about $250 from Data-Doc Electronics: (800) 328-2362; fax (512) 928-8210.
  - ExtraLine, $179 list but much cheaper from dealers. Call Lynx Automation for location of nearest dealer: (206) 775-9700; fax (206) 744-1444.
  - Versa-Link ATX-300, about $395 from Multi-Link, Inc.: (800) 535-4651; fax (606) 885-6619.
  - A more sophisticated line sharer called DataJack comes from Viking Electronics of Hudson, Wisconsin. Call (715) 386-8861 for the name of a local distributor. This device helps put idle lines to use and can save money if you program it to route outgoing calls over your least-cost lines. Some businesses may be able to eliminate multiple dedicated lines (to faxes and modems, for example) that sit idle most of the time. Priced under $700.

- Another switching device, called RINGdirector ($60 and up), can put the "distinctive ring" option available from most phone companies to work for your business. Distinctive ring links up to three or four separate phone numbers to a single line, then rings differently depending on which number is called. RINGdirector listens for the ring, then routes the call to, say, your fax, modem, voice mail, or you personally. Available from Lynx Automation in Lynnwood, Washington: (206) 775-9700; fax (206) 744-1444.

TACTIC #145
Soup Up Your Simple System on a Shoestring Budget

Instead of spending big bucks on a new system, try squeezing more out of what you have by adding low-cost optional services, available at the flip of a switch. For example, here are some of the options Bell Atlantic offers its small business customers:

Repeat Call: Keeps dialing a busy number for thirty minutes, but leaves your line open to make or receive calls. Special ring alerts you when a connection is made.

Three-Way Calling: Lets you hold a conference call with two other numbers.

Speed Calling: Program up to thirty numbers for two-digit dialing.

Call Waiting: Let's you know a call is coming in when you are on the phone. You can answer by putting the first call on hold. With *Tone Block* you can block the annoying call-waiting signal when you are on important calls or using your modem.

Caller ID: Identifies the number of an incoming caller before you pick up. Stores the numbers, dates, and times of incoming calls so you can refer back to calls you missed and pick up on every opportunity to make a sale. (Not available in some areas.)

Call Block: You can block calls from up to six numbers. A message will tell the caller you are not taking calls.

Priority Call: A special ring or tone alerts you to incoming calls from as many as six selected numbers.

Distinctive Ring: Allows up to three numbers to be shared on the same telephone line, each with a distinctive ring.

Call Forward: Send all calls to another phone when you are out of the office, or, with *Select Forward*, send only the calls you want from as many as six preselected numbers.

Return Call: Returns the last call, even if you didn't answer. If it's busy, keeps trying for thirty minutes.

Answer Call: Replaces your answering machine. Answers even when you're on the line. A stutter dial tone lets you know when there's a message so you don't have to make a special call. *Voice Mail* adds normal, urgent, or private message delivery. You can send messages to a group of subscribers with one call.

Intelligent 800: Gives you 800 service without adding new lines or equipment. You use the same lines for all of your calls—local, long distance, and incoming 800.

WATS: Saves you money by charging a flat rate for each hour of calling. As your WATS usage goes up, your costs per hour go down.

Centrex: Lets you decide which features to have on each phone in your business—for example, which will be configured for long distance. Offers flexibility to add or subtract lines and capabilities as needed without purchasing new equipment.

TACTIC #146
Put the Triple-Squeeze on Your Phone Bills

Squeeze #1: Audit Your Telecom Costs for Errors Phone companies make mistakes. But you'll never know about 'em unless you scrutinize your phone bills. Try your own audit, or bring in an outside specialist. When PepsiCo audited its phone bills a few years ago, it wound up with a refund approaching $100,000. Don't forget to include an audit of your cellular phone bill. Errors in that area are even more common.

For help in finding a professional who can audit your phone bills and suggest other ways to cut your costs, contact the Society of Telecommunication Consultants in Boca Raton,

Florida, at (800) 782-7670; fax (407) 852-9262. Sharyl Bradley-Hennard, executive director, will send you a directory listing the group's 170 members geographically.

Do-it-yourself audits work too. Atlanta-based American Flat Glass Distributors, Inc., which has distribution centers across the country, chopped 8% from an annual phone tab of about $750,000. The firm audited bills, consolidated systems, yanked unused lines, and negotiated volume rates.

Squeeze #2: Use a Telephone Cost Accounting Plan Do it yourself or outsource it—some phone companies provide this service to business customers. The idea: Group all monthly phone activity to give you a quick read on what's happening. Where are the calls going? How long are they lasting? Who's making what calls and when? An accounting plan lets you spot bad calling habits that are needlessly costing you money; and spot phone abuse too.

Squeeze #3: Get Your Phone Bill on Disk or by Modem Many cost-conscious companies are already opting to ax the old pile of paper called a phone bill and receive an easier-to-handle electronic version instead. Plug the bill into your company PC, add billing management software, and you're ready to save a bundle by analyzing your bill and, with the software's help, identifying waste and areas where you can cut costs and generate discounts. Your long-distance carrier may be able to help with software. Sprint, for example, offers a PC-based phone bill management package called FONVIEW. Flexibility's a plus, says Sprint spokesman Tom Weigman. For example, the software lets you code individual calling cards held by workers in your firm and easily allocate costs to the proper department. You can track and manage costs for 800 lines, and much more. If messing with billing management software isn't your cup of tea, however, turn it over to a telecommunications consultant (see the Follow-up File).

TACTIC #147
Get Low-Cost Comparison Shopping Help

Making the right long-distance choices for your business can save you thousands of dollars per year. But the research can be agonizing. For help, check out a Washington, D.C.–based nonprofit group called the Telecommunications Research and Action Center (TRAC). This group's Tele-Tips Small Business cost-comparison service analyzes rates in over a dozen different plans from all of the major long-distance carriers. TRAC compares costs for different levels of usage, from around $100 per month to over $6,000 per month in charges. For a copy of Tele-Tips Small Business, send $5 and a self-addressed stamped envelope to TRAC, P.O. Box 12038, Washington, DC 20005. For other information call TRAC at (202) 462-2520; fax (202) 408-1134.

TACTIC #148
Connect to Cost Savings through Resellers

Long-distance resellers, also called aggregators, are companies that buy big blocks of phone time from AT&T or other phone firms at a discount, then resell the service in smaller pieces to small businesses, passing along part of the volume discount. You typically can get 800 service as well as regular long distance from the third-party resellers. Savings vary widely and comparison shopping is crucial. With all of the competition, there's no guarantee an aggregator's price will always be the best one available. For more information on how resellers work, contact the Telecommunications Resellers Association, a national group that represents over one hundred phone service resellers, at P.O. Box 8361, McLean, VA 22106; (703) 734-1225; fax (703) 734-8572.

TACTIC #149
Beep Cheap

Compared to cellular car phones, purse phones, and now even wristwatch phones, yesterday's pager technology seems mundane. But if your on-the-fly communication needs (or bank account) require something less than what cellular phones offer, the lower-cost simplicity of a pager may be the best choice for your business. Pagers still keep you and your employees in touch, but at a vastly lower price than cellular phones.

Service pros, such as ad execs, sales reps, and real estate agents, use 'em to stay in touch with clients. Small and home-based business owners, telecommuters, and entrepreneurs rely on pagers to stay in touch while they are away or on the phone. Engineers and architects are using pagers to receive up-to-date project information while in the field. Restaurants and car repair shops offer pagers to busy customers who don't want to wait around. When the car or table is ready, the customer is beeped.

Pager prices (you can buy or rent) depend on the type you choose.

Tone-only pagers are cheapest. They simply alert you to a message, but don't tell you what it is. You have to call a predetermined number to find out. Cost: $70 to $80 to buy, or rent for $9 to $15 per month.

Numeric pagers, the most popular, have a tiny screen that displays up to twenty digits—usually the phone number of the person you're supposed to call back. For a rented numeric pager with local coverage, the average monthly cost is $12 to $23. If you buy it (around $100), the monthly service fee averages $11 to $17.

Alphanumeric pagers use a larger, eighty-character screen that lets you receive a full message without having to return the call. Some models can store up to twenty messages in memory. Average monthly rental for local coverage is $24 to

$33. If you buy ($200 to $250), the monthly fee averages $25 to $30.

For free information on paging, write to the Paging Services Council, P.O. Box 32229, Washington, DC 20007. Motorola, the first word in pagers, now offers one the size of a credit card (a quarter inch thick). Check the Yellow Pages under paging for local and national paging companies.

TACTIC #150
Sign Up for Six-Second Billing

Most giant corporations are billed for phone service in six-second increments by long-distance carriers. But most phone companies bill smaller companies in one-minute hunks. That means if your call runs sixty-one seconds, you pay for a full two minutes. Over the course of a year, six-second billing could lower your bill 20% to 40%, depending on your phone usage. Growing companies can demand six-second billing or go shopping for a phone firm that will comply. Some of the phone resellers offer this feature.

TACTIC #151
Send Faxes at Night When Rates Are Cheap

If you've ever had a fax waiting for you in the morning, that's probably what the sender did. Read your fax manual (or delegate that task) to find out how to program the machine to send faxes at certain hours. Then do it for savings of 20%, 40%, or even more on long-distance charges.

TACTIC #152
Reduce Service Time

According to *Call Center* magazine, over 80% of a phone technician's billable time on the average service call is spent trying to *find* the trouble; only about 20% is spent fixing it. To reduce the hunt time (and save money), keep a phone wiring schematic available along with information on where key phone equipment is located within the company. This will help service folks troubleshoot more quickly.

TACTIC #153
Be Chintzier with Your Cellular Number

Not only do calls made from cellular phones in your car or elsewhere cost more than calls made from phones that are attached to Mother Earth, but every call you *receive* also costs you money. Don't give out your car phone number to the world; be a little more selective and you'll save money.

TACTIC #154
Eliminate Unused Lines

Got a separate phone line in a conference room that's not being used? How about dedicated lines to modems or faxes that are no longer in service? A couple of empty offices with their own phone lines? Each one of those phone lines probably costs you at least $150 to $200 per year even if you don't make a single call. Don't pay for lines you don't use. Remove them.

SAVE-A-BUNDLE FOLLOW-UP FILE

- Finding the phone firms:

AT&T:	(800) 222-0400
MCI:	(800) 444-2222
Sprint:	(800) 877-2000
Cable & Wireless:	(800) 969-9998
Advanced TECHCOM:	(800) 992-7564
Allnet:	(800) 783-2020
SkyTel:	(800) 456-3333
RCI Long Distance:	(800) 836-8080
Metromedia Long Distance:	(800) 275-0200

Ask your Baby Bell for ideas and services available that can help you save money on your local phone bill.

- Reach New York–based *Teleconnect* magazine (monthly, $15/year) at 12 West 21st Street, New York, NY 10010; (800) 677-3435. Request the publisher's catalog of other telecommunications publications.

- *Long Distance for Less*, a book by telecommunications consultant Robert Self, can help you understand and evaluate long-distance rates. It's $75 from Self's New York–based firm, Market Dynamics, at (800) 262-7353. Says Self: "Choosing the right long-distance plan is far more important than choosing a carrier. The key is finding the right plan out of the dozen or so that AT&T, MCI, Sprint, and others offer." Self also publishes the *Long Distance for Less* update series ($98/year).

- The Society of Telecommunications Consultants (STC) can help you locate a topflight phone consultant in your area. Write to STC, 23123 South State Road 7, Suite 220, Boca Raton, FL 33428. Call (800) 782-7670; fax (407) 852-9262.

- The AT&T Corporate Calling Card offers a variety of discount plans (savings up to 18%) for calling card calls made from just about anywhere in the world. Call (800) 637-1618.

CHAPTER 13

Save Money on Your Advertising, Marketing, and PR

TACTIC #155
Golden Savings from Your
Yellow Pages Ads

According to Yellow Pages guru Barry Maher, of Barry Maher & Associates in Santa Barbara, California, most Yellow Pages advertisers overspend—often by thousands of dollars per year. One of Maher's best money-saving tips applies to businesses that waste money on big display ads (which can cost as much as $35,000 per year in the largest directories) that *still* place them behind ads from numerous competitors.

The key to big savings hinges on where your business name falls alphabetically in a large subject category ("Lawyers," "Plumbers," or "Auto Dealers," for example). If it's high up, you can buy a supercheap in-column ad (an inch or so in size) that will appear at your company's name in the alphabetical listings. Such an ad done right (which means with just a couple of catchy words, i.e., DRAIN PROBLEM?, *not* crammed with copy) can rocket your response, says Maher. It also lets you downsize your display ad.

Maher's book *Getting the Most from Your Yellow Pages Advertising* is a super resource for more Yellow Pages tactics. See the Follow-up File.

Here are some of Maher's other money-saving Yellow Pages tips:

- Know thy competition. If you study what they're doing, you may be able to save a bundle. Say, for example, you run a toy store. Now study all the possible Yellow Pages category headings that would apply to your business (your Yellow Pages rep has a list). You find that "Games" isn't even in the book because none of your competitors has listed under that heading even though customers have told you they'd looked extensively to find some of the unusual children's games that you carry.

You buy the smallest listing—what Maher calls a "squint print" listing—under "Games" for next to nothing. That puts the heading in the book and it's all yours! Says Maher, "In your directory, that means that for $2.90 a month you dominate the heading. Your listing is as good as a full-page ad."

- Know when to *reduce* the size of your ad. If your ad is already several sizes ahead of the competition there's no reason to spend even more to make it larger still. In fact, Maher maintains that *one* size larger is usually enough. So instead, consider dropping a notch (but still keep an edge on the competition) and spending the savings on designing a better-looking ad.

- Grab an alphabetical advantage with a second, fully registered "doing business as" (DBA) name for your business. Make sure your DBA, or alternate name, starts with an *A*. That'll put you at the head of the class. You may need to prove the name serves a legitimate business purpose (other than leapfrogging the listings) to satisfy the directory publisher.

TACTIC #156
Cash In on Co-op Ads

Co-op ads are cost-sharing deals between national manufacturers of brand-name products or services and the local businesses that sell those products and services—Bausch & Lomb, CNA Insurance, Bridgestone, Honda Power Equipment, and Sharp Electronics, to name a few. You'll have to follow some guidelines (like not mentioning competitors) in your ads to earn the co-op bucks, and each co-op program has its own policies and rules. But that's a small concession for the financial muscle that can, in effect, boost your ad budget by 50% or more. You get the added prestige of associating your business with a national name, plus cash to add color, increase ad size, expand markets, or put in the till.

Typically, a business earns co-op ad "credits" each time it purchases eligible products or services from the national supplier. Credits commonly accrue at 3% to 5% of purchases and the local dealer can use the credit to pay for up to 50% of an ad. For example, a company that buys $10,000 worth of Bissell rug-cleaning machines and products earns a 5% credit, or $500, toward co-op advertising. If the dealer pays $1,000 for a co-op ad, Bissell would pay $500 of the cost.

In most cases, you'll have to pay the full bill up front, then submit documentation to the national co-op program sponsor for reimbursement of its share. Your Yellow Pages publisher or newspaper advertising rep will get the prior approval you need to run the ad and collect the money and should take care of all the paperwork. But some Yellow Pages reps, thinking they won't make as much money on co-op ads, don't bother to bring them up. It's up to you to ask.

TACTIC #157
Trim Your Trade Show Tab

Trade shows are a cost-effective way to strut your company's stuff. Even so, trade show costs can pick your pocket if you don't watch out. Calculate what your company has spent to exhibit at trade shows and divide by the number of leads those shows generated. If you're spending more than about $145 per lead, trade show marketing experts say you're probably spending too much.

One good move is to spend less on in-booth frills and more on preshow publicity. The greatest booth ever won't do the job by itself. Ya gotta let people know your business will be there, in advance. According to the Trade Show Bureau in Denver, an average 16% of trade show visitors will be interested in your product or service. But Trade Show Bureau research shows that a well-done preshow promotional campaign can bump that figure to over 30%.

Other ways to cut trade show costs:

- Use a "preowned" exhibit. That'll cut one of the biggest trade show costs of all—the exhibit itself. Until recently, buying used exhibits was next to impossible. But more cost-conscious companies are looking to buy used (or sell their old ones), and a new market has emerged. Typical costs run 20% to 50% of the original price. Contact:

  - World Exhibit Brokers, Long Beach, California: (800) 743-0330.
  - Exhibitgroup, Elk Grove Village, Illinois: (800) 424-6224.
  - The Exhibit Emporium, Newark, California: (800) 541-9100.

- Plan ahead. List items you'll need at your booth, then buy them in advance. That'll save you the huge markups that are charged for such items at the show.
- Vacuum the booth yourself. The at-show cleaning service will set you back a bundle. Instead, buy your own vacuum and take it from show to show.
- Generate more leads per dollar spent. Trade show expert Laurie Salgueiro, of the Learning Exchange in Walpole, Massachusetts, names these eight key steps to successful trade show selling:

  1. Qualify prospects first. Before you can sell effectively, you need to know whom you're selling to. Try to find out what the customer needs.
  2. Be brief. Enough said.
  3. Talk about benefits, not features. Based on what you

learned from Step 1, translate your product or service into specific benefits for the visitor.

4. Ask probing questions and invite feedback. Does the visitor already have feelings—good or bad—about your company, its products or services? Try to involve the prospect in your presentation.

5. Be a careful listener. Look for areas of agreement and reinforce those as you move on.

6. Use the exhibit as a selling tool. You paid for it, so use it.

7. Take notes for later follow-up. Try designing a standard lead sheet for your business. But don't write too much—that's distracting.

8. Know when to stop. End on an upbeat note if possible.

TACTIC #158
Do More of Your Marketing Work In-house

Companies both big and small are saving huge sums by doing more of their marketing, advertising, and PR work in-house. You'll still want to tap outside experts for the creative side to these endeavors, for special projects, or for valuable advice. But desktop publishing technology (see Tactic #105), along with a can-do attitude, the prospect of greater control, speed, and flexibility, and the lure of potent cost savings, is leading more and more firms to bring more and more of this work in-house. No marketing consultant, PR firm, or ad agency can have the same cost-cutting motivation that *you* have yourself. What's more, you are your only client—not number thirty-eight on a roster of fifty.

If you aren't getting results from the money you spend, or you've put off doing anything until your company grew a bit, now's the time to consider an in-house move for all or at least a part of your marketing program.

TACTIC #159
Monitor, Measure, and Dump Ads That Aren't Working

If you advertise in several places, a mechanism for measuring where your business is coming from is a must. Something simple can work—like asking customers where they heard about you. In fact, that's probably the best and cheapest monitoring device there is. If you can't ask in person, have customers fill out a simple survey card. Tally the responses and cut the ad outlets that finish last. You'll probably find that most of your business comes from a few sources. Then you can either pocket the savings from the ads you ax, boost your spending elsewhere, or do both.

TACTIC #160
Join the Great Madison Avenue Exodus

With apologies to the old Madison Avenue of lore and metaphor, times have changed. So where's the business going? To smaller firms that offer great service for a great deal less than most of the agency giants of the Avenue.

Companies like Viacom International, PaineWebber, Sony Corp., AT&T, and Quotron Systems are moving to upstart firms such as Terri Edelman's Edelman Group in New York, among others. Edelman caters to the new, more cost-conscious breed of marketing executive. Those execs are bypassing the larger ad agencies in favor of smaller, less expensive firms to fulfill many of their needs.

Though Edelman started as purely a corporate design firm, demand forced a change. "Our clients are asking us to create television and print advertising campaigns and in some cases even handle media schedules and ad placement," says Terri Edelman, who founded her ten-person, Manhattan-based firm in 1982. So Edelman has obliged, charging rates that undercut the large agencies by up to 40%. In freer spending times, many of Edelman's clients would have paid the larger agencies for those specialized services. Edelman is also willing to help clients with cost-cutting do-it-yourself projects by providing software and advice.

The same trend that's boosted Terri Edelman's firm past $2 million in revenues is doing the same for small advertising and design shops nationwide:

- Bucher & Russell is a small Los Angeles ad agency that doubled revenues to over $4 million within three years by offering business advertisers a lower-cost no-frills package. One B&R client, a restaurant, saw sales jump 7% after a B&R-designed coupon insert program was launched. That's the kind of "boring," but low-cost and get-the-job-done, idea that has worked so well for the firm.
- J. H. Berman & Associates, a ten-person firm in Washington, D.C., has taken the same tack as Edelman, adding marketing, advertising, and PR to its mix of services at prices less than those of the agency giants. And business buyers are biting.
- Sayles Graphic Design in Des Moines, Iowa, has attracted business by billing itself as a lower-cost alternative to the generalist ad agencies that try to do it all.

TACTIC #161
Banish Brochures

Each year, millions of dollars are spent writing, designing, printing, and distributing irrelevant, useless brochures that are never read by anyone other than the people who dreamed them up. "Yet, as sure as the sun rises, thousands of executives in hundreds of companies will meet today for incredibly serious and ludicrous discussions about company brochures that will require tens of thousands of hours of preparation, but will add nothing to the profits of any of those firms," says John Graham of Quincy, Massachusetts–based Graham Communications.

Graham claims that almost without exception, the brochures proposed for businesses in any given day should never be produced. "Of those produced," he says, "ninety percent will be outdated and virtually worthless by the day they are delivered."

Graham has a simple solution: Avoid brochures. "Always be on your guard. Ad agencies and PR firms love to produce brochures. Why? Because a brochure is relatively easy to produce and it's chock-full of profit. Chances are no one at the agency will worry about why you may or may not need it or how you're going to use it. And once you've paid the bill, no one will care."

TACTIC #162
Get Immediate Results with Broadcast Fax

Within three days of sending its first product promotion by broadcast fax, ICOM America, a Bellevue, Washington–based business, rang up over $100,000 in new orders. ICOM, which sells marine communications equipment, sent product promotions to a network of about three hundred dealers nationwide in minutes without tying up its own fax machine and without any special hardware or additional phone lines.

The big payoff: lightning quick customer response time. "We initially planned to do the promotion [for a special on marine radios] by direct mail," says Jim Carroll, manager of ICOM's Marine Division. "But we changed our minds after comparing the immediate delivery time of broadcast fax to the cost and time it would've taken to produce a direct-mail piece and get it to customers."

Most higher-quality fax machines have some broadcast capabilities built in, allowing you to fax the same message to multiple locations simultaneously. Or you can buy broadcast service outside. ICOM used a broadcast fax service offered by U.S. West Enhanced Services, a division of the Denver-based Baby Bell. Call (800) 945-9494 for information. The service, which can fax a single document to as few as five and as many as five thousand locations, is available nationwide.

TACTIC #163
Radio Deals
Time Your Pitch Right for Free Radio Plugs

Radio's an oft-overlooked ad and PR route. Effective and not all that expensive—except in major markets like Los Angeles (the King Kong of radio markets) and Chicago. So a small biz like Chicago-based Mama Tish's Gourmet Sorbetto has to be a bit more creative to get on the air.

When Mama Tish's delivered samples to top-rated Chicago DJs on a scorching July afternoon, the low-cost gesture snagged radio time that money can't buy. The DJs raved about the Italian ice desserts, issuing play-by-plays on different flavors as they ate. Would the response have been so hot if the temperature hadn't been? No way, says the Chicago PR firm Defrancesco Goodfriend. Timing is crucial in the quest for free radio time. By taking advantage of special events (Valentine's Day, for example) or circumstances (a heat wave), your company can reach thousands of radio listeners at a low cost. The formula, says Defrancesco Goodfriend, is a dash of creativity at the right place and the right time.

TACTIC #164
Get Down and Dirty with Cheapie Ads

Skip DiCamillo, of the seventy-three-year-old family-owned DiCamillo Bakery in Niagara Falls, New York, lives in a cost-conscious community populated by cost-conscious customers. "If people know they can get a dollar off on their next dry cleaning, they'll go out of their way to do it," says DiCamillo. No wonder his own approach to advertising is, well, cost-conscious.

DiCamillo's advertising secret is low-cost direct-mail coupon packs—in this case, Val-Pak coupons. He puts about 180,000 of the coupons in customers' hands each year at a cost of about three cents each. Redemption rates go as high as 6%. DiCamillo couldn't be happier about the results this budget approach has brought his twenty-five-employee business.

Big-bucks ads not drawing flies? Try these other cheapie routes:

- *Shoppers:* Free newspapers or tabloids distributed locally can have a loyal following of bargain hunters—and ad space is far cheaper than in the regular press.
- *Local TV guides:* A variation on a shopper, usually distributed free with local television listings.
- *Per inquiry (P/I) ads:* Publishers and radio station owners, for the most part, consider P/I ads dirty linen. But when they're hungry enough, they do it. The idea is simple: The advertiser pays a fee only for inquiries (or in most cases, actual orders) received. Major publications and stations don't do P/I deals, but many smaller outlets will be receptive.
- *Postcards:* An underused direct-mail medium. Stands out because people don't get 'em very often. Cheap too.
- *Classifieds:* For the right kind of business (discount appliances, or used furniture, for example), they are a cheap way to work advertising wonders.

TACTIC #165
Become a Community Role Model

Harold Martin, who launched his athletic shoe company, MVP Products of Wixom, Michigan, back in 1989, wrings maximum benefits from low-cost marketing strategies—a must when you're selling against shoe giants like Nike and Reebok. The Michigan manufacturer does a lot of business leader "role model" speaking to student and civic groups, helping spread the word about his company.

When Martin first researched the Detroit market, he found that virtually all 634,000 public school students wore athletic shoes and bought as many as four pairs yearly, paying up to $100 per pair for name brand shoes. But the former auto industry engineer believed that school kids had become trapped by Madison Avenue marketing that sold them high-priced names as popularity symbols. MVP's strategy was to promote educational pride rather than brand names by putting college and high school logos on its shoes and letting the schools sell direct to students for a share of the profits. MVP hangs posters in the schools, advertises in school publications, and helps schools set up special fund-raisers selling shoes—all helping boost MVP's visibility and customer base.

TACTIC #166
Take These Cost-Effective Steps
to Marketing Success

Marketing is like dieting. Everybody wants to do it, but few do it well. Would-be dieters and would-be marketers make similar mistakes: They start without a plan, they select a diet (strategy) that's not right for their body (business), and they don't stick with it. Here are some things you can do:

1. *Look in the mirror.* It's vital that you understand where your business fits in the marketplace, and where you want it to fit. If your goal is to reach the "premium," or upscale, end of the market, but current customers perceive you differently, your marketing dollars are being wasted.

2. *Round up your research.* Look for trends within your market area or industry. Get a grip on what the competition is doing.

3. *Consider* all *your options.* Don't elope with the first pretty marketing face you meet. You can advertise fifty different ways, from newspapers, magazines, and billboards to radio, TV, and the Yellow Pages. Direct mail, telemarketing, flyers, statement stuffers, videos, store displays, packaging, giveaways, and a publicity program are all areas to consider. You can give talks, seminars, parties, and put on charitable events. Or offer contests, coupons, and twofers. Ask around. Get professional advice. Develop your own unique marketing hybrids.

4. *Write a plan.* If you can't easily describe it in writing, either it's too complicated or you don't really have a plan. Include a detailed budget and clear-cut goals. Explain your plan to employees and tell them where they fit in.

5. *Get it going.* If you have your own ideas and time, or employees to whom you can delegate marketing tasks, handling it in-house may work well. But marketing firms have much to offer if your budget permits. Check the Yellow Pages and interview more than one firm if you can. Ask to see details of previous marketing programs they've conducted.

6. *Keep it going.* The only good marketing program is one that you stick with. Keep trying something—especially when times are tough. That will give your overall plan the consistency it needs.

7. *Get on the scale.* You won't know how well your diet is working until you step on the scale. Likewise, to check your marketing plan's pulse you need a way to measure

success. Keep track of response wherever possible. Feed your response data into a computer to generate your own mailing lists and at-a-glance reports.

TACTIC #167
Reduce Your News Release Costs

And here are five ways to do it, suggested by the editors of *Communication Briefings* of Blackwood, New Jersey:

- Update your mailing list. Editors, reporters, producers, radio or TV hosts all move around. A PR pitch addressed to the wrong person or sent to an old address is wasted.
- Save a page by reducing the length of your release. Most are too long anyhow. Print it on both sides of the page. You'll save on collating costs, paper, and sometimes postage too.
- Use a legal-size sheet for releases that run just a bit longer than the standard letter-size sheet.
- Don't equate fancy letterheads with successful news releases. Yes, it should look businesslike and professional to get noticed. But beyond that, editors are interested in what's *on* the paper, not how much you paid for it.
- If your releases aren't especially time-sensitive, enclose two at the same time, saving you postage and mailing preparation costs.

SAVE-A-BUNDLE FOLLOW-UP FILE

• *Yellow Pages Co-op Advertising Programs* is a phonebook-size directory of co-op programs published several times yearly by the Yellow Pages Publishers Association (YPPA), an industry trade association in Troy, Michigan. Details hundreds of co-op programs on everything from adhesives and air-conditioning to window shades and work clothing. Your Yellow Pages rep should have a copy for you to look at.

• The bible of Yellow Pages advertising is Barry Maher's book *Getting the Most from Your Yellow Pages Advertising* (AMACOM, $14.95 plus $3 shipping). It's plump with cost-cutting tips. Barry Maher & Associates, in Santa Barbara, California, consults on Yellow Pages tactics for businesses nationwide. To order the book or contact Maher call (805) 962-2599.

• *Communication Briefings,* a monthly newsletter ($69/year) published in Blackwood, New Jersey, offers a steady diet of cost-saving ideas in marketing and PR. Call (800) 888-4402; fax (609) 232-8245.

• The *Trade Show Marketing Idea Kit* is a fifty-page booklet of tips and worksheets to help you get the most from a trade show at the lowest cost. Free from Skyline Displays, 1301 East Cliff Road, Burnsville, MN 55337; (800) 328-2725; fax (612) 895-6318.

• For news and information on trade show exhibiting, try *Exhibitor* magazine (monthly, $68/year), published in Rochester, Minnesota. Call (507) 289-6556; fax (507) 289-5253.

• The Trade Show Bureau is a Denver-based organization dedicated to promoting trade show participation. Offers how-to reports starting at about $5 each. Call (303) 860-7626; fax (303) 860-7479.

• The Wisconsin Innovation Service Center is a university-linked nonprofit service that conducts low-cost market research (mainly on new products) for small businesses. It will generate an overall market feasibility report for a flat fee of $165. It also conducts workshops on developing and marketing new products. Contact WISC at 402 McCutchan Hall, University of Wisconsin, Whitewater, WI 53190; (414) 472-1365; fax (414) 472-1600.

• *The Frugal Marketer,* by J. Donald Weinrauch and Nancy Croft Baker (AMACOM, $15.95), can be ordered at (800) 538-4761. The title says it.

• Val-Pak coupon packet sales are handled by about three hundred dealers throughout the United States and Canada.

Check local listings or contact Val-Pak's national sales office in Florida at (800) 237-6266 or (813) 393-1270.

• The *Thomas Register of American Manufacturers,* a twenty-six-volume monster, is a marvelous marketing tool for manufacturers. For example, Solidur Plastics, a Delmont, Pennsylvania, specialist in industrial-grade custom plastic components, has an extensive communications program that includes advertising in magazines and directories, press releases, trade shows, and more. But about 43% of the company's leads and an even higher percentage of sales are attributed to the *Thomas Register.* The *Thomas Register* is at Five Penn Plaza, New York, NY 10001; (212) 290-7277; fax (212) 290-7365.

CHAPTER 14

Slash Legal and Accounting Costs

TACTIC #168
Bid Out Your Legal and Accounting Work

Big spenders have the most leverage. But small companies can also get red carpet treatment with the promise of more work to come as the business grows and prospers. If you've been using an outside accounting firm—especially one of the big ones—shopping for cost estimates on accounting services could be a real money saver, says John Breneman, a CPA with the St. Louis firm Brandvein, Shapiro, Kossmeyer & Co. You may be surprised by the result. According to Breneman, who works with many small companies, "You might find you are paying as much as double what you should."

If you require specialized legal expertise, you may not have as much choice. But for routine legal work, soliciting bids can also save you money.

You may simply have outgrown your current accounting or law firm, just as you've outgrown office, plant, or retail space. A small firm, even though cheaper, might be costing you money if it isn't financially sophisticated enough to handle your needs. If your needs are simple, however, you needn't pay top dollar at a Big Six accounting firm when a local CPA can do the work for half the price. Here's how average hourly rates for an accounting firm partner compare at different sized firms:

Small local CPA	$120
Midsize local firm	$150
Regional firm	$156
National firm	$210
Big Six firm	$245

TACTIC #169
Take Your Beef to Small-Claims Court

For small business, small-claims court is a great do-it-yourself legal tactic. An unpaid tab of, say, $1,500 doesn't seem worth going to "regular" court over if legal fees and other costs threaten to eat the entire amount—*if* you collect—and then some.

But small-claims court could be the answer if the amount you're owed falls below the maximum small-claims ceiling in your state. Those maximums range between $1,000 and $10,000 (see the list below).

By sluglike judicial standards, small-claims court is swift. Cases can be scheduled and resolved in weeks, not months or years. And it's cheap: Filing fees are between $5 and $50, depending on the state.

But the biggest money saver of all is this: *You don't need a lawyer to go to small-claims court.* In fact, some states— Arkansas, California, Colorado, Idaho, Kansas, Michigan, Montana, Nebraska, North Dakota, Oregon, and Washington—*ban* lawyers in small-claims cases. In other states you can have one if you want, but it's not necessary.

Compared to regular court, small-claims courts are informal, almost relaxed. The rules are not strict and the whole process is far less intimidating. But you still must be prepared. Gather your documentation and prepare your arguments. Keep it simple. See the Follow-up File for several good books on preparing for small-claims court.

Maximum claim ceilings differ by state and are subject to change. At this writing they were as follows:

Alabama	$ 1,500	Colorado	$3,500
Alaska	5,000	Connecticut	2,000
Arizona	1,500	Delaware	5,000
Arkansas	3,000	District of Columbia	2,000
California	5,000	Florida	2,500

Georgia	5,000	New Mexico	5,000
Hawaii	3,500	New York	2,000
Idaho	3,000	North Carolina	2,000
Illinois	2,500	North Dakota	3,000
Indiana	6,000	Ohio	2,000
Iowa	2,000	Oklahoma	2,500
Kansas	1,000	Oregon	2,500
Kentucky	1,500	Pennsylvania	4,000
Louisiana	2,000	Rhode Island	1,500
Maine	1,400	South Carolina	2,500
Maryland	2,500	South Dakota	4,000
Massachusetts	1,500	Tennessee	10,000
Michigan	1,750	Texas	5,000
Minnesota	5,000	Utah	2,000
Mississippi	1,000	Vermont	2,000
Missouri	1,500	Virginia	10,000
Montana	3,000	Washington	2,500
Nebraska	1,800	West Virginia	3,000
Nevada	2,500	Wisconsin	2,000
New Hampshire	2,500	Wyoming	2,000
New Jersey	1,000		

TACTIC #170
Choose "Brand X"

Though it makes most legal beagles barf, the trend in business law, as in groceries, is (gasp!) *pricing*—buying Brand X when the name brand is too costly. With senior partners at smaller regional firms going for as little as $100 to $150 per hour, compared to almost $400 per hour for some partners at the big-name firms in New York, Los Angeles, Chicago, and elsewhere, businesses that buy these legal services are shopping price. Pre-1990, price didn't matter much. Most companies, and especially the faster-growing firms, didn't figure that shaving $10 or $20 per hour off their lawyer's tab was worth the risk of receiving inferior service.

That's changed. Not that companies will tolerate crummy service—it's more a discovery that *good* legal advice isn't always the *highest-priced* advice.

Allstate, the Sears Roebuck insurance unit, knocked 25% off its legal tab in a year by aggressively doling out more of its $10 million worth of annual legal work to lower-cost regional firms. Allstate is even paying its in-house lawyers a bonus when they ring up savings by rolling out legal work to regional firms.

TACTIC #171
Demand Detailed Billing and Challenge Questionable Costs

Every day, companies pay invoices for accounting and legal services that contain all the specificity of a politician's promise in an election year. "Prepare contract correspondence: $1,500." Something like that. Companies that demand detailed billing at least have a shot at monitoring and lowering their legal costs. Those that have no idea what they're paying for, really, have no way to make cost-cutting adjustments, since they don't know what they might be.

Ask for bills that state what work was done, how long it took, who performed the work, and what that person's hourly rate is. With those details, your company can more easily spot errors, see where the money's going, and pinpoint areas for savings.

Don't be afraid to challenge costs. Legal and accounting work shouldn't be treated any differently than other services you buy.

Monitoring legal and accounting bills can have two other happy side effects:

- The mere threat that you are scrutinizing costs (which implies you might take your business elsewhere) can spur the firm you're using to watch more closely what it does or even lower its costs.

- A closer look at what legal and accounting advice costs you can be sobering; you may think twice the next time you hold a lengthy telephone chat with your lawyer or ask your accountant to stop by for a talk.

For microscopic scrutiny of legal and accounting bills, look for an independent firm that specializes in auditing such bills. With cost-cutting efforts reaching into company legal and accounting departments, such bill auditing services are in much bigger demand these days. They'll take the bills, examine 'em bit by bit, and look for errors, waste, and inefficiencies that can more than justify the expense of the audit. See the Follow-up File for names.

TACTIC #172
Get Creative on Fees

First rule to remember: Fees may be negotiable—despite a reluctance by many lawyers and CPAs to talk about the matter up front.

- Negotiate flat rates for routine work.
- If you put a lawyer on retainer, look for a price break over the nonretainer rate.
- Suggest a contingency arrangement where the lawyer gets a cut if you win, either in court or via settlement, but gets a lesser fee or just expenses if you don't.
- Barter for legal services (see Tactic #7).
- Use a retention letter or litigation engagement contract that details the work to be done, what your business expects, and what you will and won't pay for.

The book *100 Ways to Cut Legal Fees and Manage Your Lawyer* (see Follow-up File) includes suggested letters and contracts for engaging lawyers.

TACTIC #173
Do Some Routine Work Yourself, or Hire a Different Level of Professional

Some types of legal work—research, filing forms, writing letters—don't require an attorney. You can save a bundle by performing routine legal chores in-house or by hiring a lower-priced paralegal to help. The self-help legal resources listed in the Follow-up File can get you started on the road to legal savings.

Ditto with some of your tax and accounting work. One of the biggest money savers of all when it comes to accountants is good record keeping. The cleaner your information is to start, the less time an accountant will need to complete your taxes. *Disorganized records waste money; organized records save money.*

You might also consider using an "enrolled agent" for some of your tax work. Enrolled agents are licensed to advise or represent businesses in tax matters, but their rates are often lower than those of CPAs.

TACTIC #174
Run, Don't Walk, from Litigation Expense

Litigation costs American business some $20 billion per year, says an estimate in the *National Law Journal.* Zounds! The best way by far to avoid litigation costs for your company is to stay the hell out of court in the first place.

How? John Landrum, an attorney in New Orleans, has a four-step recipe for dodging the litigation bullet. Mind you, Landrum is an unusual lawyer. He's a business litigator who actually speaks English and has a knack for translating legalese into terms that us plain folk can grasp.

"Litigation is war," says Landrum. "Just as shooting wars

can destroy a country, litigation can bankrupt your business."
Here's Landrum's advice:

1. *Do the right thing.* That means doing business ethically, following the law, and honoring your contracts.
2. *Don't hang around with jerks.* By that he means don't deal with the types of people who are likely to drag you into litigation.
3. *Don't be a jerk yourself.* "Avoid creating the emotional atmosphere that leads to litigation."
4. *Do the thing right.* That is, structure your business relationships to reduce opportunities for disputes or incentives to litigate.

For more hands-on advice, read Landrum's book *Out of Court: How to Protect Your Business from Litigation* (The Headwaters Press, $14.95). Call (800) 926-1286.

TACTIC #175
Write Arbitration Clauses into Your Company's Contracts

Arbitration and mediation are huge money savers for business (see Tactic #2). But to ensure that disputes go the private justice route, you need to include standard language in your contracts that obliges both parties to arbitration before any other legal action is taken. This simple step could save your company thousands of dollars in legal costs later on.

The American Arbitration Association in New York can provide all the information you need to install private justice bulletproofing in your company's contracts, including booklets on how to draft a dispute resolution clause for your business. Call (212) 484-4000. See the Follow-up File to Tactic #2 for more on arbitration and alternative dispute resolution (ADR) in general.

TACTIC #176
Penny-pinch Out-of-Pocket and Overtime Expenses

Faxes, phone calls, overnight delivery, photocopies, secretarial services, data or word processing, on-line research, and transportation are a few out-of-pocket expenses you can expect a law or accounting firm to tack on to your bill. If rush work under deadline is involved, you may also be charged for eats and overtime. All are legitimate charges. But you still need to watch what you're paying for to make certain (1) that the expenses were actually incurred on your behalf; and (2) that the prices you're being charged are reasonable.

If lawyers travel on your behalf, make it clear that you don't pay for first-class airfare, limos, or other expensive perks. And if overtime is charged, make certain it was the result of a deadline out of the law or accounting firm's control and not merely a result of the firm's own backlog of work or inefficiency.

On-line research—where the law firm accesses a computer data base—can be expensive. Such services can cost several dollars per minute and the firm should be asking your permission to spend money on this before going ahead. Also, some documentation of the time spent hooked in to the computer data base should be included in your billing. These charges should be billed roughly at actual cost—the firm shouldn't be adding a profit margin on top.

TACTIC #177
Make Tightly Scripted Calls

Whenever possible, talk to a lawyer by phone. Meetings tend to ramble on, especially if several people are involved, and can be vastly more expensive.

If others at your company need to be involved, gather the

essential people for a teleconference, but put one person in charge of "moderating" what is said. List all questions ahead of time, in order of importance. That'll help organize the conversation and keep it shorter. Several people should take notes so there's less chance of anyone forgetting or misinterpreting what was said.

Set a policy on who is allowed to contact lawyers directly. The fewer people the better, and the cheaper. Funnel everything through a single contact if possible.

SAVE-A-BUNDLE FOLLOW-UP FILE

• Two publishers that specialize in self-help legal books are (request a catalog):

- · Nolo Press, Berkeley, California: (800) 992-6656.
- · Nova Publishing, Boulder, Colorado: (800) 748-1175.

• Firms that specialize in auditing legal bills for business include the following three. (Check phone listings for similar firms in your area.)

- · Law Audit Services, Westport, Connecticut: (203) 221-2810.
- · Legalgard, Philadelphia, Pennsylvania: (800) 525-3426.
- · Stuart, Maue, Mitchell & James, St. Louis, Missouri: (314) 291-3030.

• *100 Ways to Cut Legal Fees and Manage Your Lawyer* by Erwin Krasnow and Robin Conrad is the best treatment of this subject around. Krasnow is a partner in the Washington, D.C., law firm Verner, Liipfert, Bernhard, McPherson & Hand, while Conrad is director of litigation for the National Chamber Litigation Center, a unit of the U.S. Chamber of Commerce. The book is $10.95 plus $1.95 shipping from the National Chamber Litigation Center, 1615 H Street, N.W., Washington, DC 20062; call (800) 638-6582.

• *Everybody's Guide to Small Claims Court* by Ralph Warner (Nolo Press, $15.95). Call (800) 992-6656.

- *Small Claims Court: A User's Guide* ($8.95) from HALT: An Organization of Americans for Legal Reform. Call (202) 347-9600.
- *The Complete Book of Small Business Legal Forms* by Daniel Sitarz (Nova, $17.95). Call (800) 462-6420.
- *How to Get the Best Legal Help for Your Business at the Lowest Possible Cost* by Mead Hedglon (McGraw-Hill, $16.95). Call (800) 2MCGRAW.
- *It's Legal* ($29) is a self-help software program many small businesses use for routine legal letters and contracts. Call Parsons Technology, Hiawatha, Iowa, at (800) 223-6925.
- *Dancing with Lawyers* (Royce Baker Publishing, $19.95) by Nicholas Carroll offers some hard-hitting advice on getting the most for your legal dollar. Call (800) 733-7440 to order.

CHAPTER 15

Cut Insurance Costs to the Quick

TACTIC #178
Save Money with Safety

Spruced-up safety awareness ranks near the top of nearly every insurance cost-control list. If your company doesn't have an *aggressive* employee safety program, install one now. You need a two-pronged approach, focusing both on workplace conditions (i.e., safe equipment and procedures) and on people (motivating them to work safely).

Your insurance carrier can be a good resource. For example, CNA, Aetna, Kemper, and others have moved to help companies control insurance costs through better worksite safety. Your insurer's safety experts may even do a safety "audit" of your business to detect problems. Ask. One company that saved big on safety is Aspen Imaging International, a Lafayette, Colorado, firm with about three hundred employees that makes supplies for computer printers. A safety program at Aspen Imaging helped cut the firm's workers' comp costs in half (a six-figure sum) over a two-year period.

These safety resources can help:

- Don Brown Productions, in Orange, California, produces industry-specific safety training videos for hundreds of different types of businesses. Most range between seven and thirty minutes. Prices average $70. Call for a catalog: (800) 359-7910; fax (714) 771-9713.
- American Safety Publications, Inc., in Hebron, Indiana, offers the *Job Site Safety Inspection Program* ($55.75), geared mainly toward the construction industry. Call (800) 262-6701; fax (219) 988-7355.
- If your employees drive on the job, driver-safety training can be a terrific money saver as well. Monsanto's accident

rate dropped 51% in less than three years after the chemical company began a safety program offered by Inner-Action Safety, Inc. (ISI), of San Jose, California. ISI's S.A.F.E. Plus driver-safety program costs about $20 per driver to complete and works for small companies as well as big ones. Call (408) 297-9183; fax (408) 297-9442.

- The National Safety Council, an eighty-year-old nonprofit group dedicated to safety issues, offers boatloads of safety information, including consulting services, workplace safety programs, industry-specific safety newsletters, videos, slide shows and more. Write to Public Relations Department, 1121 Spring Lake Drive, Itasca, IL 60143. Call (708) 775-2307; fax (708) 775-2310.

- The National Council on Compensation Insurance (NCCI) publishes *Safe Workplace* magazine and offers other products and services aimed at lowering the cost of workers' comp insurance through greater safety. Request NCCI's free Products & Services Catalog from NCCI Order Processing, 750 Park of Commerce Drive, Boca Raton, FL 33487; call (407) 997-4607; fax (407) 997-4233.

A safety program will help your bottom line in other ways. For example, fines for OSHA (Occupational Safety and Health Administration) violations have increased some 700% in the 1990s. A hazardous condition you don't notice or correct can mean penalties when inspectors show up. Mandatory fines: $7,000 to $70,000 per offense. Companies with more than ten employees are subject to periodic OSHA inspections; smaller firms can still be visited and fined if complaints are made.

Tap the free safety-compliance help available from your state's version of OSHA (twenty-three states have 'em). These agencies will usually help callers comply with safety rules without danger of any fines. The *OSHA Handbook for Small Business* ($4) lists OSHA-sponsored consultants around the country who can provide free on-site safety consulting. Call the Government Printing Office, (202) 783-3238. If the inspectors find problems, you will be given a chance to fix them without being cited or fined.

TACTIC #179
Work Wonders with Wellness

Many companies with worker wellness programs have found them to be powerful cost cutters. Each dollar invested in workplace health promotion yielded $1.42 in savings due to lower absenteeism and insurance costs at Du Pont. Absences from illness unrelated to the job among blue-collar workers dropped 14% at sites where the wellness program was offered.

At Johnson & Johnson, in New Brunswick, New Jersey, an in-house employee wellness program has been such a success that J&J formed a separate division, Johnson & Johnson Health Management, Inc.—(800) 443-3682—to market the concept to other companies. J&J estimates its wellness strategy is netting the company annual savings of $178 per employee. Elsewhere, Minneapolis-based General Mills estimates savings of $3.90 for each $1 the food giant spends on its wellness plan, and Colorado-based Adolph Coors claims to have saved $1.4 million over a six-year period from its healthy-heart program alone.

It works for smaller and midsize firms too. Springfield Remanufacturing Corp., a 650-employee engine rebuilder in Springfield, Missouri, gave wellness a stab. A $4,000 outlay produced long-term savings of about $40,000. For companies like Springfield that self-insure all or a portion of their coverage, wellness is especially crucial. Savings go directly to the bottom line.

Wellness programs come in all sizes, shapes, and colors, including company-sponsored heart disease and cancer screening; stop-smoking, nutritional, and stress-management seminars; physical fitness classses; in-house workout facilities; educational handouts; and more. Wellness programs can be run cheap, with bottom line–boosting results. The most successful programs include financial incentives (like cash for not smoking) for employees to participate.

To get started: Contact Omaha-based Wellness Councils of

America—the premier source of worksite wellness information—at (402) 572-3590. WELCOA is a nonprofit association of twenty-eight regional wellness councils (call for a list), which are membership organizations your business can join and which offer a variety of wellness activities for your employees. Ask if there's a wellness council in your area and request WELCOA's catalog of publications. Among the outstanding selections:

- *Healthy, Wealthy and Wise,* a how-to manual on planning, implementing, and evaluating a wellness program, is their best-seller. Around $95.
- *Healthy People at the Worksite 2000* ($5) is an information kit outlining general wellness activities.
- *Worksite Wellness Works* is a quarterly newsletter for $16 per year.

Wellness programs can even lower life insurance costs. Sun Life, a $60 billion multinational insurance giant, was one of the first major insurers to offer a discount (of up to 5%) on group life premiums to companies with wellness programs. Call (800) 882-4786 for information.

TACTIC #180
Check Out Self-Insurance Savings

In some cases, self-insuring a risk can be cheaper and more effective than buying from an insurance carrier. The trick is knowing when to self-insure and how to set it up right if you do. The Self-Insurance Institute of America, Inc., a nonprofit educational group in Santa Ana, California, is a good source of information on the pros, cons, and methods of setting up do-it-yourself insurance in a variety of areas. The institute also conducts self-insurance seminars for business and publishes a newsletter on regulatory and legislative changes affecting companies that self-insure. Annual dues are $595. For a free membership package call (800) 851-7789; fax (714) 261-2594.

TACTIC #181
Discover Do-It-Yourself Dental

Direct-reimbursement dental is a well-kept employee-benefits secret. If you set it up right, it's a simple and cheap way to provide coverage. No insurance companies. No middleman profits to pay. You decide the limits. With companies large and small dropping benefits due to skyrocketing rates, you can be among the few to expand coverage while limiting costs.

Under this type of plan, employees present their signed dental receipts and you reimburse them up to a set percentage, either directly or through a trust set up for this purpose. The costs can even be lower than buying a group policy.

The American Dental Association (ADA) has a splendid (and free) booklet on direct reimbursement that tells all, including details on how to calculate costs, set up the plan, and put it into action. Contact the ADA, Council on Dental Care Programs, 211 East Chicago Avenue, #1753, Chicago, IL 60611. Call (800) 621-8099, ext. 2746, and ask for the publication *Direct Reimbursement: Tailor Your Own Employee Dental Benefit Plan.* Be sure to ask for their sample claim forms as well.

TACTIC #182
Adjust Attitudes Before and After a Claim

Before: Your company's attitude toward its workers—and vice versa—plays a large but often overlooked role in determining insurance costs. Disgruntled employees are more likely to be injured *and* more likely to sue. Happy workers get injured less and when injured, they return to work more quickly. Paying attention to the little things—like keeping the place clean and praising worthy employees—can produce startling results. Let employees know they are important to the company and that their satisfaction is important too. Make an effort to boost employee morale.

After: A major cost in most workers' comp claims is lost wages. Try working with an injured worker (and probably his or her physician too) to bring the employee back to work as quickly as possible—perhaps in a lighter or part-time slot. Some companies taking this tack have seen workers' comp savings of 40% or more.

The idea is to *manage* claims once they occur. Most companies shrug and wait to hear when the employee is ready to return. Other firms get involved immediately. They contact the employee, look for ways to show the firm cares, and perhaps offer a more limited-duty job during recovery (with a doctor's permission). An out-of-sight, out-of-mind worker can cost your company a ton. Many insurance carriers offer premium discounts for companies that have their own return-to-work programs for injured employees.

The right insurance carrier can play a role here too. For example, ITT Hartford's Return-to-Work program is one of the most comprehensive in the field. Aetna's nurse consultants contact injured workers soon after lost-time injuries are reported. These efforts can keep injured workers from hiring attorneys and can get benefits to workers quicker, saving time and money for everyone.

TACTIC #183
Fight Back against Fraud

If the old TV game show "Password" were still around, getting your partner to say the word *fraud* would be easy: Just say "insurance" and "fraud" immediately comes to mind. By taking a stand against a slew of suspect claims, companies and their insurance carriers stand to save millions each year. When an insurance company goes ahead and pays a suspect claim, it's *your* premium that goes up.

Bill Kizorek, owner of InPhoto Surveillance in Naperville, Illinois, is one of a growing number of fraud investigations experts, especially in the workers' comp area. Kizorek's firm does a booming business tailing claimants whose cases are considered suspicious. InPhoto's covert videos and photos showing "injured" workers climbing trees and water-skiing have saved employers and insurance carriers millions.

According to Kizorek, being your own claims detective could save your business some serious money. Businesses generally presume that their insurance carrier will investigate employee injury claims, especially those involving more serious, long-term disabilities. But Kizorek says that presumption is wrong. "Claims adjusters may be saddled with over two hundred files. With the trend toward telephone adjusters and away from street investigators, it's possible that your insurer may never even visit the employee's neighborhood," he says.

Don't hesitate to pass along information you have to the insurance carrier. Says Kizorek, "Be as specific as you can. It makes it easier for the claims adjuster to get permission to investigate more intensively." If the insurance company is not responsive, call your insurance broker or agent and demand action. If there's still no response, consider hiring a licensed investigative firm operating in your area and forward findings to the insurance carrier.

For a free booklet listing phone numbers in each state for reporting suspected workers' compensation fraud, request the *Fraud Hotline Directory* from the National Council on Compensation Insurance (NCCI), Order Processing, 750 Park of Commerce Drive, Boca Raton, FL 33487; call (407) 997-4607 and ask for order processing.

In California (fraud heaven), Fremont Compensation Insurance Co. offers a fraud-fighting video package with practical steps your company can take. Write to Fraud Investigation Unit, Fremont Comp., 500 North Brand Boulevard, Glendale, CA 91203; (818) 549-4591; fax (818) 549-4628.

One good way to avoid insurance fraud is to find out as much as possible about the new people you hire. Unearthing a trail of past employee dishonesty can quash fraudulent claims. Here are some helpful resources:

- *The Sourcebook of Public Record Providers* lists ninety companies that conduct employment screening. Some services operate on-line and can provide your company with reports quickly via computer and modem. It sells for $18 plus $2 shipping from BRB Publications, Inc., 1200 Lincoln, Suite 306, Denver, CO 80203; call (800) 929-3764; fax (800) 929-4981.
- A nationwide screening service is available from the Credit Managers Association of California. CMAC provides verification on a job applicant's employment history, including past employee misconduct, criminal convictions, falsification of past employment, and reasons for terminations. Call (800) 447-3998.
- *The Guide To Background Investigations* ($124.50) is a source directory for employee screening published by National Employment Screening Services, 8801 South Yale Avenue, Tulsa, OK 74137; call (800) 247-8713; fax (800) 232-9074.

TACTIC #184
Get Help to Lower Your Liability and Manage Your Risk

This is pure self-defense. By managing your risks—that is, exposing the business to fewer of 'em—you lessen the odds of suffering a loss. And the fewer losses you suffer, the less your insurance should cost.

Risks differ dramatically from business to business. A real estate management company, a restaurant, a country inn, a retail store, a manufacturer all have different liabilities and risks. The important thing is to get risk-savvy; to spot the liability pitfalls that lie in every company's path—crime, accidents, fire, natural disasters. That may also mean bringing in an outside risk management or liability consultant to have a look and make suggestions for your business. One such firm, Liability Consultants, Inc., in Framingham, Massachusetts, publishes a quarterly newsletter spotlighting specific legal cases. Call the company for a list of available publications at (508) 872-5222; fax (508) 872-5241.

Sean Mooney, senior vice president of the Insurance Information Institute in New York, says that the two biggest risks facing most businesses today are property loss due to fire, wind, or theft, and liability loss due to injury. Mooney suggests these basic risk management tips:

- Make sure the wiring in your building is in good shape.
- Keep stairways, handrails, carpets, and flooring repaired.
- Train workers to lift heavy items properly (use your legs, not your back) and to wear safety masks and gloves.
- Install a sprinkler system and a fire alarm.
- Keep only a small amount of cash in the register. Deposit the rest in a floor safe that employees can't open.
- Store inventory in two locations. A loss at one still leaves you in business.
- Make sure that all of your drivers have good driving records. Provide additional driver-safety training. As noted above, InnerAction Safety, Inc., of San Jose, California, offers a helpful driver-safety program for about $20 per driver. Call (408) 297-9183; fax (408) 297-9442.

TACTIC #185
Dissect Disability Details

Disability coverage is one of the most important fringes a company can offer. Expensive, too. To lower the cost, go for a longer "elimination period." Basically, that's the length of time the policyholder must wait for benefits to kick in after the onset of a disability. A wait of only thirty days makes the policy expensive. Selecting a ninety-day wait or even longer can lop hundreds off the annual premium.

Policies that automatically increase benefits in line with inflation are unnecessarily expensive. Review coverage levels periodically and adjust as needed.

Some insurance carriers let you secure further savings with a Social Security integration clause. In short, that means the policy's payments are reduced if the insured also becomes eligible to receive benefits under Social Security's disability provisions.

TACTIC #186
Monitor and Review Your Coverage

Yeah, yeah, you've probably heard it before: Review your company's insurance coverage regularly—at least every two or three years. Confess: Did you actually do it? Probably not. It's a surefire money saver if you do.

Gather all of your policies. Sit down with your agent. Eyeball your coverage point by point. Has your business changed? Is there coverage you don't need anymore? Look for overlapping or extraneous coverage to eliminate. Ask about the premium-lowering effect of raising deductibles. Have an independent agent get quotes from other companies. Small and midsize businesses may be able to save money with a special package policy known as a business owner's policy or BOP.

Check it out. Investigate specialty insurance coverage for your particular line of business. The latest trend is for insurance carriers to write customized policies for risks unique to certain businesses—whether it's a funeral parlor, muffler shop, or law firm.

SAVE-A-BUNDLE FOLLOW-UP FILE

• *Insuring Your Business* by Sean Mooney (Insurance Information Institute Press, $22.50) offers savvy advice on what you need to know to get the best insurance coverage for your business. This book leaves scarcely an insurance stone unturned. It's one of many publications available from the Insurance Information Institute, 110 William Street, New York, NY 10038. Call (800) 331-9146 and ask for the publications department.

• The National Insurance Consumer Helpline (NICH) is a toll-free telephone information service sponsored by several insurance-industry trade associations. NICH can answer general questions about insurance and send brochures on request. Call (800) 942-4242. Hours are 8:00 A.M. to 8:00 P.M. Eastern Time, Monday through Friday.

• *Business and Health* ($99/year), a monthly magazine from Medical Economics Publishing, P.O. Box 3000, Denville, NJ 07834, looks at health insurance coverage from a company's point of view. Good ongoing advice and cost-cutting ideas. Call (800) 562-1973.

• *Workers' Compensation Cost Control* is a monthly newsletter ($94.50/year) from Northeast Publishing Group, Marine Industrial Park, P.O. Box 1659, Boston, MA 02205; (800) 229-2084. A steady diet of solid ideas for reducing workers' comp costs.

• *Maximizing Coverage, Minimizing Costs* by Richard Clarke is a terrific (and concise) collection of cost-saving insurance ideas published by the Society of Chartered Property and Casualty Underwriters. The cost is $19.95 from the Society of CPCU, 720 Providence Road, Malvern, PA 19355-0709. For information call (215) 251-CPCU.

• The Washington Business Group on Health, in Washington, D.C., is a nonprofit educational group whose two hundred or so members are mainly large U.S. corporations. The National Resource Center on Worksite Health Promotion, sponsored by the Washington Business Group on Health, can provide information on worksite wellness programs. Both can be reached at (202) 408-9320; fax (202) 408-9332.

• The National Council on Compensation Insurance (NCCI) offers a *Loss Control Program Package* designed to help smaller and midsize firms cut workers' comp costs. It costs $5.50 from NCCI, Order Processing, P.O. Box 025445, Miami, FL 33102-5445; (407) 997-4607.

• Bill Kizorek, a onetime criminal investigator for the U.S. Army and owner of InPhoto Surveillance in Naperville, Illinois, has written several books on how surveillance has cut workers' comp costs. They include *Claims Detective* ($40), *Disability or Deception* ($40), and *Psychological Claims Investigation* ($35). Call InPhoto at (800) 822-8220.

• Here are two other sources for wellness products and programs: Krames Communications, 1100 Grundy Lane, San Bruno, CA 94066; call (800) 333-3032 for a catalog. Says Krames, "When employees are healthy, your bottom line stays healthy." The other is Great Performance Inc., 14964 N.W. Greenbrier Parkway, Beaverton, OR 97006; call (800) 433-3803 for a catalog of books, videos, tapes, posters, and other info.

CHAPTER 16

Cost Savings in Banking and Finance

TACTIC #187
Pay Down/Refinance Your Debt

Debt's a drag. Especially in these turn-on-a-dime times for business. Interest expense is like lead overshoes for your balance sheet. Now's a good time to claw your way out. Take some of the savings you're ringing up from the other tactics in this book and use the money to pay down, maybe even pay off, your debt.

Say your company's paying an average 8% interest on its debt. Think of a paydown as an immediate—and *guaranteed*—8% return on your money. Not bad. While debt may be necessary for fast-growing firms, the payments can smother a small business that needs scarce cash for other purposes.

You can also cut costs by refinancing outstanding debt when rates are low. Review your debt picture. Ask your banker if there are lower-cost ways you could be borrowing. Then, once you've refinanced, use the savings on monthly payments to pay off the debt early.

TACTIC #188
Think like a Banker When You Want a Loan

If you do, you're more likely to get a better deal on a business loan. Rule number one when you go knocking on doors asking for money is to be prepared. That means knowing your company's numbers inside and out. No need to masquerade as a CPA when you're not. But a thorough knowledge of the basics will help. That includes financial projections, how the money will be used, and—most important—how you will pay back the loan.

To think like a banker you have to read what bankers read. And when it comes to comparing business numbers, the banking best-seller is a sizzling tome called *RMA Annual Statement Studies* (see the Follow-up File for how to get it). Okay, so it's not exactly *Monica Meets the Hunk*. But reading this piece of homework can put you in good stead with your banker and may save you money as well.

Annual Statement Studies is published yearly by Robert Morris Associates (RMA), an association of bank loan and credit officers. It contains composite balance sheets and income data on hundreds of different industries—from autos to apparel, marinas to motels, vegetable farms to video stores. This is the book that bankers read when they want to compare *your* company's numbers against others in your industry to see how you stack up financially.

TACTIC #189
Look for Special, Discounted, or Free Banking Services

Banks are madly courting business accounts these days—especially small business—with long lists of perks: free financial advice by phone, discounted bank services, business seminars, helpful publications, networking groups, and a host of others. Some of the most progressive (and aggressive) banks when it comes to small business services are Wells Fargo, Chemical Bank, Banc One, Barnett Banks, and Shawmut National, among others.

Larger companies already receive special treatment through their bank's commercial banking group. But most small businesses end up in the bank's retail division. A $1 million business gets the same treatment and services as the guy with $200 in his checking account. If your bank doesn't offer anything geared specifically to your size range of business, split. In some areas, community banks may be the answer. They've *always* been attuned to the small business market.

Get to know your account officer. Find out what services are available (phone transfers, payroll services, banking by computer, small business credit lines, cash "sweeps" to interest-bearing accounts, etc.) and what discounts are available for your size of relationship. The more you put into your banking relationship—personal accounts included—the better deal and the more breaks on fees you'll be able to get.

Contrary to current thinking that says banks and businesses are parting ways, they will be forging *stronger* ties in the years ahead. Many banks believe this is where their bread will be buttered, and small companies have much to gain by making their bank a "partner" in the business.

TACTIC #190
Link Loan Costs to Company Performance

Since the banking and S&L debacles of the late eighties and early nineties, lenders have become more prudent with their pennies. One way to loosen the purse strings is to push for a kicker in the loan terms that ties the cost of the loan to how well your company does. The better you do, the lower the bank's risk and the less your loan should cost. Often such loan triggers are tied to your company's debt-to-equity ratio (as it declines, so should your loan costs). This increasingly popular tactic, known as "performance-based pricing," has helped some growing companies lower their borrowing costs.

Lenders often balk at putting specific cost reductions in writing based on performance benchmarks. But they should at least be willing to talk about loosening your loan terms or lowering costs once certain performance levels are met. That much you and your lender can agree on ahead of time.

The key will be your ability to deliver bottom-line improvements. Bankers may also insist on the ability to *raise* costs if your earnings head south, so don't try this tactic unless you're reasonably certain your finances are on the upswing.

TACTIC #191
Look Before You Lease

Looking for a way to free up cash and generate possible tax write-offs? Tired of dumping dough into lumps of metal and plastic (cars, trucks, computers) that lose value with each tick of the clock? If so, leasing could be a smart move. With companies looking to cut costs at every corner, vehicle and equipment leasing has taken off in a big way.

One key reason: The gap between what you pay to acquire a vehicle plus spend to operate it, and what you get back when you sell it, keeps widening, says Runzheimer International, a Rochester, Wisconsin, firm that tracks vehicle ownership costs. To make leasing work as a cost-cutting tactic, however, you have to look closely at the *total* cost of leasing versus the *total* cost of owning.

Leasing's bottom line changes from company to company. "The moment you sign a lease you acquire two assets: tax benefits for the equipment and the resale value," says Thomas Steinke of El Camino Resources, a major lessor of IBM and Digital mainframes with offices nationwide. "Either you or the lessor can use the tax benefits during the lease period. If your company is new or faces marginal profitability in the years ahead, the depreciation benefits are of little value to you. Better to let the lessor retain those benefits and lower your lease payments accordingly."

Some leasing benefits and resources:

- Simpler tax write-offs. Nothing with the word *tax* in it can really be simple. But compared to the complexities of claiming tax deductions for depreciation on vehicles you own, claiming your lease payment write-offs is a relative snap. In a few states (check with your accountant or a leasing firm in your area), the vehicle sales tax can be paid over the life of the lease rather than 100% up front.

- With a "full-service" truck lease your company can be assured of a fixed cost for acquiring and operating its vehicles. Basically, all you and your employees do is drive; the leasing company handles everything from maintenance to license plates.

- Leases are flexible, especially for businesses that lease multiple vehicles. The length of the lease, mileage limits, vehicle options, maintenance provisions, and other items can be tailored to your needs—within limits. Delivery vehicles that log upwards of forty thousand miles per year, for example, may be cheaper to own than to lease. Making sure any lease fits your needs is crucial to making leasing work best for your business.

- If you have an American Express Corporate Card, check out the Small Business FleetPlan—an exclusive deal offered through GE Capital. This program offers all the usual leasing advantages plus the power of group buying that can knock 20% off the lease price you'd pay elsewhere. GE Capital is the nation's largest independent auto lessor. Under the deal with American Express's FleetPlan, GE Capital buys cars in big volume, then passes along some of the savings to small business owners who lease even a single car through the plan. It's also convenient: You "shop" for your cars through the plan's toll-free number.

  Small business owner Robert Knowles of Rye Brook, New York, leased three cars elsewhere, then moved to the Small Business FleetPlan. Says Knowles, owner of Video Occasions, "Not only are my monthly payments twenty percent less than I'd pay elsewhere, but the process is easy. Car specs are done by fax and phone. Once credit is approved, you then receive a call from the dealer. In my case, both the agent from GE Capital and the dealer were consummate professionals. I would recommend the service to anyone." To reach a FleetPlan counselor call (800) 451-3796.

TACTIC #192
Focus Your Finance Functions

Does your company have more than one division? And does each unit handle its own invoicing, receivables, freight payments, payroll, T&E reports, fixed-asset accounting? Companies such as Xerox, GE, Alcoa, AT&T, Hewlett-Packard, NYNEX, Scott Paper, Shell Oil, and Digital Equipment have cut the cost of processing those financials by 50% to 75%, according to a study of financial operations at fifteen Fortune 500 companies conducted by A. T. Kearney, a management consulting firm. And companies of considerably less bulk than those giants can do the same. How? By focusing and sharing financial operations.

"Conventional business wisdom shies away from such centralizing," says Earl Landesman, head of Kearney's finance practice. But the path to cost reductions here is unconventional, and the rush to decentralize in the 1980s has produced bloated finance department overhead due to duplicated operations. "The companies we studied [including the ones named above] are reaping the cost benefits of sharing financial functions traditionally duplicated in each business unit," says Landesman.

TACTIC #193
Seek Conventional Loans First

SBA-backed loans through the popular 7(A) program can be great. They're flexible—the money can be used for working capital, equipment, real estate, or to refinance other debt. And repayment terms are generally more liberal than conventional small business loans.

But going this route *first*, without checking the alternatives, could cost you money. These are *not* subsidized loans. The SBA agrees to make the bank whole if your business goes bust, so lenders are more willing to make these loans. Uncle Sam doesn't guarantee this debt for free, however. There's a fee (2% at this writing) that you'll wind up paying one way or another. So an SBA loan can be *more* costly to you than conventional financing. What's more, most banks levy higher interest rates on these loans—on average, about a full percentage point more than on similar commercial loans without SBA's involvement.

If you do seek an SBA loan, definitely look for a lender that has earned "Preferred" status from the SBA. These lenders are permitted to make loan approvals on the spot. That cuts paperwork, speeds your loan, and lowers costs. Fewer than two hundred lenders have been granted Preferred status, so you may have to look around, or ask for a list of lenders from a local SBA office.

TACTIC #194
Buy Your Checks by Mail

U.S. companies and consumers will write 60 billion checks this year (about 1% will bounce). Do you buy your checks from the bank? If so, no matter what type of checks you use—including computer checks—you can probably get 'em cheaper direct from a specialty check supplier through the mail.

For example, Checks in the Mail is a 70-year-old check printing company that now sells direct to consumers and businesses. According to this firm, a typical bank charges $89.95 for 500 computer checks while Checks in the Mail charges

$39.95. Want selection? Checks in the Mail offers 300 designs. They're just as good (all banks accept them), just as secure, but cheaper. Call (800) 733-4443 or write to Checks in the Mail, 5314 North Irwindale Avenue, Irwindale, CA 91706.

Another firm, American Check Printers, specializes in checks for software programs such as Quicken, QuickBooks, Microsoft Money, CA-Simply Money, MyBusiness Checkbook, Managing Your Money, Dollars & Sense, and others. Prices average 40% to 60% less than what the software companies charge and are kept low because customers supply the check-printing information on a computer disk.

The American Check Printers kit is available at Egghead and CompUSA for $19.95 (retail) and includes a coupon for $20 off the first check purchase. You can order the kit by mail (add $4.95 shipping; no $20 coupon) from American at (800) 257-3838 or write to 2197 East Bayshore Road, Palo Alto, CA 94303.

SAVE-A-BUNDLE FOLLOW-UP FILE

• You may be able to borrow a copy of *RMA Annual Statement Studies* from your accountant or banker or find it in the library. Or order your own for $99.50 from RMA, One Liberty Place, 1650 Market Street, Suite 2300, Philadelphia, PA 19103; (215) 851-0585; fax (215) 851-9206.

• *A Consumer Guide to Vehicle Leasing* is a free booklet available from the Federal Trade Commission, Public Reference Branch, 6th Street and Pennsylvania Avenue, N.W., Room 130, Washington, DC 20580; call (202) 326-2222.

• Miami-based Ryder Systems will conduct a free lease-versus-own analysis for your business. Ryder also has special leasing plans for small business truck users, including one called EasyLease. Call Ryder Systems at (800) RYDER-OK.

• Rollins Truck Leasing, in Wilmington, Delaware, offers literature on truck leasing. Call (800) 752-2677.

• Other major vehicle leasing firms include Penske Truck

Leasing in Reading, Pennsylvania, at (215) 775-6000; Ruan Transportation Management Systems in Des Moines, Iowa, at (515) 245-2500; NationaLease in Oakbrook Terrace, Illinois, at (800) 729-6857; GE Capital Fleet Services in Eden Prairie, Minnesota, at (612) 828-1000; and United States Fleet Leasing in San Mateo, California, at (415) 572-2000. AMTRA-LEASE, in Haddon Heights, New Jersey, can refer you to an affiliated truck leasing company in your area. Call (609) 547-7720.

• It's helpful to know the leasing lingo when you shop for a lease. For a free *Glossary of Leasing Terms*, write to ADVANTA Leasing Corp., P.O. Box 1228, Voorhees, NJ 08043-1228, or call (800) 235-5330.

• A terrific way to keep the cash flowing, and lower your costs, is to have your customers pay for your products or services via electronic funds transfer (EFT). Many small businesses are already using commercial EFT services from Checkfree Corporation, a leading electronic payment processor, to reduce costs and provide better service. Example: Peapod Delivery Systems, a Chicago-based computerized grocery shopping and delivery system, offers a free electronic payment card to members to make ordering easy. Cash flow is increased and the number of checks the company must handle is reduced. For information on how it works, call Checkfree's Commercial Division at (800) 882-5280; or write to Checkfree Corporation, 720 Greencrest Drive, Westerville, OH 43081.

CHAPTER 17

*Cost-Cutting Tax Tactics**

The only difference between death and taxes is that death doesn't get worse every time Congress meets.
—WILL ROGERS

Tactic #195: Let Uncle Sam Pay Now for Part of Your New Equipment

Tactic #196: Convert Flabby Inventory and Obsolete Computers into Fat Write-offs

Tactic #197: Trim Estimated Payments If Income Has Dropped

Tactic #198: Carry Back or Carry Forward Current Losses

Tactic #199: Grab the Golden Opportunities to Cut State and Local Taxes

Tactic #200: Challenge Your Property Taxes

Tactic #201: Try a TRI Business Tax-Reduction Workshop

Tactic #202: Capture the Keogh Connection

Save-a-Bundle Follow-up File

* Tax laws change. *Often!* Check with your tax pro before proceeding on any tax matter. They are all subject to lawmaker whim.

TACTIC #195
Let Uncle Sam Pay Now for Part
of Your New Equipment

Rules for depreciating business property are Byzantine, at best. But here's one bit of welcome tax-cutting simplicity for now. Your company can write off immediately—no questions asked—the first $17,500 of new tangible property (capital equipment) that you buy and place into service this year. In CPA-speak, this immediate write-off is known as "expensing." And it's allowed under Section 179 of the Internal Revenue Code. One catch: The write-off is phased out in any year that the business puts more than $200,000 worth of equipment into use.

This would apply to computers, printers, and a host of other equipment or machinery intended for use over several years. Amounts over $17,500 must be depreciated according to IRS rules for the type of property involved—anywhere from three years (some types of computers) to thirty years or more (for real estate).

TACTIC #196
Convert Flabby Inventory and Obsolete
Computers into Fat Write-offs

Stuck with slow-selling inventory? Has the season for your seasonal items come and gone? Got any unused computers or audio equipment growing mold? Here's a way to convert all of the above, and then some, into a money-saving payoff: Do-nate the stuff to a qualifying organization—one granted 501(c)(3) status by the IRS—in return for a federal tax deduction allowed under a little-known 1976 tax law.

Here's what's so nifty about this write-off: Regular C corporations can deduct the full cost of the inventory donated, *plus* half the difference between cost and fair market value, *up to twice the cost.* S corporations, partnerships, and sole proprietorships earn a straight cost deduction. Four nonprofit organizations that can handle your donations are the National Association for the Exchange of Industrial Resources (NAEIR), the National Cristina Foundation, the Gift-in-Kind Clearing House, and Educational Assistance Limited. Donated items are redistributed to thousands of qualified schools and charities across the United States. See the Follow-up File for details.

TACTIC #197
Trim Estimated Payments
If Income Has Dropped

If your business had under $1 million in taxable income in any one of the last three years, you can keep more cash this year by trimming estimated tax payments, according to David Jessen, head of entrepreneurial services at Ernst & Young in Raleigh, North Carolina. Your estimated payments must equal only what you paid last year—even if profits are up. Yes, you will owe tax later (no penalty), but at least you, not the IRS, can use the money until then. Beware: If you owed nothing last year, the rule doesn't apply.

Companies that have overpaid their estimated taxes may qualify for a special IRS quick refund program that can put the cash back into your hands even before the business files its regular income tax return. To get the money, file a Form 4466 and wait by your mailbox.

TACTIC #198
Carry Back or Carry Forward Current Losses

Business showing a net operating loss (NOL) this year? If so, and your company has previously paid income taxes, you may be able to carry back your current losses for up to three years, says David Jessen of Ernst & Young. Under some circumstances, this could even trigger a refund for your company.

Start-ups have a similar opportunity to use tax carry*forwards*—losses that can be applied in the future against three years' worth of revenues.

IRS Publication 536, *Net Operating Losses*, will tell you how to calculate an NOL deduction. Call (800) TAX-FORM to get it.

TACTIC #199
Grab the Golden Opportunities to Cut State and Local Taxes

When it comes to tax-saving tactics, the spotlight's usually on Uncle Sam's hand in your pocket. But many U.S. companies now pay more in state and local taxes than they do in federal taxes, says James Sweeney, a state and local tax specialist with Arthur Andersen & Co. in New York.

"State and local tax planning is a golden opportunity for savings," adds Bob Wood, a multistate tax services partner with Coopers & Lybrand in New York. "These [tax-saving opportunities] have been neglected, ignored, or misunderstood. Company resources are not typically applied to state and local tax planning."

For example, taxing authorities often use prescribed depreciation schedules to value property such as machinery, furniture, computers, and tools, says Jeremiah Lynch, a partner in KPMG Peat Marwick's state and local tax section in New York. "But they may use a twelve-, fifteen-, or twenty-year life when the actual useful life of the equipment is only six or eight years. What constitutes real property for tax purposes may also be at issue. We've helped companies obtain significant refunds by having property reclassified." Also note: Inventories that are taxable in many states may be tax-exempt when interstate or foreign commerce is involved.

Wood says that growing companies in particular can nab savings by paying more attention to sales taxes. "Companies are frequently unaware of exemptions that are available to them. In most states, if you purchase equipment for manufacturing there is a specific exemption."

TACTIC #200
Challenge Your Property Taxes

Property taxes are plump with possible savings. In this, the decade of declining property values, opportunities to reduce the assessed value of your commercial property (and thus your taxes) abound. It takes a little effort to pursue it, but the payoff can be big.

Accountants are amazed at how *few* businesses challenge their assessments. Yet overvaluation and other mistakes—due largely to overly complex valuation formulas—often result in excessive property tax assessments. Start by conducting your own review. Assessment records are available to the public. Check the worksheet on your property and compare your valuation with similar properties. "Such a review by a research and development facility owned by a specialty products concern produced annual tax savings of $167,000," says Jeremiah Lynch of KPMG Peat Marwick.

James Sweeney, of Arthur Andersen, notes another opportunity to save. "Businesses that lease property often have the right to challenge an assessment on the property under the terms of the lease. That's because they pay property taxes through the lease. Don't overlook this opportunity." Sweeney also issues a warning on timing: Challenges in many areas must be made within thirty days of receiving the annual valuation notice. You should prepare in *advance* to challenge your property tax bill when it arrives.

TACTIC #201
Try a TRI Business Tax-Reduction Workshop

Tax-reducing seminars come and go, but this outfit—Bethesda, Maryland–based Tax Reduction Institute, Inc. (TRI)—puts on some of the best in the business and with a money-back guarantee. Since 1979, over half a million small business owners and professionals have attended TRI seminars. At $230 to $330, these full-day affairs are money well spent if you're looking for tax-saving strategies that work. TRI also has offices in Edmonds, Washington. Call (800) TRI-1040 or write to 511 Walnut Street, Edmonds, WA 98020.

TACTIC #202
Capture the Keogh Connection

No matter how small your business, it has the same basic rights the giants have to install and fund a pension plan for you and your employees.

The basic pension for small-business owners and self-employed individuals is often called a Keogh plan, named after Donald Keogh, the congressman who created it. But some plan purveyors may simply call it a defined-contribution pension. With a defined-contribution plan—today's most popular variety—your business (even a one-person business) can set aside a percentage of earnings each year. By whatever name, it's a sweet deal. Contributions are tax deductible and earnings go untaxed until you withdraw the money.

Those tax breaks come with a catch: Since this is retirement savings, you have to agree not to dip into it early. There's a 10% penalty if you tap the account too soon, and the law says that's generally anytime before you reach age fifty-nine and a half—or, if you leave or close the business, age fifty-five.

Contributions to your business pension are always fully tax deductible, no matter how high your income and regardless of whether you or your spouse are covered by another retirement plan. There's no such thing as a nondeductible contribution, as there is with an IRA. And you can have an IRA in addition to your small-business plan. (While IRA contributions won't be deductible, once inside the account the money grows tax-free.)

How much you can shelter depends on your income and the type of Keogh you choose. If you have employees, they must be included in the plan. There are three kinds of Keoghs:

1. *Profit-sharing for maximum flex.* You can put as much as 15% of your net self-employment earnings, up to $22,500, into a profit-sharing plan. Here, "earnings" means your net business income minus the amount you contribute to your Keogh, minus one-half of any Social Security tax you pay on your self-employed earnings. To dodge the math, simply use 13% instead of 15%.

   The advantage to profit-sharing is flexibility. You need not contribute the same percentage each year. Put in 13% one year, 6% another, even skip a year if you want. A profit-sharing plan lets you roll with the self-employment punches, putting in more in good years, less in bad ones.

   Flexibility is one reason that Batteries Inc., a battery wholesaler in Upper Marlboro, Maryland, switched to a profit-sharing plan. The eight-employee company, owned by brothers Steve and Charlie Hall, had a defined-*benefit* plan for about twelve years. But such plans require the business to kick in large sums annually and are generally more expensive and complex to operate. Steve Hall is happy with the switch. "We simply figure our profit at the end of the year and base our contribution to the plan on that," he says.

2. *A plan with higher limits.* In a "money-purchase" plan you can contribute up to 25% of net earnings. Again, net is the amount that's left after you subtract your contribution, making the effective limit 20% instead of 25%. The ceiling is $30,000. The big plus with a money-purchase plan is that you can shelter more money. This is a good choice if you can afford to devote a large portion of your business income to retirement savings and you expect to be able to continue funding your plan at the same level year after year. Once you decide what percentage of income you want to set aside, you must contribute that percentage each year. You trade the flexibility of profit-sharing for the ability to shelter a greater amount.

3. *Have both!* A superb strategy to capture the flexibility of profit-sharing and the higher limits of a money-purchase pension is to have both. It's perfectly legal. First, set up a money-purchase plan and commit 7% of your earnings. That's your minimum bite. Then, set up a profit-sharing plan that can be funded for up to 13% more of your income. As long as contributions to the two plans together total no more than 20% of earnings, you're okay.

SAVE-A-BUNDLE FOLLOW-UP FILE

• For a free, no-obligation information kit on inventory or equipment donations, contact the National Association for the Exchange of Industrial Resources (NAEIR) at (800) 562-0955;

fax (309) 343-0862; or write to 560 McClure Street, Galesburg, IL 61401. NAEIR takes donations of excess inventory and redistributes the material to schools and nonprofit groups that can use it. Thousands of different items can be donated, but NAEIR must first see a list and give you the nod to proceed.

• The National Cristina Foundation funnels old and surplus computers, software, and peripherals to educational and training facilities for people with disabilities and students at risk of failure. Call (800) 274-7846; fax (203) 622-6270.

• Gift-in-Kind Clearing House is a Davidson, North Carolina–based nonprofit group that takes donations of furniture, equipment, merchandise, and supplies and then distributes the donations to universities, community colleges, schools, and other nonprofits. Call (704) 892-7228; fax (704) 892-3825; or write P.O. Box 850, Davidson, NC 28036.

• Educational Assistance Limited (EAL), in Wheaton, Illinois, will also turn excess inventory into a business tax break, using donated goods to help send needy kids to college. Call for a free guide on how it works, (708) 690-0010; fax (708) 690-0565. Or write to P.O. Box 3021, Glen Ellyn, IL 60138.

• The *Kiplinger Tax Letter* (biweekly, $54/year), published by the Kiplinger Washington Editors, Inc., can keep you up to date on the latest tax law changes. Call (800) 544-0155.

• For a booklet called *Simplified Employee Pensions: What Small Businesses Need to Know*, send $1 to Superintendent of Documents, P.O. Box 371954, Pittsburgh, PA 15250-7954. Ask for Publication 045-000-00256-0.

• *The Small Business Owner's Guide to Keogh Plans* is a free booklet available from T. Rowe Price Associates. Call (800) 638-3006. Most of the other major no-load mutual fund families also offer helpful booklets on setting up a Keogh plan. A few to consider: Dreyfus, (800) 373-9387; Fidelity, (800) 544-8888; Vanguard, (800) 962-5086; Scudder, (800) 225-2470; and INVESCO, (800) 525-8085. A discount brokerage firm such as Charles Schwab can also be a great place to establish a SEP or Keogh. Schwab has a good selection of free booklets explaining the plans. Call (800) 435-4000.

• Chicago-based Willamette Management Associates is one of the oldest and largest independent valuation consulting firms in the United States. Works with small family-held firms and Fortune 100 corporations. Specialist in helping companies contest their property taxes. Call (800) 933-0288.

Acknowledgments

They might not know it, but Paul and Margaret Kehrer, my father and mother, wrote this book. For them, thrift has always been second nature. Mom clipped enough coupons to carpet California, though money was never a problem. (Naturally, she credits her coupons for that.) And as a top savings industry executive, Dad helped generations of midwestern families handle their money wisely. Together, they embody an old-fashioned value that is being rediscovered in America today by both consumers and commerce: Saving money is the only certain path to financial security—for a household, a business, or a government.

My partners at Group IV Communications, Inc.—Don Phillipson, Mike Carpenter, and Tom Sargent—deserve credit for this book as well. Since its launch on April Fool's Day 1989 at the brink of recession, our enterprise has survived harrowing times to emerge as a leading publisher of small business magazines, with an award-winning network reaching over a million businesses nationwide. Nobody could ask for a more talented and congenial trio of friends and colleagues.

I am also indebted to the fine folks at the National Federation of Independent Business (NFIB), the nation's oldest and largest advocate for small business. Group IV publishes *IB* (*Independent Business*) *Magazine* for the more than 600,000 small business owners who belong to the NFIB. The tireless efforts of this group, in Washington, D.C., and fifty state capitals, have saved millions of small businesses billions of dollars over the decades. In particular, I want to thank NFIB's president and CEO Jack Faris, and vice president for public affairs David Cullen for their encouragement and support of *IB Magazine*, which I edit.

Any book with as many names, addresses, phone numbers, and other facts as this one needs a nose-to-the-grindstone individual to help weed out the inevitable clinkers. That person is Ethan Blumen, a stand-out information sleuth who spent countless hours tracking down and checking information for *Save Your Business a Bundle*.

My grateful thanks also go to Fred Hills, vice president and senior editor at Simon & Schuster. Fred is the person who first saw promise in my idea, then made sure it became a reality. He's the kind of tough yet supportive editor every author likes to have. Laureen Connelly, his assistant, proved a flawless facilitator, helping manage the Right Coast–Left Coast flow of paper between S&S in New York and the author in Los Angeles.

And even after seven books, I can't sign off without saying thanks, yet again, to my tolerant and talented wife Kaye Kittrell, and my son Walker, for standing pat while I spent still more nights, weekends, and holidays stitching together *Save Your Business a Bundle*.

—DANIEL KEHRER

Index